# Praise fo

"A delicately crafted, absorbing account of an American past seldom encountered in conventional histories... meticulously researched."—*Kirkus Discoveries*

"Dr. Schake presents a highly detailed, but easy to read, characterization of La Charrette's long neglected significance. It is a worthwhile read for anyone interested in American History."—**Harry Windland**, Treasurer, Illinois Lewis and Clark Bicentennial Commission

"For both the scholar and the avocational historian, La Charrette adds much-needed pages to the history of the westering experience and the Missouri River."—**Clive G. Siegle**, Southern Methodist University, Executive Director, Zebulon Pike Bicentennial Commission

"One might question whether a village of seven houses rates a book, but to do so would be to underestimate both Lowell Schake and La Charette. This was not just any village, but for nearly a half-century in the late 1700s and early 1800s, it was the last outpost of European settlement on the Missouri River, the natural highway to two thousand miles of Indian country, everyone's last stop on the way out and the first stop on the way back. Lowell Schake has done a remarkable job of digging in French, Spanish, and territorial records to reconstruct the multi-racial, multi-lingual, and multi-ethnic society of his hometown, the intriguing frontier village of La Charette."—**Walter Kamphoefner**, Director of Graduate Studies, Department of History, Texas A&M University

"Schake's book documents the intimate life and history of a village that helped serve as a launching point into the territory and its role in American frontier life."—**Brad Urban**, *St. Louis Post-Dispatch Suburban Journals*

"*La Charrette* is highly recommended not only as a result of the impeccable research by the author, but also his talent for bringing the village of La Charrette to life in print."—**Timothy Forrest Coulter**, descendant of John Colter

"If you are a history buff—or even if you're not—*La Charrette* will make a valuable edition to your personal library."—**Stephen E. Smith**, *My Missourian*

"At last...'Charrette Village' is put in its universal, national, and territorial place. For the strong interest now in the Lewis and Clark Expedition this book should be useful matter."—**Ralph Gregory**, President, Franklin County Historical Society, *Washington Missourian*

"This is an important book and recommended."—**Leo E. Oliva**, *Santa Fe Trail Quarterly*

"If you have ancestors who moved to and settled in Missouri when it was still the edge of the American frontier, you will be interested in...*La Charrette*...I think you will find it an interesting historical and genealogical source."—**Martha Jones**, PhD, *Victoria Advocate*

"Boone descendants will be happy to see this new and original book pertaining to a part of Daniel Boone's life, and the lives of his family members, that has not been written about before... If you are interested in learning more about the earliest life of those who moved to and settled Missouri when it was still the edge of the American frontier, you will enjoy this book."—**Margy Miles**, Boone family descendant

# La Charrette

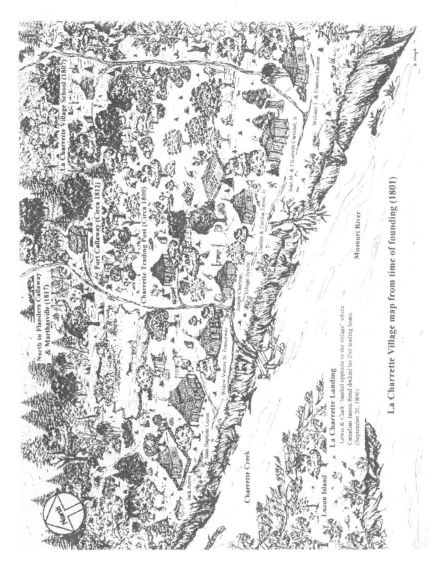

La Charrette Village map from time of founding (1801)

Missouri River

Luzon Island

La Charrette Landing
Lewis & Clark "landed opposite to the village" where Canadian James Reed docked her five trading boats.
(September 20, 1806)

Charrette Creek

Jack Aimes

Jean Baptiste Luzon

Widow Venice St. Francoway

Joseph Chartran

Charles & Cecilia Tayon, Jr

Petit Village Stofle

Jean M. & Elizabeth Chartran, Jr

William T. & Frances Latime

Charrette Trading Post (Circa 1800)

Fort Callaway (Circa 1812)

North to Flanders Callaway
& Marthasville (1817)

La Charrette Village School (1807)

Timelines for historic La Charrette Village (1801~1825)
by Dorothy E. Meyer

# La Charrette

A History of the Village Gateway
to the American Frontier Visited
by Lewis and Clark, Daniel Boone,
Zebulon Pike

*Lowell M. Schake, PhD*

iUniverse Star
New York  Lincoln  Shanghai

# La Charrette

A History of the Village Gateway to the American Frontier Visited by Lewis and Clark, Daniel Boone, Zebulon Pike

iUniverse Star
an iUniverse, Inc. imprint

iUniverse books may be ordered through booksellers or by contacting:

iUniverse
2021 Pine Lake Road, Suite 100
Lincoln, NE 68512
www.iuniverse.com
1-800-Authors (1-800-288-4677)

*Departing From the Village of La Charrette*,
painting by Billyo O'Donnel Copyright 2004

ISBN-13: 978-1-58348-483-8 (pbk)
ISBN-13: 978-0-595-80603-4 (ebk)
ISBN-10: 1-58348-483-3 (pbk)
ISBN-10: 0-595-80603-1 (ebk)

Printed in the United States of America

To all early families of Charrette Creek

"I have come to look upon the Missouri as more than a river. To me it is an epic...haunted with great memories. Perhaps never before in the history of the world has a river been the thoroughfare of a movement so tremendously epic in its relation to development of man."

John Neihardt (1881–1973),
*Epic Poet of the American West*
Instructor and poet-in-residence,
University of Missouri, 1949–1965

"By the time the United States acquired Louisiana, Charrette had become a thoroughly mixed village of back-country Americans, French-speaking Creoles, emigrant and native Indians, free and enslaved African-Americans, and the growing progeny of their various combinations."

John Mack Faragher, *Contact Points* (1998)
Professor of history, Yale University

# Content

# List of Illustrations

# Foreword

While attending the University of Missouri at Columbia during the late 1970s, I would often travel home to St. Louis along State Highway 94 rather than Interstate 70. The scenic old two-lane road wound through the hills and bottomlands just north of the Missouri River, providing a view of the state that was completely different than the one offered by the antiseptic modern four-lane route. As a history major in college, I was aware that Lewis and Clark had gone up the Missouri River in 1804, but I knew almost nothing else about the region. I certainly did not realize that Euro-Americans had settled upstream from St. Louis prior to the famous expedition that was said to have opened up the West, nor was I aware that Frenchmen had established the village of La Charrette on the north bank of the Missouri River, near Highway 94, in the late eighteenth century.

Thankfully, the notion that the history of the American West began in 1804 has passed. As Colin G. Calloway noted in his most recent book, "Lewis and Clark did not bring the West into U.S. history; they brought the United States into Western history." Lowell M. Schake's book, which details the activities of French trappers who traded in the vicinity of La Charrette four decades before the Louisiana Purchase, as well as the people of various nationalities who settled in the region in the 1790s, is part of an exciting new historical trend that gives the proper due to the French and Spanish colonial effort in North America, placing it on par with that of the British.

Until very recently, most historians have either overlooked or dismissed the accomplishments of non-Anglo-Saxons in the Louisiana Purchase region north of the state of Louisiana. Schake, however, illustrates these accomplishments, following in the footsteps of authors such as Morris Arnold, who has written three works on colonial Arkansas, and Carl Ekberg, who covers French Illinois and Missouri in his impressive *oeuvre*. These historians, as well as Daniel Usner, Gilbert Din, and Gwendolyn Midlo Hall, who have written extensively about colonial Louisiana, have demonstrated that the French and Spanish had founded viable communities in the Mississippi Valley prior to the arrival of Anglo-Americans. As these authors have shown, these colonies were not failures, as prior historians have portrayed them, but settlements that merely differed from the British experience in North America.

As Schake notes in this highly informative and entertaining book on La Charrette, the history of North America is that of various peoples—Asian, African, and European—coming together in many different settings, none of which are any more or less valuable than the others.

F. Todd Smith, Dallas, Texas, June 2005
Associate professor of history, University of North Texas, Denton

# Preface

Why should you—or anyone else—bother to read about an old Missouri River village of only seven indigent families? The question is entirely natural and appropriate, especially when alternatives competing for our attention and resources constantly bombard our senses. While you may hold innate suspicions about La Charrette, compelling reasons to proceed do exist. *La Charrette* reveals the process by which we became the culture and society today known as the United States of America.

La Charrette Village is central to two national bicentennial celebrations of the twenty-first century. The expedition of Lewis and Clark as well as Zebulon Pike departed civilization at La Charrette, establishing it as the nation's first launchpad into the vast unknown. Beyond these celebrated events are the daily happenings at this crossroads of culture and expeditions, offering the reader the most vivid understanding possible of what frontier America was really like before novels, movies, and television distorted it. Here, Native Americans, squatters, slaves, the village citizens, their children (including nine orphans), their guests, and neighbors all held dreams and aspirations of success. Their pluralistic society—and those following in their footsteps—paved the path to a dream all of us share as our birthright, the American Dream. Knowing that this compelling story of Americanization has never been told before only adds to its intrigue.

Not one book or scholarly journal article has ever addressed the sole topic of La Charrette Village. What is published on Missouri's westernmost village of the Louisiana Purchase are mostly newspaper articles or footnotes to larger works. Its span of life was short. It never grew to become a great metropolitan center. Even the nearby creeks and river channels where La Charrette Village once stood have since undergone extensive change. Only meager shreds of physical evidence document its existence. If professional historians and editors are not interested in the topic, what possible reason should motivate others to attempt the task of chronicling the lives, times, and activities of its residents and their guests? Why bother?

"Because the village was once there" is perhaps a sufficient reason to proceed. As a Charrette Township youth, I became fascinated by Indian culture, western exploration, and settlement activities, even though I was unaware of the village's extensive role in these matters. The compulsion to study and record what fascinates one is a unique, powerful force across society, especially when it involves one's heritage. For three or more generations, all of my maternal and paternal families lived on and farmed the lands once associated with La Charrette Village.

As you will see, the village history is rich, far-reaching, and informative. Retrospectively, one may ask why the events of La Charrette Village from two centuries ago have remained secluded in footnotes and archives for so long. Perhaps we will develop a greater appreciation for extinct, old villages because of this study. As we know from science, the more we learn to focus and concentrate our efforts, study the intricate, and explore minute details and functioning of things, the more fully we may comprehend the whole. Many history books tackle expansive themes. This is not one of them. *La Charrette* represents a thin slice of social history associated with the founding of two little fur-trading villages leading the way in the development of the American West.

It is my desire—as well as that of my collaborator—to present a comprehensive, technically accurate history of La Charrette Village, sometimes called Village Charrette. To this end, I pursued all potential sources and leads in a wide range of published works, archives, and other materials. This lifetime interest involves nearly 1,000 documents and untold miles of searching. Our objectives include enhancing interest in local history as well as validating the old village site while capturing as much evidence regarding the village and related epic events as possible. In addition to history, I have made an effort to emphasize the village citizenry and their everyday lives circa the Lewis and Clark Expedition.

This book might be most interesting to those who are somehow associated with the creek or township sharing its name. However, anyone who ever contemplated why people chose to settle a remote village or wondered what may have transpired there in the olden days is also a prime candidate to enjoy this village history. Likewise, those interested in the study of present-day multiculturalism will find these village residents blessed with all types of diversities. Obviously, those with a specific interest in events surrounding the Corps of Discovery and subsequent expeditions should enjoy this read. Should you wish to visit this region and study specific details of the individuals and events represented on the western edge of the American frontier, you may also find those opportunities here. One could certainly not ask for a more diverse, famous, and colorful cast of characters to portray life on the Missouri frontier when it was still known as Louisiana.

# Acknowledgments

Jerome and Lucille Holtmeyer of Washington, Missouri, initiated this undertaking. For years, they were interested in documenting the precise location of historic La Charrette Village and pinpointing where the Lewis and Clark Expedition members camped overnight in 1804 and, again, in 1806. Due to health reasons, it was not possible for them to proceed as desired. The Holtmeyers and I corresponded. We discovered our mutual interests, which then culminated in their collaboration on *La Charrette: A History of the Village Gateway to the American Frontier Visited by Lewis and Clark, Daniel Boone, Zebulon Pike.*

I would like to express my deepest gratitude to Jerry and Lucille for their roles in this effort. A special acknowledgment, with thanks, is extended to Jerry for all his diligent work to document the village site, share numerous documents, and provide his valued support throughout the preparation of the manuscript. Likewise, portions of this manuscript have benefited from review comments offered by several scholars of history. Special thanks to John Mack Faragher, professor of history at Yale University, for sharing his note files on Charles "Indian" Phillips and Daniel Boone; Walter D. Kamphoefner, professor of history at Texas A&M University, for his contributions on the migration of Germans to Charrette Township; and Leo E. Oliva, editor of the Santa Fe Trail Association's *Wagon Tracks,* for his comprehensive editing skills. I value and greatly appreciate the willing assistance of Dr. F. Todd Smith, associate professor of history at University of North Texas at Denton, for preparing the Foreword. His broad-ranging professional interests and training in western-frontier America uniquely prepared him to offer insights.

Local Missouri historians interviewed in person include the following: Kenneth A. Kamper of Hermann, president of the Daniel Boone and Frontier Families Research Association and charter member of the Boone-Duden Historical Society. Ralph Gregory, my youthful, ninety-five-year-old friend from Marthasville, who actively serves as president of the Franklin County Historical Society, faithfully offered perspectives on local history along with his file on Charrette Village. Boone researcher Margy Miles of Marthasville was always helpful, as was

Dorris Keeven Franke of Washington and Deanne Purcell, gifted and talented fifth-grade teacher of Flour Bluff, Texas, ISD. W. Crosby Brown of Washington opened his private library resources to me. James Denny, state historian for the Missouri Department of Natural Resources in Jefferson City, also offered comments. Each is due thanks for his or her valued inputs during the preparation of the manuscript. As part of the local Lewis and Clark Bicentennial Celebration of 2004, La Charrette Committee Members Pam Jensen and Rita Hoelscher of Marthasville, graciously arranged for the Marthasville Chamber of Commerce to provide pictures of the La Charrette commemorative medallion shown on the front cover of the first issue.

Many others also assisted and encouraged me, to whom I extend my gratitude. Included are my wife, Wendy; my sister, Dorothy Meyer of Washington, Missouri, for her illustrative sketch of the village; and my sister, Helen Hoertel of Rolla, Missouri, for introducing me to the collaborators. I am also immensely grateful to my dear friend, Yolanda Pepper Miller of Corpus Christi, Texas, as well as to the staff members of the Corpus Christi city libraries who faithfully assisted me during many years of intense research activity.

# Introduction:
# Dreams and Legacies

More than 200 years ago, on a bold frontier of a vast, unexplored wilderness, La Charrette Village flickered into existence. Within thirty years of its founding, it would vanish without fanfare...without making any headlines or newscast. A rich, vibrant heritage with an abundance of unanswered questions remained in its stead. This remote, impoverished Creole village holds legacies deeply rooted in local, state, and national history. As one of the earliest settlements on the Missouri River, it was documented by early explorers. It was a modest, fur-trading outpost with a river landing. These explorers later constructed a school and a fort or two to serve the settlement's frontier families. The village soon began fading from existence for reasons largely unknown. Following the loss of the village, Marthasville Landing emerged via the renaming of Charrette Landing to serve the needs of the many settlers arriving by steamships, boats, and skiffs to Charrette Township of Warren County, Missouri.

Marthasville was spawned in a narrow valley immediately to the north of where the village once stood. Today, it stands as the oldest town of continual habitation in Warren County. However, its neighboring ancestor of La Charrette Village holds at least an equivalent historical distinction as it attracted the region's earliest residents, who serve as this work's primary subjects. The village would host many celebrated expeditions, frontiersmen, scientists, scholars, legendary heroes, wilderness men, and a famous Indian hunter...all before Marthasville was founded.

However, work was to be done to develop half a nation, including taming the wilderness, trapping for furs, raising cabins, clearing land, farming, merging cultures, and establishing commerce and communities. La Charrette residents would experience these and other challenges, and would assist others in accomplishing the same as part of a monumental westward migration. La Charrette Village emerged upon the very cusp of a vast expanse of westward-looking potentials, civilization's last outpost on its super information "river network" of the day.

People of diverse origins sought to exploit wealth from La Charrette Village's surroundings as their lives became intertwined.[1] The first Europeans to join the Native Americans were those of French ancestry. The Spanish were soon in control. Then, once again, the French and, eventually, Americans controlled the region as old, Southern planters arrived with their slaves. Later, those of German descent came in excess. All were searching for new lives and opportunities. A giant fur-trading industry was the initial motivation. Later, ownership of land and farming provided the incentives to settle. Less fortunate ones were forced to settle on Indian reservations or to toil as slaves. Spanning more than a century of frontier life, most settlers left behind an incomplete trail to document their influence and contributions to Charrette Township and beyond. Today, even after this tiny, remote village was lost to cartographers, it continues exerting its influence far beyond those closely linked to the township, creek, and local businesses sharing its name.

Beyond these local interests, there is history. La Charrette Village's presence, though lost before the formation of Warren County, somehow remains with us as it provides a vital link to past events in the development of Upper Louisiana, the Missouri Territory, and the state. Neither the exact details of its founding, nor the reason(s), nor the date this early crossroads of culture and history became extinct are known with certainty. Perhaps its most notable role in world history is the entry, "the last settlement of whites on this river," which was recorded in Sergeant Floyd's journal on May 25, 1804, as the Lewis and Clark Expedition proceeded westward through the Great American Desert in search of the Pacific.

However, to revisit that eventful day in May 1804 now is getting ahead of how this event and others unfolded at La Charrette Village. Join me as I recount exploring the mysteries and discovering the details of some of the more eventful happenings at this historic site where Charrette Creek empties into the mighty Missouri River. It was this location where La Charrette's long, powerful frontier tentacles would labor.

By means of comparison, I am reminded of the late Stephen Jay Gould's 1995 book, *Dinosaur in a Haystack*. Gould rightfully bemoaned the loss of one species of antelope, the blaauwbock of South Africa. These "blue bucks" were known to scientists for less than fifty years before an ill-placed bullet exterminated them in 1799. Four mounted hides, bone fragments, and perhaps some yet undiscovered petrified remains are all that document the species today. La Charrette

Village has experienced much of the same ill-fate as the blue buck. Known to exist for less than thirty years, the village has precious little tangible evidence to document its existence—just bits and pieces scattered over many historical documents, oral history, family genealogies, and related sources. Future archaeological studies may identify buried artifacts to enhance our understanding of this riverbank village. After all, history is written not in concrete, but in sand. *La Charrette: A History of the Village Gateway to the American Frontier Visited by Lewis and Clark, Daniel Boone, Zebulon Pike* attempts to partially re-create the life and times of La Charrette's residents, all from scant fragments of past happenings; it is the only treatise solely devoted to La Charrette Village history and genealogy.

# Part One:

## Engaging the Wilderness

"In spite of its early beginning, La Charrette never grew to be very large or important."

Collins and Snider, *Missouri, Midland State* (1955)

# Chapter 1:

## Louisiana, a Historical Sketch

French, English, and Spanish empires greatly influenced events related to Louisiana's development. Their expeditions, forts, trading posts, and missions established a substantial buttress supporting subsequent squatter and settlement activities. Their prime motivations were political and economic gain, typically expressed in their aggrandizing, expansionist, near feudal-like, destiny-driven cultures. Also in play were the elements of national pride and honor and, for Spain, the desire for a controlling monopoly. In some manner, all were competing with one another, predictably placing one or more parties at odds with another. At the time of the Louisiana Purchase in 1803, two-thirds of Americans lived within fifty miles of the Atlantic Ocean. The United States ended at the Mississippi River. Only four roads crossed the Allegheny Mountains. However, within a few decades, the great westward expansion would be underway, pushing Native Americans farther westward. The magnificent Louisiana wilderness would never again be as it once was before transforming into the world's largest, most productive agricultural complex of today.

New Spain, stretching from Texas to California, was to the southwest of Louisiana. To the north, England controlled Canada, and Russia soon erected a fort on the northern coast of California.[1] An immense, largely uncharted landmass, named Louisiana by René-Robert Cavelier, Sieur de La Salle in 1682, resided in between. Within its present-day bounds, stretching from the Gulf of Mexico north along the Mississippi River into Canada and westward to the Rocky Mountains, reside the states of Arkansas, Missouri, Iowa, South Dakota, Nebraska, Kansas, and Oklahoma in addition to major portions of Louisiana, Texas, New Mexico, Colorado, Wyoming, Montana, North Dakota, and Minnesota. At one time or another, Spain, France, England, and the United States each sought to expand its sphere of influence across

Louisiana to acquire wealth by developing—and controlling—new trade routes. The vision, motivated primarily by economic interests, was the discovery and control of a Northwest Passage and its associated waterways. Ultimately, the dream was to trade furs and other valuables on the Sea of California providing access to markets in the Orient. Control of the waterways was paramount and none was more important than the Mississippi-Missouri River system. English author Daniel Coxe[2] was typical of those who fostered this dream. He confidently penned the headwaters of the Missouri "proceeds from a ridge of hills somewhat north of New Mexico, passable by horse, foot, or wagon in less than half a day." On the westward side of this ridge, according to Coxe, was "a large lake called Thayago, which pours its water through a large navigable river into the boundless sea." Everyone envisioned fabulous profits, making them protective of their land claims and ambitions yet suspicious of the same ambition in others.

Many notable expeditions contributed to the general knowledge of Louisiana and the neighboring territories that eventually led to permanent settlement. New lands were subject to new jurisdiction by the "right of discovery." New Spain established claim to her territory by the exploits of gold seekers, like Francisco de Coronado and contemporary explorer Hernando de Soto, who discovered the Mississippi River in 1541. Other explorers, including Juan de Onate, ventured into the southwest as well resulting in the 1598 founding of the mining and trade center at Santa Fe.[3] These explorers were the first Europeans to set foot in what would become the Louisiana Territory.

On the opposite end of the continent, French seaman Jacques Cartier discovered the St. Lawrence River and took possession of New France for King Francis I in 1534. In 1608, Samuel de Champlain founded Quebec, establishing French dominance along the St. Lawrence River. Maisonneuve founded Montreal, the ancestral, North American home of many La Charrette villagers, thirty-four years later. New France's fur industry rivaled New Spain's mining and cattle industries. Spanish officials generally considered the lands between New France and New Spain as an effective barrier. Besides, where were the wealthy cultures comparable to the Inca or Aztec with their gold and silver? The French thought differently, wishing to occupy the western wilderness peaceably or, if need be, by force. Both Spanish and French authorities occasionally sent out expeditions to learn of the others' activities, focusing on military strategies to control the river routes for purposes of colonization and trade. La Louisiane came under French control when, amid much ceremony, La Salle turned a spade full of earth and placed a cross somewhere in the swampy delta near the mouth of the Mississippi in 1682, claiming all land drained by her waters for King Louis XIV.[4] The Frenchmen planted the banner, fired a volley of musket shots, and prayed as they annexed "this country of Louisiana...The most high, mighty, invincible and victorious Louis the Great, by the Grace of God, King of France and Navarre..." proclaimed a priest as part of this April 9 ceremony, officially giving Louisiana its name.[5]

Previously, in 1670, Father Jacques Marquette, a French Jesuit missionary, learned of a mighty river, the Mississippi, eight or nine days south of St. Ignatius, on his mission at Michilimackinac on Lake Michigan. The French hoped the Mississippi emptied into the Gulf of California, offering a shortcut to China. Marquette, along with Louis Joliet and five others, floated down the Mississippi in 1673. According to Marquette, they entered the Mississippi near present-day Prairie du Chien on June 17. A little Indian corn and dried meat made up their entire stock of provisions. By early July, they arrived at the mouth of the Missouri, becoming the first Europeans to see "la riviere Pekitanoui," the longest river in America. At the confluence of these rivers, they recorded that "entire trees" and "floating reefs" gushed from the violent Missouri, making their passage very hazardous. They noted that enormous Indian nations using wooden canoes lived on this river. Before returning north, they continued down the Mississippi to the Arkansas River, concluding that the Gulf of California was not part of this river system. By 1698, missionaries like Father St. Cosme and other Frenchmen began interacting with the Native Americans along the lower Missouri. Several years before, St. Cosme had been instrumental in founding Cahokia as part of the American Bottoms. It was located on the east bank of the Mississippi near what would later become East St. Louis. Next, Pierre-Charles Le Sueur reached the Missouri in 1700. By 1703, twenty men from Illinois Country attempted an upriver voyage, but no report of their venture has survived.

It was not until 1714 that a Frenchman, Commandant Etienne Veniard, sieur de Bourgmond (sometimes Bourgmont or Bourgmounte), became the first to chart the lower reaches of the Missouri River. By 1720, Bourgmond was commissioned as captain and commandant of the Missouri. He constructed Fort Orleans in 1723, the earliest European structure on the Missouri.[6] Today, its location is verified as having been on the north bank of the Missouri River, near Malta Bend in Saline County.

Bourgmond was a flamboyant character. Before his arrival in Missouri, he escaped from an assignment at Fort Detroit in eastern Michigan and lived among Missouri and Osage Indians for several years. Marrying an Indian maiden, he fathered a son named Petit Missouri. He then returned to his family in France with Petit Missouri and other Native Americans, serving as exhibits to the court. Dashing as always, Bourgmond then married a wealthy, young French widow and gained a French nobility title. His most significant contribution to the history of La Charrette Village was a map apparently depicting Charrette Creek as one of the north-bank streams entering the Missouri. His journal entries are dated April 6 and 7, 1714:

> Friday, 6. West-southwest three-quarters of a league: to the east, a chain of islands about one league in length.-northwest a quarter of a league; to the east, some hills; to the west, an island.

> Saturday, 7. West an eighth of a league. West-northwest three-quarters of a league; to the east, an island of half a league; the channel form west to northwest. Northwest half a league; to the east, rocky escarpments, at the end is a little island, concealing the river which we call the Fourchure [L'Outre River].

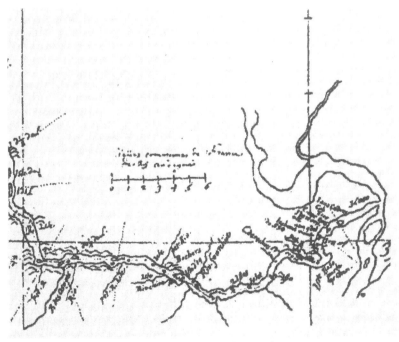

Figure 1. The Bourgmond map of 1714.

Thus, Bourgmond became the first European to attempt documenting what later became known as Charrette Creek (Figure 1). His map gives "Riv. Fourchure" as L'Outre River (Otter Creek), approximately twelve miles west of Charrette Creek's mouth. Fort Orleans (Figure 2) was farther upriver. The map, drawn by French cartographer Guillaume Delisle circa 1716, is a document in the public domain at the Service Historique de la Marine in Vincennes, France. Regrettably, notations assigned to future Charrette Creek and to most other landmarks are illegible. His map also depicts the Osage River to the west as well as other streams along the lower Missouri. Later, I will explain how some of these streambed configurations have changed since Bourgmond attempted recording them.

French, English, and Spanish control over these North American landmasses continued experiencing administrative change. Extensive efforts, like those of Bourgmond and a few scattered traders and missionaries, gave France full claim to Louisiana. By 1744, traveling the Missouri, some French fur traders went upriver into North Dakota and Colorado. However, French dominance in Canada was about to conclude. For three years (1629–1632), the English controlled New France before relinquishing it back to France. Once again, the French and English were soon fighting over control of the upper Ohio Valley. Additional European involvement combined with these and related conflicts culminated in the French and Indian War, known as the Seven Years' War in Europe. This sealed the fate of New France in Canada, leaving many Americans with the impression the British would forever hold influence over North America. By 1760, England was once again in control of Canada.

Loss of French control over Louisiana also resulted from the French and Indian War as Spain took all territory west of the Mississippi River, including the Isle of New Orleans (as stipulated in the Treaty of Fontainebleau signed in 1763). Simultaneously, via the Treaty of Paris, France lost control of lands east of the Mississippi to the British. These secret negotiations were not known to the French living in the territory until October 1764, causing great uncertainty in the minds of those living along the Mississippi. Not only were they concerned about the future of their fur-trading ventures, but they feared for their security because they greatly distrusted the British. The Spanish finally arrived in New Orleans to administer their new territory two years later. However, it was not until 1769 that their complete administrative authority became established.

Louisiana's administration changed twice more, causing much concern for those residing along the Missouri and Mississippi Rivers. First, French power was restored under the leadership of Napoleon Bonaparte, forcing

Spain to cede Louisiana—including the Isle of New Orleans—back to France by a secret treaty in 1800. Other secret sessions took place, as well, but this time, it was the United States Senate's turn. Before the March 4, 1801 presidential inauguration of Thomas Jefferson, the Senate held a secret session on February 16, 1801, to authorize his desire to purchase the Isle of New Orleans. The Senate appropriated monies, crafted strategies, and planned negotiations. They authorized Robert R. Livingston and James Monroe, American foreign representatives, to negotiate the purchase of the Isle of New Orleans from France. While negotiations were underway on April 11, 1803, in Paris,[7] French foreign minister Charles Maurice de Talleyrand-Perigord limped into the conference room on his clubfoot and suddenly asked, "What would you give for the whole?" Astounded, Livingston cautiously asked what the boundaries of "the whole" might be. "Whatever it was we took from Spain," the French minister answered with a shrug. Talleyrand congratulated the Americans after the deal was struck and curtly exhorted them, "And I suppose you will make the most of it." Even Napoleon was pleased with the terms, "The sale assures forever the power of the United States, and I have given England a rival who, sooner or later, will humble her pride."

News of the $11.25 million Louisiana Purchase, as well as its actual administrative control, reached local citizens months later. The total purchase price, including interest and concessions involving the French and Indian War, became $27.27 million. Alexander Hamilton, American statesman and political rival of Jefferson, approved of the acquisition, but he thought seizing it would have been much cheaper. Even though the transaction did not have approval of the United States Congress, they ratified it by a twenty-four to seven vote on October 20, 1803.

# Chouteau Town

In the meantime, scattered settlements along the Mississippi had been underway since the early 1680s.[8] French fur traders and trappers, farmers, slaves, and priests came from Canada, New Orleans, and elsewhere to establish a community of settlements below the mouth of the Missouri on the Illinois side, collectively known as the American Bottoms. Soon, Father Gabriel Marest, along with a band of Kaskaski Indians, established the first mission on the Mississippi at the mouth of River des Peres. Initiated in 1700, it was disbanded by 1703. This community of Mississippi River residents, as well as those at Arkansas Post, established trade routes through the Great Lakes and the Gulf of Mexico to sell the highly valued beaver pelts used in the manufacture of fashionable men's hats in Europe.

In 1762, Pierre Laclede Liguest and his partner, Antoine Maxent, obtained an exclusive eight-year trading license from French Governor D'abadie, general of New Orleans, to trade with Native Americans in Missouri Country. Lured by the prospect of profits in the fur trade, Laclede and his flotilla navigated from New Orleans to Fort de Chartres near the American Bottoms in the fall of 1763. Here, they learned France had relinquished all of her claims east of the Mississippi to England. Laclede then decided to select a bluff on the west bank of the Mississippi for his post. Here, but not until late in 1764, several months after the founding of St. Louis, these French settlers learned of the secret French treaty ceding her claim to lands west of the Mississippi to Spain. St. Louis was now a French settlement in the Spanish District of Louisiana, also known as Upper Louisiana. French families by the name of Chouteau, Cardinal, Chartran, and Tayon joined Laclede and others to found St. Louis near the union of the Missouri and Mississippi Rivers. These same families would soon be trading at Charrette Creek.

While Laclede led in the construction of the trading post at St. Louis, a band of about 150 Missouri Indians, mostly women and children, offered to join the settlement. They assisted in digging the foundations for the major buildings, anticipating the future benefits of intermarriage and related interdependence.[9] Laclede accepted their short-term good-will, but he was disinterested in their long-term desires:

> You Missouris, you will not be eaten by eagles; but these men who have waged war against you for a long time past, who are in great numbers against you who are few, will kill your warriors, because they will offer resistance, and will make your women and children slaves.

Even so, each summer, Missouri women continued visiting what they called "Chouteau Town" to assist with construction. Smaller bands of Osage came more frequently to trade with their furs, while the Sac and Fox purportedly came with their maple sugar and pecans to barter.

At about this same time, events around Charrette Creek began unfolding. Squatters and fur traders supposedly first operated there when St. Louis was still in its earliest embryonic stages, perhaps even before. Once again, fur trading provided the primary motivation. Being located about sixty miles up the Missouri from St. Louis undoubtedly offered some competitive advantages for them. Why these squatters and fur traders chose the wilderness setting on Charrette Creek in comparison to other alternatives logically resided in local geographic features and ready access to furs. Desirable waterways and a Native American population willing to trade in furs were paramount considerations. Whatever the attractions, one may assume the options were carefully pondered before squatter and settlement activities proceeded at the westernmost frontier village of Upper Louisiana (Figure 2).

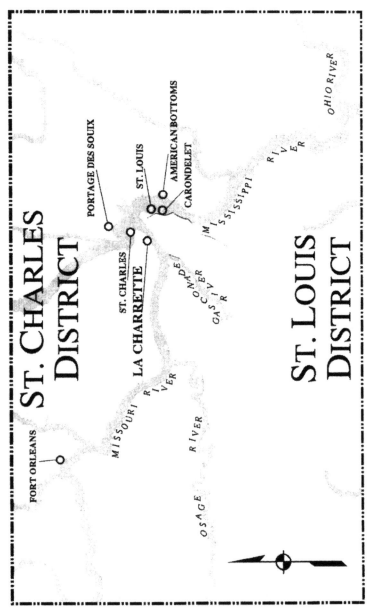

Figure 2. Upper Louisiana with La Charrette as its westernmost village, 1801–1808. Its two northernmost districts were west of the Mississippi River, separated by the Missouri.

For these and related reasons, the reader will be introduced to the surroundings of Charrette Creek before proceeding with settlement activities. Events preceding village founding in 1801 include the naming of Charrette Creek, fur-trading activities, and the adventures of early squatters. But of singular importance are those who lived there before, the Native Americans. Not only were they essential to trading in furs, but they were the wives and mothers of many casually referred to as Frenchmen or French-Canadians. While some served as expedition guides, others were helpful to the settlers. Without their contributions, La Charrette Village would have never existed. Portraying a clearer picture of these relationships will enhance our understanding of village founding.

# Chapter 2:

## The Geographic Landscape

Charrette Creek, a small, meandering stream, has been variously described. One author simply described it as a beautiful stream. Meriwether Lewis recorded it in practical terms: twenty yards wide at its mouth, sixty-eight miles from the Mississippi, and watered a tolerable country well-covered with timber, but of no great extent.

"The country along the banks of this river [referring to the Missouri River near Charrette Creek] surpasses in beauty and fertility the rest of the colony, possessing a happy climate which, without fail, produces everything in abundance," was the 1717 assessment of Sieur Hubert, a future St. Louis merchant.

An early German settler named Gottfried Duden compared the local river bottoms to his native Germany.[1]

> The forest presented a wilderness more beautiful than Germania, as described by Tacitus. Days of wandering in the Missouri River valley...one can travel hundreds of miles between gigantic tree trunks without a single ray of sunshine falling upon one's head.

This abundance of trees created a canopy of shadows and shading upon the waters of this creek of many moods. Its mood changes could swing from tranquil to rampant within hours, causing devastating floods altering the course of the stream and destroying whatever else lay in its path.

During the prehistoric past, the processes of continental glaciation during the Pleistocene epoch of some two million years ago greatly influenced the configuration of the Missouri River and its north bank tributaries. The melting of a succession of several great sheets of packed ice as recent as 400,000 years ago—some more than 5,000 feet thick—caused the resulting water to seek its escape over the existing landmass, beginning the processes of shaping these streambeds. These ice sheets progressed as far south as the prairies above Hopewell Hill, near the headwaters of Charrette Creek. The Missouri River starts at the meeting of the Jefferson, Madison, and Gallatin Rivers in the Rocky Mountains of Montana. On average, 64,000 cubic feet per second passed by the site once anchoring La Charrette Village. Sediments from its floodwaters produced deep, fertile bottomlands. The fine, windblown loess soil transformed onto the nearby uplands, forming a tier of uniquely sculptured hills resembling sandy dunes.

In 1687, Henri Joutel first recorded the word *Missouri* as we spell it today to denote the local Native Americans from which the river—and subsequently the state—acquired their name.[2] However, Louis Joliet first recorded the word with two alternate spellings in 1673. The precise meaning of the word *Missouri* still remains obscure. Houck reports two possible alternatives for the river, either "smoky water" or "drowning of people in a stream." Most accept the smoky or muddy water choice as being most descriptive.

Charrette Creek meanders twenty miles from the north, rising in the southwest part of Hickory Grove Township of Warren County. At least four tributaries and many springs feed the stream. The most prominent one is approximately seven miles upstream, locally dubbed as Engemann's Spring. Waters at the lower reaches of the stream are murky, gradually giving way to clear, spring-fed waters cascading over a streambed of rock and gravel. As is typical of its neighboring streams, including the Bear, Loutre, Tuque, Lost, and Little Lost, it has assumed different routes across its floodplain at various times, including its entry into the Missouri.

Around the turn of the nineteenth century, La Charrette Village would emerge on this floodplain at the joining of Charrette Creek and the Missouri River. Land surveys indicate, sometime between 1806 and 1817, the entry of Charrette Creek into the Missouri changed. The number of intervening changes that may have occurred is not known, but it now enters the Missouri a few miles farther east than before. In doing so, it joined with Tuque Creek southeast of Marthasville. This combined channel continues southeasterly, paralleling the Missouri River, until it joins with Lake Creek near Dutzow in Hancock Bottoms. Today, the waters of these three streams empty into the north bank of the Missouri immediately west of Washington Bridge, which supports Missouri State Highway 47.

# Place Name La Charrette: Chorette or Charette?

The abundance of aquatic and forest life, timber, and fertile land must have attracted Native Americans, French fur traders, and others to the stream soon to be allied with the village. What is known of its name origin? French settlers variously referred to it as Chorette's (Charette, Cherrette, Charet, Choritte) Creek or simply Charrette Creek, its present name.[3,4] The stream likely acquired its name from Joseph Chorette, a French fur trapper working there in 1795. Chorette and seven others accompanied Jean-Baptiste Trudeau (Truteau) from St. Louis since July 7, 1794, on an expedition entitled the Missouri Trading Company for the Discovery of the Nations of the Upper Missouri.[5] From the published translation of Trudeau's journal, the following unfolds:

> On the tenth of July, I unfortunately lost one of my Frenchmen, named Joseph Chorette, who was drowned, while bathing alone at dusk, in the Missouri.

Born in Montreal, Trudeau was a distant cousin of Don Zenon Trudeau, then-lieutenant governor of St. Louis, and the first, although intermittent, schoolmaster of St. Louis from 1774 to 1827. He continued chronicling events of the first of three expeditions for the newly formed Missouri Trading Company. They had been traveling with trade merchandise to acquire furs from the Mandan and other Indian nations in a large pirogue propelled by eight oars, but they were now returning to St. Louis a year later:

> Two little Indians aged about ten and twelve years old, came running to us to say, that they had seen a white man, who was washing his body on the bank of the Missouri, and while playing had wandered a little farther away from him; a few moments later, they looked towards the spot where he had been and had seen him no more; then going to the spot where he had gone into the water, they found his clothes, which were still there.
>
> Accompanied by the other Frenchmen and several Indians, I ran to the edge of the river; we found his clothes, just as these children had told us. The Indians jumped into the river just at this spot, also some distance below, to make a search, but without avail. For the last few days this man had taken the habit of going to bathe in the Missouri, in spite of all we could

say, telling him that the bed of the river being uneven, full of holes and precipices and he being unable to swim, he would undoubtedly be drowned; but incredulous to the last, he obstinately continued his bathing and unfortunately was drowned. I was most unhappy over this misfortune. During the twenty-six years and over, in which I have been making my trips, neither I, nor anyone of my companions, has met with a serious accident. I had him searched for, during several days, but without success.

Chorette, thirty-seven years old, was the son of Jean Chorette, who lived on the Mississippi below Carondelet in 1787, about the time Joseph entered the fur trade. By 1791, he and his family were listed as St. Louis residents. Less than a month before his death, Trudeau sent Chorette and "Quebec," a fellow expedition member, on a mission to recover stolen horses from the Arikara Indians, with whom they had been trading furs. Chorette was obviously a valued member of the expedition because of his recognized abilities to interact successfully with Native Americans, but he did not have a full understanding of the dangers associated with swimming near the stream that would soon acquire his name. Indeed, as many swimmers have since verified, the unseen currents and eddies swirling about within these streams could behave treacherously.

Trudeau's informative account further reveals his party remained in the area for several days in close association with the Native Americans, but the remains of Joseph Chorette were never recovered. As usual, Trudeau and his men traded with the local Native Americans and squatters in the area, as they worked from temporary trading posts or "forts" all along the Missouri. Trudeau's statement he was "accompanied by the other Frenchmen" to locate the remains of Chorette seems to confirm French squatters were there. Based upon this account, the earliest either of them would have traveled up the Missouri River was 1787 for Chorette and 1769 for Trudeau, thereby offering trade opportunities with local Native Americans and squatters well before 1795. However, Trudeau's bosses in St. Louis did not consider him an effective trader and soon replaced him with John MacKay to lead the next expedition later that same year.

Another viable name origin alternative frequently cited for the stream—and subsequently the village and later still the township—involves the unique, two-wheeled wooden cart the French settlers used. *La charette*—sometimes improperly called *la charrette*—in French becomes "the cart" when translated to English, thereby explaining the usage of the definite article *la* as part of the village name.

University of Missouri historians suggest the Chorette surname to be the most probable origin for the name of the stream. Chorette (or Chorette's Creek) was a place name commonly used in early local documents, including the 1805 District of St. Charles tax records designating both the creek and its associated bottomlands. Despite one account varying with the previous rendition, suggesting Chorette drowned among the Arikara nation farther upriver,[6] that account also inappropriately gave the age of Chorette as twenty-nine, not as thirty-seven.

The etymology from the surname Chorette to the feminine noun *charette* remains obscure. As early as 1797, the map of de Finiels[7] shows the stream as R(iver) a Choret. By the early 1800s, variants of La Charette were in common usage by Lewis and Clark and others. In 1997, I even chose that spelling for my "Schakes of La Charette" genealogy Web site. Of course, the stream and village name origins could represent independent events. The stream could originate from Joseph Chorette, and the village could derive from "the cart." Subsequent renditions shared today's common spelling of Charrette. The many alternate spellings of the two words scattered across numerous documents suggest as much. The stream was sometimes improperly designated as either Wood River or St. Johns Creek. A 1762 map of Louisiana—with scant details—offers tenuous identification of the stream as R(iver) al Ruey.[8] Native Americans and early squatters may even have referred to it as Wolf Creek.[9] Nearby to the east is Tuque (often Duke) Creek in Charrette Bottoms. It likely derived its name from the French hat or flat cap called a toque. The de Finiels map shows Tuque Creek entering the Missouri a short distance below Charrette Creek, before the two streams formed their present-day confluence.

Trudeau was not the only fur trader operating in the area by the late 1760s; however, his is the only surviving account giving evidence of trade at Charrette Creek between Native Americans and Frenchmen. His account supports the notion that Charrette Bottoms had a long-standing reputation as a suitable fur-trapping/fur-trading location. At least one experienced fur-trading squatter named Cardinal must have thought so.

# Chapter 3:

## Adventuresome Squatters of 1763

Jean-Marie Cardinal Sr. likely represents a typical squatter in Charrette Bottoms. He and his family had a long-established history of intrigue and adventure. His North American patriarch, Jacques Cardinal, was among the first to come down the Wisconsin River after its discovery and held the third license to go to Ottawa in 1683.[1] Since 1619, as early as the French record of trade extends on the St. Lawrence River, Cardinal family members are noted. Jacques was of French ancestry, but he was born in Lachine, Montreal, Quebec, Canada, to Simon-Jacques Cardinal (Cardinault) and Michelle Garnier (Grenier) in 1659. Jacques must have been eager to explore the continent because he appeared at the French Poste aux Arkansas (Arkansas Post), the oldest settlement in the Lower Mississippi, by 1685. An accomplished oarsmen and trapper, he traveled the Mississippi and its connecting waterways to include the early settlements associated with the American Bottoms in Illinois Country immediately south of present-day St. Louis. Arkansas Post, a stockade and trading post on the Arkansas River, was approximately fifty miles above the Mississippi. In 1687, while at Arkansas Post, Jacques encountered Joutel, Pierre, Jean-Baptiste Talon, and two others of the ragtag remnant of the party belonging to the most famous French explorer in the annals of the American frontier. Joutel and his party had been part of La Salle's ill-fated 1684 expedition.[2] Earlier, they had mistakenly sailed across the Gulf of Mexico, somehow overlooking the mouth of the Mississippi River, and had landed instead in Matagorda Bay, Texas. Now Joutel, La Salle's nephew, and his party of Frenchmen were on their way north in a forty-foot boat. Fifteen Native Americans accompanied them up the Mississippi as they headed to Fort St. Louis, on the Illinois River, seeking Canada. On August 30, 1687, they passed the mouth of the Missouri. By late November 1688, they finally arrived in France.[3]

By 1689, Jacques' branch of the Cardinal family resided in Illinois Country at Fort St. Louis. During the 1700s, other family members resided all along the Mississippi. Jean-Baptiste Cardinal farmed at St. Phillipe in the American Bottoms until 1764 when he joined Pierre Laclede Liguest; his stepson, Auguste Chouteau; Joseph Tayon Sr.; and others to establish St. Louis later that year. Jean-Baptiste Cardinal arrived on the second boat from the American Bottoms.

Jean-Marie Cardinal Sr., a restless man in the mold of his American patriarch, had other plans. Previously, circa 1754, he left the American Bottoms to establish the historic French settlement of Prairie du Chien (Plain of the Dog) near the Wisconsin River's mouth. He was then among the first permanent white settlers in what was the second-oldest settlement in today's Wisconsin. He later departed Prairie du Chien for Missouri to reside in both Charrette Bottoms and St. Louis.

Of Jean-Marie himself, our primary subject of this family, we know he was born around 1730. His likely parents were Pierre Cardinal and Marie-Catherine Matou dit Labrie, he the son of another Pierre Cardinal, one of four sons of Jacques.[1] Ironically, someone among the 1,600 British, Indian, and French-Canadians from Prairie du Chien was responsible for Jean-Marie's death in St. Louis on May 26, 1780, in a fur-trading dispute as part of the American Revolution. His death represented the first American killed in this surprise attack on St. Louis settlers, compelling them to form their first militia. He was buried in an unmarked grave on his property, where he was killed. Today, this site is associated with Cardinal Spring and Cardinal Avenue near Fairground Park. At the time of his death, he had resided in St. Louis for probably three years, where he had purchased property in 1777. Jean-Marie apparently accumulated considerable material wealth as a fur trader. His five half-Indian daughters all married into "good" families among the French in St. Louis. His sons-in-law possessed prominent surnames of the time, including Valle, Marechal, Vifarenne, Girardeau, and Desnoyer.

The Cardinal family genealogy compiled by Dr. Scanlan provides further details into Jean-Marie's adventuresome lifestyle. It indicates Jean-Marie had a mining lease along the west side of the Mississippi near the Tuque River by 1769. Some have placed Jean-Marie near present-day Dubuque, Iowa, but two revealing footnotes follow:[1]

> Some historians have located Tuque River, not on the Mississippi, but on the north side of the Missouri River, higher up than St. Charles, near the village of "Chorette," where Paul Cardinal did live in 1804.

The Cardinal estate was settled in 1799, and division made of the property held in common with his partner, one William "Lemme."

The references to Tuque River (Tuque Creek), Chorette (Charrette Creek), and William Lemme provide interesting leads in tracing Jean-Marie and his family to Charrette Bottoms. It will be later shown the Cardinal farm at La Charrette Village, which bordered Tuque Creek, was sold to William T. Lamme in 1806. In addition, Jean-Marie's sons, Paul and Jean-Marie Jr., did live at La Charrette Village. As indicated previously, Charrette Creek derived its name from Joseph Chorette. However, his partnership with William Lemme—perhaps W. T. Lamme of La Charrette Village—may have not been the case. Lamme, born in 1777, was a native Virginian; however, Lamme may have somehow purchased property from the Cardinal estate before his 1803 arrival in what was to become Warren County.

Jean-Marie's mining interest on Tuque Creek has not been revealed. However, Indian Phillips once acquired a shot pouch full of lead ore within an hour when at La Charrette. After heating it, he pounded it into bullets to support a moonlight hunting junket with his Boone family friends who had lived in the area since 1799. An 1837 *Missouri Gazetteer* account claimed deposits of iron ore in the streambed of Charrette Creek and elsewhere in Warren County. The submission of Cardinal's mining claim in 1769 could have been related to two local events in that year: the founding of St. Charles and the establishment of Spanish administrative control over the district. Cardinal, along with Nicholas Colas, his Osage (some claim Mandan) Indian slave, was perhaps working this claim before 1769, but formalities were postponed until authorities were in place to allow him to legally pursue his aspiration for mineral wealth, like the lead miners had on the Meramec River. In 1777, Auguste Chouteau and Juan Cardinal (Jean-Marie Cardinal Sr.) were both granted trading rights with the Osage.

In 1776, Jean-Marie and his unnamed, common-law, Panis Maha (Omaha) Indian wife were married in a unique ceremony in St. Louis. At the same time, their eight surviving children, born between 1755 and 1775, were baptized.[1] However, a Bordeau genealogy file at the St. Charles County Courthouse records Jean-Marie Cardinal marrying Angelique Brugiere on May 30, 1776. Most certainly, this is the same event, providing both the name of the bride/mother and the specific date of this dual marriage/baptism. What prompted the Cardinal family to depart Prairie du Chien? Were mining, fur trading, and formalizing the wedding and children's baptism the only motives? Had something else forced the Senior Cardinal and his young family to leave? The answer further supports his early squatter status in Charrette Bottoms preceding the establishment of Village Charrette.

In the winter of 1762–1763, Messieurs Cardinal and Tebeau participated in a clash between two British traders on the Wisconsin River at English Prairie (now Muscoda, Wisconsin, approximately twenty miles from Prairie du Chien). Abraham Lansing and his son James were British fur traders from Albany, New York, who had engaged Cardinal and Tebeau for their services. For years, in both Europe and America, the French grew to detest the British. However, for whatever reason, Cardinal and Tebeau killed the Lansings. The next spring, the local French and Native Americans of Prairie du Chien told Lansing's partner the two men left Prairie du Chien to avoid capture and punishment by the British. Both reportedly crossed to the western side of the Mississippi River.[1] Evidently, sufficiently strong motivations prompted Jean-Marie Cardinal Sr. and Jose Tebeau Sr. to seek new lives for themselves, which supports their arrival at Charrette Bottoms, perhaps later in 1763, a year before the founding of St. Louis. What better alternative might exist for escaping British authorities than relocating on a remote, western wilderness frontier outside British jurisdiction? Besides, turmoil was in the American Bottoms, allowing them to further disguise their identities as they passed by, at least until the air had cleared. Cardinal would "seek a location which in addition to supplying wood and water and tillable soil for his home would provide good opportunity for fishing and hunting," all attributes of Charrette Bottoms. Because both his common-law wife and Indian slave originated from farther up the Missouri, there is every reason to assume Cardinal had at least been informed of—if not acquainted with—Charrette Bottoms before he left the American Bottoms for Prairie du Chien.

As further collaborative evidence to support this move, Jose Tebeau Sr. (often corrupted as Tabo, Thebeau, Tabeaux, Tebaut, Thibaut, Thibault, or otherwise), "a Canadian born rower" also has his common-law marriage to a Pawnee Native American named Marianne (no surname listed) confirmed in St. Louis in 1776. By 1779, he appeared as a thirty-seven-year-old enlisted man in the Second Company of Captain Pure at San Luis de Illinueses. His name may also have appeared when recorded as Pedro Tibo in the first census of St. Charles in 1787. He likely greeted the joyous Lewis and Clark Expedition in St. Charles on September 21, 1806:

> We received invitations from Several of those gentlemen a Mr. Proulox, Taboe, Decett, Tice Dejonah & Quarie.[4]

The *Territorial Papers* later reported a pair of Ioway Indians on the Missouri killed an "old French trader" named Joseph Thibault in 1808. Additionally, Jean-Marie Cardinal Sr. family members allied with La Charrette Village continued interacting with his son, Jose Tebeau Jr., on the Santa Fe Trail and in the founding of Cote sans Dessein.

As early as 1763, other squatters, trappers, and drifters might also have found motivation to join Cardinal (and perhaps Tebeau) at Charrette Bottoms in Upper Louisiana. The most obvious motivation was the ongoing uneasiness of the French residing in the American Bottoms toward the English. One source indicates even the American Bottom missionaries, including their attendants, returned to France in 1763. Reports indicate most left the American Bottoms for western frontier locations, but the absence of land claim or other records precludes any conclusion as to where they relocated. Their status at Charrette Bottoms is far less assured than Cardinal.

As we shall subsequently see, the sons of Jean-Marie and Angelique Cardinal as well as Jose and Marianne Tebeau continued these adventuresome family lifestyles shortly before the founding of La Charrette Village. It is not known with certainty if these young men resided in Charrette Bottoms at the time of their overland adventures or not. Nonetheless, both Cardinal sons would reside at the village within a few years of crossing the Santa Fe Trail.

## Santa Fe Trail: Its First Map

The Cardinal and Tebeau sons next appeared as a small band of overland traders, applying their travel experiences gained from the fur-trading business to exploit the potential of trading in these and other products on new markets. Besides, St. Louis merchants were also anxious to develop new markets in the face of a sharp downturn in local peltry prices during the late 1790s.[5] Brothers Paul and Jean-Marie Cardinal Jr. were twenty-six and twenty-two years old, respectively, when they purportedly ventured into the far Southwest circa 1797. Jose Tebeau Jr., born sometime before 1776, was their partner and contemporary in age on this historic mission. According to his 1795 St. Charles marriage record, Jose Tebeau Jr. was the illegitimate son of Jose Sr. and Marie (Marianne). These young men all had Indian mothers. Two were

known to have married Native Americans, and the Cardinal sons even
had Nicholas Colas, their father's Indian slave, as their stepfather early
in life. Without a doubt, these circumstances provided many opportunities for them to learn—by way of Indian lore—about an old Indian trail
crossing the plains to the New Spain trade center at Santa Fe. After all,
for centuries, the Osage, Pawnee, Kansas, and Caddoes had traded over
an impressive network of trails leading into the Southwest.[6]

Legends about Santa Fe as a potential trade center started early in the
1600s and eventually spread all along the lower Missouri. Mysteries
about the town grew as "occasional strangers appearing from the east"
came to Santa Fe before returning to tell of their experiences. Like others before them, the Cardinal-Tebeau trio must have reasoned that not
all commerce had to be conducted on the highly conventional water
routes of the day. Later, their knowledge of this old trail would prove
useful to the leader of an American military expedition, but it would be
a source of much concern to New Spain authorities.

Captain Zebulon Pike was leading his expedition into the Southwest
when Spanish troops arrested him there early in 1807. These New Spain
officials became greatly disturbed upon discovering a small map Pike
carried. It outlined a route to Santa Fe that Pike had only partially traveled. How could Pike possibly have acquired knowledge of this alternate route? What did it portend? The Spanish thought it might be a
future military attack route. Since then, scholars like Jackson have concluded the small sketch Pike carried is the earliest known representation
of the Santa Fe Trail.[7, 8] As the eighteenth of twenty-one documents in
the Secretariat of Foreign Relations archives in Mexico City,[9] the map is
described as

> a small rough drawing, on a torn sheet, of lands situated
> between the Misuri and Santa Fe, with information, acquired
> in this villa, regarding its population, commerce, etc.

These papers were first housed in Chihuahua before Mexican
authorities presented the bundle of Pike's twenty-one papers to the
Texas-Louisiana Boundary Commission.

Next, it is explained that the key to the origin of Pike's alternate
route to Santa Fe may reside in the three names in the lower right-hand
corner of his little map. Here, immediately below the scale notation,
appear the names of Polite (Paul) Cardinal, Jno. (Jean) Marie Cardinal
(Jr.) and Jose Tebeau (Jr.). Figure 3 shows the name of Jose Tebeau Jr.
only faintly legible below the two Cardinals. As collaborative evidence,

Jackson indicates Jean-Marie Cardinal Jr. had married a Pawnee woman and noted the Santa Fe Trail on Pike's little map started at the Grand Pawnee village. The implications are obvious. Because Cardinal was a member of the Pawnee "family," not only could they help provision this trio of explorers with horses and other essentials for travel, but they could also have guided them over this trail that was familiar to them. Pike's complete map (not shown) provides dotted lines to indicate the trail with the best places to ford streams. The number of days it took to complete the journey indicated distance.[7,10] According to Wheat, "This little sketch-map is a precious memento..."[8]

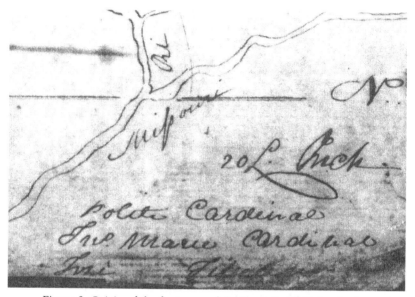

Figure 3. Origin of the first map of the Santa Fe Trail sketched at La Charrette Village.

Next, it was postulated Pike had obtained this little map from these three men shortly after departing on his expedition in 1806.[7] Because the map is drawn in Pike's hand, one or more of these three men presumably described it to him. As we will later see, Pike spent three days in July 1806 at La Charrette Village, allowing ample time for this exchange when the Cardinals were known to have lived there. Jackson thought ill-defined, illegal, and private trading ventures of 1797 coincided with the Cardinal-Tebeau trio crossing the trail. It is frequently reported that French traders were sufficiently prevalent in Santa Fe by 1795, resulting in New Spain's governor ordering their arrest and the confiscation of their goods.[11] Bolton, the first to describe the 10.25×6.50-inch map in 1908, indicated "no useful conclusions can be drawn from it."[12] Today, Library of Congress historians describe it as "the earliest representation of the Santa Fe Trail...[10] These revelations directly link the map acquired at La Charrette Village to two of its documented citizens, thereby establishing their rightful role in the early chapter of Santa Fe Trail history. The presence of Charette Mesa and Charette Lakes at the convergence of the various routes of the Santa Fe Trail approaching Santa Fe offer further support of their travels, although these place name origins are reported as "unknown."

This trio might also have been encouraged to explore this overland trade route by several other sources, including the Frenchman residing in New Spain named Vial. Pedro Vial claimed he had crossed the trail from Santa Fe and had traveled on the Missouri River perhaps as early as the mid-1770s. It is widely acknowledged Vial did indeed travel on the Missouri River; knew of the Osage, Kansas, Missouri, and many other Indian tribes; traveled to Illinois Country before 1792; arrived in St. Louis from Santa Fe on October 6, 1792.[13,14] In his diary in June of that year, Vial reported on his capture and protracted torture by Kansas Indians and indicates his party stopped frequently to hunt deer and bear on the Missouri as they approached St. Louis. News of his arrival in St. Louis "was widely circulated among the traders on both sides of the Mississippi." He then returned to Santa Fe and crossed the trail again in 1794. By 1799, Vial lived at Portage des Souix, just north of St. Charles (Figure 2). He then remained in Missouri for several years before returning to Santa Fe, where he died in 1814. Even before Vial, the Mallet brothers stayed nine months in Santa Fe after crossing portions of the trail in 1739 and 1740. Before them, the Missouri River explorer Etienne Bourgmond tried negotiating the trail with Native Americans sometime between 1712 and 1717, but he failed. Any number of these and similar events could account for the families of Paul, Jean, and Jose learning about the trail and arousing their interest beyond that provided by contacts with contemporary Native Americans on the Missouri. Regardless, Paul Cardinal, Jean-Marie Cardinal Jr., and Jose Tebeau Jr. share credit in providing the first cartographic documentation of this 800-mile international trade route, thereby helping establish new trade opportunities with the Spanish Southwest. Later, but before residing at Cote sans Dessein, Jose Tebeau Jr. became licensed to trade with the Pawnee Indians on the Platte River in Nebraska in 1807.

However, commercial trade over the newly mapped route would be slow to develop. Initial attempts at trade were not highly successful. In 1804, Jean-Baptiste La Lande was engaged to deliver goods to Santa Fe. However, he absconded with the proceeds. Auguste-Pierre Chouteau, second cousin to La Charrette Village landowner Don Carlos Tayon, traded over the route in 1817 with his partner, Jules de Mun.[15] All twenty-six of his men were jailed for forty-eight days while Chouteau and de Mun lost more than $30,000 in goods. Captain William Becknell of Franklin, Missouri, often cited as the Father of the Santa Fe Trail, would first fully capitalize upon the trade route.[16] Becknell, previously an ensign in James Callaway's Company (son of Flanders Callaway of La Charrette) and his party successfully negotiated the trail in 1821 with a train of pack mules loaded with trade goods. The first trade wagons departed Franklin for Santa Fe in 1822.

Later still, the route would serve forty-niners during the days of the gold rush, settlers seeking the Oregon Trail, and Mormons on their way to Salt Lake City. Eventually, modern railroads and highways would follow much of the old route. On February 9, 1880, the Atchison, Topeka, and Santa Fe Railroad arrived at Santa Fe, effectively spelling the end to wagon caravans crossing this historic overland trade route. However, long before then, Missouri's famous mules had distinguished themselves, the first of which jacks brought across this trail intimately connected to Mexico had sired.[17] As a result, Missouri became the nation's leading mule-producing state with 34,500 foaled in 1889 alone. By 1924, Boone and Callaway counties were leading the state in the sale of mules. Indeed, the spirit of exploration the Cardinal-Tebeau trio from La Charrette demonstrated contributed to the annals of history by documenting a unique route of commerce across the American West, while simultaneously continuing the adventuresome traditions of their families. For the Cardinal family, this tradition had extended across vast frontiers of North America since at least 1619.

# Chapter 4:

## Resident Native Americans

Obviously, the Cardinal family was not the first thought to be associated with Charrette Bottoms. They and the Tebeau family had successfully lived and intermarried with members of various Native American tribes for successive generations. Their ventures into trading of furs and other products—as well as those of others—promoted interdependency between Native Americans and them. They understood their role in joining with cultures as ancient as their own in which cultural learning was an acknowledged two-way street, much to the harmony of everyone. They—and others like them—became active participants in the continuing process of cultural assimilation soon to unfold at La Charrette Village. A general knowledge of Native American life on the Missouri River becomes essential to the understanding of these relationships. It was fundamental to the development of the village, the region, and the state. However, in all likelihood, neither the Native Americans nor the French-Canadians possessed much knowledge of their distant heritage.

## Native Americans on the Lower Missouri

We now know Native Americans resided in Montgomery County, Charrette Village's initial county, in Graham Cave State Park some 10,000 years ago when mastodon, mammoth, and prehistoric bison still roamed the region. Missouri University archaeologists recently unearthed a cluster of ten wooden huts south of Highway 94 in the river bottoms, eight miles east of Jefferson City, the state capital of Missouri. These 5,000- to 6,000-year-old village huts of the Early Archaic period were typically fifteen feet in diameter, were supported by ten-foot-long poles, and housed a community of 100 to 150 individuals. The Little Osage in Saline County still inhabited similar structures during the early 1800s.

Numerous Indian artifacts scattered across the hilly regions north of La Charrette Village and at least seven Indian mounds document the presence of Native Americans in Warren County. During the Late Archaic period (3000–1500 BC) in present-day Warren and St. Charles counties, the hub of the "Titterington Focus," whose members introduced a greater number and variety of tools to their society, including a highly effective spear thrower known as the atlatl, lived.

During the three Woodland geological periods (1500 BC–AD 900), local Native Americans traded across a vast region extending from the Gulf of Mexico to the Great Lakes and from the Rockies to the Appalachian Mountains. During these times, they also began placing greater emphasis upon the use of pottery and agriculture. People of Hopewellian origin influenced this culture sometime during the Middle Woodland period as they joined with the local residents. Others from the south and east emerging into the Early Mississippi period later joined the people of these merged cultures, resulting in still greater cultural amalgamation.

It is accepted that the Osage nation of Native Americans resided on the lower Missouri since before recorded history. However, during the squatter settlement era of whites, no single Native American tribal identity was affiliated with Charrette Bottoms. Nor did the immediate area serve as a tribal community lodge headquarters. Even so, as soon to be revealed, Native Americans of various affiliations lived in the area and freely interacted with the squatters and settlers living there. The first historical record of Osages appears on a 1673 map belonging to Marquette. By oral tradition, the origin of these Central Siouan people is claimed to have been east of the Mississippi in Virginia. They later retold of their coming down the Ohio River, taking their Dhegihan branch of the Siouan language with them.[1,2] Today, most— but not all—scholars agree their origins were in southwest Missouri in the tribal heartland of their nation in the Osage River basin.[3,4] By the time of European exploration and settlement, members of this linguistic family lived west of the Mississippi River between the Missouri and Arkansas rivers. Any mention of the Osages before 1700 refers to them as a single tribe, though not always functioning as one unit across most of the future state of Missouri. Starting in 1717, multiple tribes formed. The Grand Osage eventually became associated with the Osage River. The Little Osage became associated with the Missouri River. The Osage of the Oaks became associated with the Arkansas River, representing some of the first to attempt to trade at St. Louis.

They were variously described as an enterprising, intelligent, pugnacious, relatively sophisticated, and totally unprincipled people who frequently fought with their neighbors but sought amicable relations with the French and Spanish.

Missouri Indians were most prominent north of the Missouri River. They were part of the Chiwerean linguistic division of the Siouan language. They became neighbors and allies of the Osage with some overlap in tribal hunting grounds upon their arrival in Missouri from west of Lake Michigan during the 1670s.[5] They eventually occupied numerous villages from the mouth of the Missouri westward for several hundred miles. While at Fort Detroit, Bourgmond recorded the presence of Missouri Indians before visiting them in Missouri in 1712.

Because of white settlement activities in Illinois Country, members of the Sac (Sauk or Saukee) and Fox (Rennards) tribes of the Algonquin linguistic family from the upper Mississippi Valley were forced to cross the Mississippi. Upon arrival in Missouri with their superior weapons, they soon overwhelmed the Missouri Indians with repeated and ferocious raids. The Fox and Sac generally acquired their arms from the British while the Missouri and Osage Indians acquired their guns and ammunition from French and Spanish sources. The Missouri Indians were reduced to a weakened state by the 1760s. By 1792, Pedro Vial noted the Sac Indians had forced both Osage and Missouri Indians to abandon their villages on the Lower Missouri. By then, the region around Charrette Bottoms had become a no man's land, subject to chronic raids by slavers and war parties.[6] These circumstances, combined with a smallpox pandemic in 1781–1782, forced many Missouri Indians to join with the Osages by 1790. Others allied with tribes farther to the west, thus concluding their existence as a distinct Indian nation.

Conflicts over tribal hunting lands on both sides of the Missouri caused much unrest at the same time that Native American lifestyles became more dependent upon American trade. Protracted disputes over the lands surrounding Charrette Bottoms continued for years between the territorial governors and the Osage, Fox, and Sac tribes, even after the Sac and Fox had ceded these lands to the United States in 1804. Around the 1790s, remnants of other eastern tribes also appeared near Charrette Bottoms to include the Pottawatomis, Shawnee, and Kickapoo, who became active in fur-trading ventures and joined the Fox and Sac tribes in their dislike of the Osage and their adopted Missouri cousins. Thus, the identity of Native Americans around Charrette Bottoms during the interval under study represented something of an overlapping progression of all these amorphous bands, somewhat like a westward progression of falling dominoes. Jean-Baptiste Trudeau traded with them in 1795. However, by 1804, Lewis and Clark noted only a few detached bands of Kickapoos when they visited the village.

American authorities eventually removed the Osages and other Native Americans to reservations in present-day Oklahoma, Kansas, and Nebraska. Because the Osage, along with their Missouri cousins, were among the first historical tribes known to claim land, hunt, and trap in Charrette Bottoms as well as play such a prominent role throughout the region's fur-trading history, a glimpse into their lifestyle will be portrayed. With approximately 8,000 estimated souls, they represented the largest tribe in Missouri. However, in essentially all cases, their individual identities remain as nameless tribal members in this zone noted for its transitory tribal affiliations. Even the name of the Osage wife of the La Charrette Village syndic, Joseph Chartran, goes unrecorded.

## Osage Heritage and Lifestyle

The Osage, like most other tribes of the region, lived in multi-clan, riverine villages where they cultivated crops, hunted game, and gathered food from the forest. Cultural sharing and amalgamation between tribes was common, a process destined to continue at La Charrette. Preceding the tribal identity of the Osages, Native Americans inhabited the greater Mississippi-Missouri-Ohio River valleys and are known today as Temple Mound Builders.[7] The focal point of their society during the Early Mississippi period was located at Cahokia by the American Bottoms, south of present-day East St. Louis, Illinois. Their culture reached its apex circa AD 1200, serving as the basis for subsequent Native American lifestyles in the vast heartland of the Midwest. Those who became known as the Osage were clearly within this sphere of influence. Hunting techniques, the growing of corn, rites of passage, artistic styles, ceremonial life, and spiritual beliefs were all rooted in this prominent culture prior to the Osages of Missouri encountering recorded history.

Osage woodland culture emerged within a forest blessed in abundance. Serving as a classroom, the forest provided a virtual hands-on laboratory, challenging their creativity; providing food, clothing, and shelter; and simultaneously offering esthetic wonders to the eye. Each resource and living organism was scrutinized for its potential role in support of life. The unique characteristics of the wood, bark, nuts, pods, leaves, and sap from oak, cottonwood, hickory, black walnut, ash, and willow—among other varieties of timber and shrubs—were contemplated. During season, they enjoyed the blossoms and fruit of the dogwood, Osage orange, redbud, locust, chokecherry, and persimmon, each adding its contrast of beauty and fragrance to the forest floor. The contrasting colors of fall foliage often became stunning, contributing to the pleasures of Osage life in this engaging environment. Intermittent meadows and prairies, offering an abundance of grasses and legumes that provided life's essentials for many wild animals to be engaged in the hunt, were scattered within the forest. On a summer evening, the air filled with fireflies offering an illusion of electrical magic, rhythmically blinking on and off and offering amusement for the children. Compensations to these amenities included wood ticks, excessively troublesome gnats and mosquitoes, fearsome copperheads and rattlesnakes, bumblebees, aromatic skunks, poison oak, poison ivy, ragweed, a tempting raw persimmon (a strong astringent quality), or an Indian turnip (a pungent acid flavor) to the novice. Charrette Creek with its associated landmass embraced all of these attributes in a typical Midwestern climate, often simply described as changeable. Osage society not only derived its material resources from this environment, but its character as well. The forest was home to the Osages, and they would soon instruct others in their unique classroom.

Explorers approaching an Osage village would first glimpse long, rectangular houses coming into view. Theirs was largely a sedentary society. The houses Zebulon Pike encountered in 1806 had one or more fireplaces. A smoke hole in the ceiling accommodated each fireplace. Entrances were located on the eastern (long) side of these multifamily structures, reported to be as large as 40×100 feet. Storage pits were dug into the earthen floor to serve as cellars, aiding in food preservation.[3] These permanent, wooden lodges were tribal headquarters. The interior of a typical lodge is described, reflecting an air of cultural superiority common to the times:

> The walls are covered inside with reed mats and are hung here and there with arms and Implements of husbandry. Both ends are piled up with luggage and harness; there they keep bundles containing provisions of dried meat and most precious caskets of hardened bison-skin in which they keep with equal care, but separately, the ornaments of the warriors and garments worn by the Osage beauties, with cakes of red and

verdigris so necessary for the adornment of the Savages. Also at the end of the hut are hung the shield, the quiver and the favorite bow, the famous war mat of the brave, the trophy that contains his titles to glory.

Trappers and settlers were frequently invited into the lodge during an Osage feast by, "Come and eat." These hospitable Native Americans considered refusing such an invitation an insult. On such an occasion, the Native Americans served sweet corn boiled in buffalo grease, beans, pumpkin, and meats. The feasts often featured sausages of various game animals and were prepared from the small intestines of buffalo, deer, or other large game. Turned inside out, washed, and filled with strips of meat, the Native Americans cooked the sausage over coals and seasoned with rock salt and herbs. Little regularity of mealtime was apparent. When food was plentiful, they consumed three or four meals daily. They practiced fasting when the supplies were exhausted or the hunt was unsuccessful. They sometimes used wooden dishes and spoons as eating utensils. As the Native Americans became more dependent upon trade with Americans, they used knives and metal cooking utensils as well as guns, needles, traps, and fishhooks to make life easier. Conversely, the new commodity of liquor, "the root of all evil," greatly complicated life for many Native Americans.

Not only did they hunt and gather to acquire food, but they were also the region's first farmers. Food procurement emphasized hunting, agricultural production, and gathering...in that order of importance. April and August were exclusively devoted to planting and harvesting, respectively. Corn, beans, pumpkins, and squash were primary crops. Plums were also cultivated. The most fertile and tillable lands were sought for village garden plots. Burning of the forest was a planned activity to support hunting and farming and expedite overland travel.

A wide variety of foods was available. Gathering activities relied upon fruits, berries, tubers, "greens," and nuts when they were in season. Wild grapes, strawberries, plums, mulberries, papaws, sassafras, blackberries, walnuts, and hickory nuts represented only a portion of the forest abundance, then as now. Hunting and fishing offered additional variety. Animals living in streams like Charrette Creek included clams, carp, catfish, bass, sucker, sturgeon, and garfish shared with many beavers, muskrat, mink, and raccoons. On land were all sorts of game, including possum, foxes, wolves, deer, bear, elk, and bison. Flocks of partridges, quail, woodcock, pigeons, ringneck doves, and water fowl flew overhead. The crafty, difficult-to-stalk wild turkey would often form huge flocks, sometimes approaching 5,000 birds ranging together.

Osage time was reckoned from one full moon to the next. Their year started at the vernal equinox.[8] Days started at sunset. The first month (March) was designated as the bird or singing month because birds began pairing and singing. Flower month was next. The planting month followed. The salt month, when game gathered at the salt licks, was after that. Buffalo month represented the breeding season of this ever-increasingly important staple in Osage life. Corn month, indicating the earliest possible harvest of roasting ears, came next. Harvest was the seventh month. Months designated as bear, buck, freezing or snow, dead, and finally the thaw or rain month—each describing signifying events of nature—followed.

Men of the Osage tribe were frequently cited as tall, handsome, and robust. They were often credited as being six feet or more in height. Their dress consisted of moccasins, leggings protecting the legs and thighs, a breechcloth, as well as an overall or hunting shirt seamed up the side and slipped over the head. All was made of leather. They shaved their heads except for a center strip called the scalp lock. Women wore decorated moccasins and leggings with cloth garments wrapped about the waist and over the shoulder. Unmarried women braided their hair. Osage men and women also adorned themselves with elaborate tattoos and wore necklaces, armbands, bracelets, and finger rings. Whites often adapted many of these articles of clothing, even though the appearance of Osage women unimpressed some.[3] As part of a society in which cleanliness was difficult and women engaged in never-ending drudgery, they aged quickly. Nonetheless, one observer named Charles Joseph Latrobe summed up his unflattering bias of Osage women:

> As to their personal appearance, with very few exceptions I can only specify three degrees—horrible—more horrible—most horrible.

Physician Eldon Chuinard studied Indian medical practices at the time of the Lewis and Clark Expedition and concluded white men had great respect for their health practices.[9] He indicated Native Americans universally rendered equally good care in the treatment of fractures as whites. Likewise, they employed the old, reliable remedies of bleeding, purging, sweating, and vomiting in treatment of diseases. The value of heat, applying poultices, rest, and cleanliness was common knowledge among them. The pharmaceutical use of plants, based entirely upon empiricism, was crude, but extensive. As influenced by the type of plants available to them, it differed from tribe to tribe. Chuinard states:

> While ritual played an important part in Indian curing procedure, there was also extensive use of what has been called rational therapy. The Indians possessed a good degree of knowledge about basic physiological processes, such as sweating, constipation, emesis, menstruation, and parturition.

In addition to traveling great distances by canoe in the streams, tribes shared numerous forest trails. When departing the trading post in St. Louis, the trail to the Village of the Missouri was crossed by proceeding westward along the north bluffs at St. Charles across Charrette Creek, perhaps stopping by the little trading post there to trade before returning to their lodges. The trail continued along the north bank of the Missouri River to Cote san Dessien. From there on, it went to present-day Carroll County, where it joined other trails.

Runners conveying messages during war or peace also crossed these trails. War with other Indian nations is noted, including an aborted plan to exterminate the Osage nation in 1794, but their relationships with whites was typically more harmonious than that of most other tribes. The continuing process of diminished access to traditional hunting lands associated with white settlement activities caused so much strife for the Osage. Consequently, they also participated in raids and defended themselves, often taking the customary scalp of a settler. If a warrior proved himself unworthy in battle, he was stripped of his social status. In 1811, John Bradbury observed a former Little Osage warrior dressed as a squaw working among the women.[10] Upon inquiry, Bradbury was informed the warrior had demonstrated insufficient bravery in battle. Once this sentence was passed, the punishment continued for life to include ostracism and bachelorhood.

Osage ceremonial life was rich, structured, and complex, represented by many songs and dances, usually performed around the campfire. Customs and laws were passed from one generation to the next through a strict oral tradition. Among the more important of tribal events was the child-naming ceremony. Only the first three sons and daughters of an Osage family were named in these ceremonies; subsequent children were considered named if the first three of each sex had been properly named. Surnames were assumed the same as the clan name, largely derived from the interpretation of local floods intertwined with legends of the "Great Flood." The assigned ceremonial (given) name was chosen from a legendary sky or earth name event, each representing the concept of life before or after people descended to earth. Adopted and personal choice names were also used. In all cases, names were ceremonially bestowed to maintain tribal organization and prevent inter-clan marriages. Related families formed clans. Related clans formed subdivisions. Related subdivisions became divisions. The tribe then represented a union of numerous divisions. Kinship was the basic link in all social identities.

Only persons of high hereditary rank owned sacred items such as pipes and medicine bundles. Pipe smoking and the painting of one's skin with hematite were important ritual components of many ceremonies. Smoking of fired clay pipes, which predate historical records, offered a means for communication with the spirits. Days of singing, dancing, and feasting to aid in the hunt or support a peace treaty negotiation augmented the pipe dance. Wagering one's most valued belongings was another long-standing custom. It is said the Osage played for days at a time, losing all of their most precious possessions.

Plate 1. Charrette Indian artifacts from the author's boyhood collection.

Game hunting in the strongly paternal society was also a highly organized event. Not only did this subsistence activity provide food, it was also a means of attaining social stature within the community.

Women would accompany men on hunts, but they only participated in the support roles, including butchering, preparing hides, and other camp duties. Three hunting seasons prevailed: one in March for bear and beaver, another in May, and an extended hunt from September until December for deer. They later became more dependent upon buffalo as the tribe was pushed westward. Hunting tactics varied. They used ceremonial songs and ambush as traditional deer-hunting techniques; however, by 1800, deer were "run down" as mounted horseman chased them to exhaustion. Black bear was hunted with bow and arrow or speared while hibernating in caves. Using grease-soaked wooden torches providing lighting made this possible. The bow and arrow was everpresent and used in all hunts. Bows were about four feet long, while the arrow, approximately two feet in length, had a triangular flint or metal head stabilized with half-ribs of turkey wing feathers attached at the nook. Relative success of Osage hunts may be approximated from the 1809 report of William Clark. While in charge of Indian Affairs, he documented the following pelts obtained that year: 30,128 deer; 2,215 bear; 2,071 beaver; 1,415 raccoon; 338 otter; 260 muskrat; 43 wolves; 30 fox; and 1 wildcat. By this time, horses, metal traps, and guns were highly favored adjuncts, offering more efficient game procurement than traditional techniques.

Obviously, Native Americans contributed greatly to the development of North America throughout history. Not only did they socialize, intermarry, and work together with whites and Africans in the fur trade, but they also taught them how to function in the wilderness. They shared knowledge about native plant and animal life, guided explorers across the wilderness, shared pemmican as a survival food, and significantly influenced the naming of objects, events, and geographic locations. Over time, this sharing of cultural knowledge has been fully amalgamated into American society to include academic studies in Native American culture at major universities. A few missionaries working among the Osage first offered schooling to them in the early 1800s. By 1819, the United States Congress passed an annual appropriation of $10,000 to assist the missionary organizations in instructing Native American children in agriculture and teaching reading, writing, and arithmetic.[11] However, Latrine, who traveled the region in the early 1830s, considered the effort misdirected.[12] In his haughty manner, he records the "squaw is cajoled to send her son to school; but what is the consequence of all these well-meant attempts to civilize them?" Today, the answer resounds fully in the affirmative.

# A Famous La Charrette Indian and His Friend, Daniel Boone

Another Native American resident in Charrette Bottoms was the elusive and colorful Indian Phillips. Not a local resident by birth, he was a representative of the Native Americans recently displaced from east of the Mississippi. His presence at La Charrette Village spanned as much as forty years as a visitor, a famous trapper, hunter, hunting guide, and local resident. In fact, he lived to see the initiation of present-day Marthasville. By 1805, he and his Osage wife lived on United States Survey 975 near the mouth of Little Boeuf Creek in Franklin County, immediately across the Missouri from La Charrette. John Colter, his friend and America's first mountain man of the west, lived nearby. Some claim Phillips once lived even closer to La Charrette Village. Phillips was possibly of French-Indian heritage. Sibley described him as "pretty much of an Indian."[13] He was at least bilingual—or more so—as he is known to have interacted with French, German, English, and other Native Americans. People possessing these talents were in high demand by fur traders and explorers. Sometime in April 1816, La Charrette Village resident Daniel Boone hired Indian Phillips to assist him on his last extended hunt up the Missouri River. This hunting party also included Boone's black slave, Derry, as they traveled by canoe from La Charrette to Fort Osage. They stayed at the fort for two weeks before continuing upriver toward Fort Leavenworth, Kansas, and perhaps farther. While at Fort Osage, Indian Phillips was described on April 29, 1816, (probably by Indian agent and frontier leader George C. Sibley, later of St. Charles) as a noted woodsman who frequently went and lived among the Native Americans. Sibley also stated Phillips was lazy and indolent, "a dirty fellow—of no account & only fit for the woods as servant or campkeeper."

However, the relationship between Boone and Charles "Indian" Phillips was not of Missouri vintage. Phillips, a Shawnee, came to Missouri around 1780, which portends his arrival at Charrette Bottoms sometimes later, perhaps interacting with trappers and traders like Joseph Chorette, Jean-Baptiste Trudeau, the Cardinals, Tebeaus, and others first associated with Charrette Bottoms. However, the first reported encounter in Missouri with Phillips was at Rogerstown while Boone was trapping nearby on the Bourbeuse in 1800. The following passages chronicle the meeting of old friends on the Missouri River.[14]

When Boone removed to Missouri, a small village of Native Americans was across the river from St. Charles, where the western St. Louis suburb of Bridgeton now lies. There, he encountered many friends from his days as a captive, Delawares and Shawnees from the town of Chillicothe on the Little Miami who emigrated during the 1780s. The village included several former captives who had chosen to remain and had raised Indian families, like Joseph Jackson, a former salt maker; Charles "Indian" Phillips; and Jimmy Rogers, now the village chief. In the area surrounding Sainte Genevieve to the south, larger concentrations of "absentee" Shawnees lived. There appeared to be little difference between the village of Rogerstown and that of Charrette, where Boone spent most of his time after 1813. Farming people who loved horses and hunting settled both. The Rogerstown people were determined to get along with the Americans. They served as guides for local militia companies during the war. William Clark called them peaceable and well-disposed people, "of great service to our frontier settlements."

The dialogue continues, indicating Boone was a frequent visitor at the Shawnee village. In the years before giving up hunting entirely, he often joined his Indian friends for short hunts in the woods, according to members of Boone's family:

> The winter following the conclusion of the war in Missouri, Boone and Derry went trapping once again, accompanied this time by Indian Phillips, a Shawnee who lived with his Osage wife in Charrette, one of a number of mixed families there. 'All the grandchildren were afraid of him.' One of Nathan's daughters remembered, for there were rumors that he was a murderer, and he played up this sense of menace by adopting a ferocious demeanor. Nathan and Jamima opposed Boone's going out with Derry, but with Phillips along they worried all the more. He was 'pretty much a savage in feelings and appearance,' one man remembered, and thought Boone took him along only because 'his services, such as they were could be easily obtained.'

At the very least, Daniel Boone entrusted Charles "Indian" Phillips with his life. If need be, he was instructed to return his eighty-five-year-old mortal remains to La Charrette if Boone had died on the upriver trip during April 1816. Their days together as prisoners of the Shawnee in Ohio in 1778 had apparently formed a bond. "I am very sorry to say that I ever killed any for they have always been kinder to me than the whites" was how Boone expressed his sentiments regarding his life among the Native Americans.[14] Obviously, the friendship between Boone and Phillips was built on mutual respect. Once his captors, the Shawnee became his second family.

During the summer of 1819, R. W. Wells recalled engaging Indian Phillips for approximately three weeks to assist him with surveying a town site, "carrying the chain," at the mouth of the Osage River.[15] Wells thought Phillips lazy. He threatened his pay to keep him modestly productive. He sometimes faked a loud groan, claiming he was sick, but Wells knew he was "possuming." Phillips then commenced, threatening by telling of his killing a white man or two. At which Wells laughed in his face. Phillips worked on. Yet everyone, including Wells, acknowledged the exceptional hunting skills of Indian Phillips. When others could not even find any deer in the heat of summer, Phillips would bring them to camp. Some said, if there were no deer, Phillips would *make* them and kill them. What unique hunting technique Phillips employed remains a mystery, but his success was legendary. It was said, "He seemed to know the habits of the deer." A man of about five foot ten or eleven inches tall, not strong, Phillips had his reputations. Wells acknowledged the two parted as excellent friends.

Phillips was unlikely to share his hunting techniques with many, except for the likes of his confidants, Daniel Boone and John Colter. Nathan Boone, a quiet, nonimpulsive, truthful man like his father, described some of his father's hunting techniques to Lyman Draper in the fall of 1851.[16] Only a glimpse into the 294-page interview follows:

> My father would sometimes hunt all day for deer. He would not just watch the salt licks. He would start early in the morning, when the leaves were moistened with dew and thus caused no noise when walking, and deer were feeding. They are always on their feet feeding or walking about during the rising of the moon, to which hunters pay great respect.
>
> My father, Daniel Boone, practiced fire-hunting on the Yadkin River in North Carolina, but only in summers. At that time the deer would come to the river to avoid flies. There is also a tender moss in the shoaly parts of the river, which deer sought after, and they would go there also to drink. As the banks of the rivers were often skirted with thick cane, it was convenient to fire-hunt with canoes, though sometimes the hunters would wade in shallow streams and carry fire.

Nathan continued explaining his father did not use the fire-hunting technique in Missouri, but, apparently, from his vivid recalling of the skills the master hunter employed, astute powers of observation were required "to know the habits of the deer."

The Boone-Phillips relationship would soon end. By November 1817, Boone was on his last local hunting trip with grandson James Boone. They made camp overnight in the snow on the headwaters of Charrette Creek, where he became ill, initiating his decline in health. Daniel Boone died September 26, 1820, in Nathan Boone's magnificent limestone home near Defiance, even though obituary notices in the Franklin *Intelligencer* and the St. Louis *Enquirer,* among other sources, inappropriately cited "Charette Village" as his place of death. "I am going, my time has come" was his last utterance.[14] His funeral, too large to be held in the Callaway home at La Charrette Village, was instead held nearby in the barn of Flanders and Jamima Callaway. Burial was on a mound just north of La Charrette in Bryan Cemetery.

One can imagine a famous, but bereaved, Indian hunter standing in the barn, wishing the best "happy hunting" afterlife for his old friend.

Baptist minister James Craig spoke "pretty well" on behalf of Boone, according to grandson Abner Bryan. Another Boone relative, Jimmie Bryan, mounted on a horse proudly displaying an American flag, led the funeral procession from La Charrette Village. A large, granite headstone marks his gravesite, today known as Boone Monument. Boone's funeral became one of the last recorded events associated with La Charrette Village.

Within a year of Boone's death, on May 2, 1821, *The St. Charles Missourian* reported a "stray taken" by Joseph Teubeau in St. Charles Township. The stray was Charles Phillips. Was this the same Joseph Teubeau, also known as Jose Tebeau Jr., who supposedly crossed the Santa Fe Trail with Paul and Jean-Marie Cardinal Jr. in 1797? Did Jose arrest Charles "Indian" Phillips? Or does this become yet another irreconcilable village mystery? To date, these issues remain unresolved.

Within this isolated and culturally diverse setting, the village of La Charrette slowly emerged and prospered. Individuals like the Cardinals and the Tebeaus, Native Americans like Charles "Indian" Phillips, the Boone family and his friends, along with both Indian and black slaves all resided in the area before a village was established. Collectively, these early residents and their descendants participated in La Charrette Village life under the leadership of syndic Joseph Chartran. Not only did their collective influences remain in evidence throughout the lifetime of the village where they intertwined their lives, cultures, and, as often as not, gene pool, it initiated— later still—yet another westernmost frontier village farther upriver.

# Part Two:

## Frontier Village Life

"An outpost of seven poverty-stricken families existed at La Charrette, the advance guard of civilization."

Greely, *Explorers and Travelers* (1893)

# Chapter 5:

## The Village of La Charrette

### Village Folklore vs. Reality

It is implied La Charrette Village emerged through a combination of structured as well as unstructured and perhaps interrupted or seasonal ventures. Except for the status of Jean-Marie Cardinal Sr. residing there as a squatter, history suggests others, known only as "undocumented" individuals, wandered through the region. They, along with two other men named Choteau and Lozie, are reported in the earliest texts and local newspapers to have lived or worked at Charrette Creek. They reportedly lived in a village of only a few homes described as crude log cabins located at the mouth of Charrette Creek to support the harvest of furs and operation of sugar camps, both highly seasonal activities. They reportedly secured large, Spanish land grants, but the date of these events is unrecorded. An undated, unpublished German manuscript with the Missouri Western Historical Collection of Columbia offers another alternative. Authored by Reverend Daniel Irion, D.D., who was born in Marthasville, it relates a fanciful village history. It supports a founding date in 1763, but it has proven to be greatly flawed and of little or no historical value. There are various works of fiction published on Jean-Marie Cardinal Sr., Daniel Boone, and John Colter. The usual fables of heroes the likes of these accompany them.

Some reports state La Charrette Village was located on Tuque Creek, offering founding dates as early as 1762. Much uncertainty also surrounds the presence of forts constructed there, adding to the folklore surrounding village history. Most historians assert Missouri River floodwaters eventually consumed the village, but none offer a certain date of the event. Ambiguities and shortcomings such as these are predictable because there has never been a comprehensive rendering of the events associated with the village.

Settlers under either French or Spanish rule were supposedly required to seek permission from authorities to stake their land claims. However, many adventuresome trappers, squatters, and wanderers of this wide-open, fur-trading frontier era chose to conduct business on their own terms. Both French and Spanish authorities considered them "lawless." In 1683, La Salle wrote of two French traders living among Missouri Indians. By 1693, two other Frenchmen reportedly traded with the Osage Indians near Kaskaskia of the American Bottoms. As early as 1700, no fewer than a hundred trappers were noted to be living among the Indian tribes along the lower Missouri. Without religious restrictions, a tract of land five arpents wide as well as necessary tools, a barrel of corn, two piglets, two hens, and a cock was offered as inducement to each individual over twelve years of age to stake a claim for their first year in the Spanish wilderness. The intensity of early settlers creeping westward along the Missouri resulted in private land claims stretching inland 120 miles from St. Louis by 1800. While traveling down the Ohio River in 1801, Perrin Du Lac related encountering many settlers who had moved up to 600 miles to relocate.[1] One (unnamed) seventy-year-old flatboat proprietor, now married to his third wife, left his home in the Monongahela Mountains of Pennsylvania for St. Charles on the Missouri River, where one of his sons lived. Vague reference to settlement and trade activities such as these are prevalent enough around the time of La Charrette Village founding. Unfortunately, most cannot be validated further.

## Early Charrette Trade

Choteau and Lozie prove to be exceptions for Village Charrette. It is well-documented that half-brothers John-Pierre "Don Pedro" Chouteau Sr. and Don Renato Agustin Chouteau traveled the Missouri River as fur traders for months at a time to trade with the Osage Indians. Don Renato Agustin (most commonly Auguste) was a lieutenant in the first company of the San Luis de Ilinueses Militia under Captain Don Juan B. Martinez in 1780. John-Pierre became a lieutenant of the militia at Fort Osage in 1808. Auguste's last name is spelled both as Choteau and Chouteau in the official military record.[2] Thus, it may be concluded the Chouteau brothers are the same individuals referred to previously as Choteau who traded in furs at Charrette Creek.

Auguste Chouteau began trading furs with Native Americans as soon as he arrived in St. Louis, even before granted permission to do so.[3] The literature frequently reports the Spanish crown granted permission to both Auguste Chouteau and Juan Cardinal (Jean-Marie Cardinal Sr.) to trade with tribes on the "Misuri" in 1777. Chouteau traded with the Grand Osage tribe; Cardinal traded with the Little Osage. These formal trading concessions are among the first recorded on the Missouri. Those trading with the Little Osage measured their annual earnings in livres worth of deerskins: Picote de Belestre (3,100 livres), Luis Bissonette (2,200 livres), and Jean-Marie Cardinal Sr. (2,000 livres). Thus, in comparison to his contemporaries, Cardinal was a modest trader of furs. Because Chouteau and Cardinal were both granted authority to trade at the same time and on the same river system, these French-speaking traders certainly would have known one another.

Following Cardinal's 1780 death, August Chouteau seemingly positioned himself for trading in furs by providing trapping equipment and services to those in Charrette Bottoms as elsewhere on the Missouri. By 1794, he had "exclusive trading rights" with all Indian nations west of the Mississippi River.[3] As late as 1804, Nathan Boone, Isaac Van Bibber, and likely the trappers of Charrette Bottoms were still under contract with Chouteau using beaver traps carrying his identification marks.

Further, at least two La Charrette Village landholders, Joseph Chartran and Don Carlos Tayon, had other documented relationships conducive to establishing fur-trading activities with Auguste Chouteau when they lived either at St. Charles or later at La Charrette Village. Tayon, serving under Lieutenant Chouteau, was a sublieutenant in the 1780 Second Company out of St. Louis. Joseph Chartran served under them as an enlisted man. Other business and personal relationships between the Chouteaus and future La Charrette Village families also existed. Involving the founding of St. Louis in 1764, the Joseph M. Tayon Sr. family arrived on the first boat of thirty settlers from the American Bottoms with Auguste Chouteau. The Chartran family crossed the Mississippi later that same year. The Tayon family freely interacted with the more influential Chouteaus, for example, the July 23, 1783, marriage of twenty-four-year-old John-Pierre Chouteau Sr. to his first wife, Pelagie Kiersereau, a sixteen-year-old first cousin to Don Carlos Tayon.[4] These interfamily ties also included a 1799 land claim partnership between Pierre Chouteau and Don Carlos Tayon on the "River Renud."

Less is revealed of the local Charrette trapper named Lozie than the Chouteaus. However, he will also soon become identified with the village as Jean-Baptiste Luzon, a probable resident of Montreal as recent as 1791. Thus, both early historical accounts as well as village folklore support the notion the Chouteaus traded at Charrette Creek with members of their extended family and other long-standing acquaintances.

From what is known, the probable chronology of those trading in furs at Charrette Creek proceeds as follows: Jean-Baptiste Trudeau (1769–1795), Jean-Marie Cardinal Sr. (possibly earlier than 1777 to 1780), and Joseph Chorette (1787–1795). Auguste Chouteau possibly eclipsed this entire span of time into the early 1800s as well as any undocumented trappers like Indian Phillips. Secondary commercial activities to those trading in furs included mining, sugar camps, and, a bit upriver, salt works. The earliest structures erected probably represented some combination of squatter camps and a modest fur-trading post associated with Trudeau's activities as well as some means of docking boats at the river-creek interface.

## Uncertain Dates of Village Founding

A long-standing, perplexing question surrounds the founding date of La Charrette Village. Unfortunately, the earliest reports seemingly fail to distinguish between the presence of squatters and those wishing to establish a village with an eye toward permanency. 1876 authors simply state some French emigrants were the first settlers in what became Warren County.[5] They indicate a village was initiated at the mouth of Charrette Creek at a date so early that no records remain, a fort was constructed during the Indian War, and both the village and fort washed away many years ago. Another typically vague report follows:

> Charette-A village founded by French settlers, on the Missouri River, at the mouth of Charette Creek, not long after the establishment of Laclede's trading post at St. Louis. This was the first settlement of white men within the limits of what is now Warren County. The village existed for a number of years and a fort was constructed there for protection against the Indians. The encroachments of the Missouri River long since destroyed the site of this early town.[6]

One report offering a founding date of 1763 refers to Choteroau, Lozie, and Indian Phillips and gives village details that others frequently chronicled.[7] These authors further indicated early settlers often found the relics associated with the sugar camps of La Charrette villagers. One such camp remained in use into the early twentieth century by the

Schake family of the author. It was adjacent to the farm of widow St. Franceway near the corner of sections number 23, 24, 25, and 26 on the limestone bluffs north of Charrette Bottoms.

Based upon more recent published literature, La Charrette Village founding dates tend to cluster into two time frames: those claiming dates in the 1760s versus those of the late 1790s. One early settlement supporter claims "La Charrette was founded early in the Spanish regime (probably about 1766), and for many years maintained a precarious existence."[8]

Missouri historians allied with the later time frame place village founding either at 1796 or 1797.[9] One map gives a 1797 village founding date, establishing it as one of sixteen Missouri settlements by 1804. Those supportive of these later dates may have assumed the first documented settlers formed a village there before 1801. They sometimes assumed La Charrette Village was contemporary with the short-lived (or perhaps nonexistent) Fort San Juan del Misuri. Some indicate the fort was constructed at the village.[10] These authors could not have been referring to Callaway's Fort because it was not constructed until 1812. Additionally, some authors have wrongly claimed Marthasville was initiated to replace the lost village of La Charrette. Another source has proposed perhaps an even slightly later founding date:

> Fifty miles up the Missouri from St. Charles lay the tiny settlement of La Charrette, near present day Marthasville in Warren County, where several French families resided in the late 1790's.[11]

The primary reason for the literature's disparity on the founding date must reside in the definition of what constitutes "founding." Those supportive of late-1790 dates must have assumed the first documented settlers formed a village. On the other hand, those allied with 1760 dates obviously credited the first squatters, such as the Cardinal family, with establishing a village. However, there is no known evidence that either group initiated a village with permanency. Curiously, one source supportive of the 1796 founding date refers to it as La Charrette Village, but then states "the original French name of the settlement has disappeared."[2] From this rendition, one could conclude pre-1796 settlement activity is at least inferred, but its name had not survived. A poorly hand-drawn 1795 map of Soulard, published by Nasatir,[12] gives what appears as St. Feadiana (perhaps Feediann) for a north bank location at an appropriate distance above the village of St. Charles to be on

Charrette Creek. However, the second volume of Nasatir's book gives place names on the Missouri as of 1797, as recorded by Missouri River authority James MacKay, without mentioning any north bank settlement describing activity on Charrette Creek.

Acknowledging the above realities, one useful technique to resolve village founding issue may be to contrast the extremes. Certainly, more happenings in the area occurred than what came down to us as recorded fragments of local history. However, the big picture assessment suggests, if a village was established before 1800, Pedro Vial, Jean-Baptiste Trudeau, Perrin du Lac, John MacKay, the Chouteau brothers, or other early river travelers like Captain John Armstrong, Joseph Berger, Victor Collet, and Jacques d'Eglise would have almost certainly recorded it in some manner. On the other extreme, too many recorded happenings appear to be occurring around Charrette Bottoms before the late-1790s to deny fur traders and squatters were active in the area.[13]

Thus, in conclusion, the 1763 date offers what may be thought of as the first, perhaps tenuous, squatter activity in Charrette Bottoms. However, it is not settlement activity indicative of a village with permanency. Because the village syndic acquired his grant to initiate the village from Governor Trudeau in 1801, that founding date seems most assured.

Adding further potential confusion to local village history, a second Charrette community was initiated in 1900 (perhaps 1899). This one was spelled with only one "r," as was common for its namesake. Undaunted by the loss of the previous La Charrette Village, the citizens of Charrette Township were apparently discontent without an address they could designate as Charette. This modest settlement was located southeast of present-day Hopewell, approximately five miles upstream from the original village. By 1907, it was without a post office, thus concluding its short life. Consistent with village tradition, nothing remains of this second Charette Village of Warren County.

# Earliest Documented Settlers

The first fully documented settlers arriving at Charrette Creek under Spanish rule were not expected to pay for their land. The government considered the hardship, danger, and isolation associated with opening the Missouri frontier as enough compensation. However, settlers were expected to seek permission from the post commandant before settling.

Their land claims had to be confirmed in New Orleans to be deemed as complete. The French had a similar policy.

The policy sufficiently enticed approximately a dozen families to settle at Charrette before the founding of the village in 1801. They represented the first wave of pioneers of the great western expansion. Robert Ramsey settled in the hills north of Charrette Creek in 1798, but he was not part of the village settlement. Those arriving in 1799 and settling nearby the future village were Joshua Stockdale, Thomas Worthington, Abraham Darst, John Haun, and Francois Woods. William Hancock and his sons, Forest and Stephen, also settled nearby as future village neighbors that year. William was a salt maker in Kentucky, where he and Stephen fought against local Native Americans alongside Daniel Boone. Today, their farms are still known as Hancock Bottoms. James and David Bryan settled on Tuque Creek by 1800. It is not known when these early settlers began using the name Charrette to describe this frontier location. Most likely, they considered themselves residing in Charrette Bottoms—or perhaps on Chorette's Creek—because their farms, unlike those of the French, were rather widely dispersed across the countryside. A bit farther to the east on Femme Osage Creek, Morgan Daniel Boone initiated land grants for his family in the fall of 1798. He left three of his black slaves in charge to farm and build a double log or "dog-run" cabin before his extended family arrived. La Charrette villagers would soon join these families.

When the United States acquired Louisiana in 1803, policies soon changed. The United States did not actually purchase the land known as the Louisiana Territory. According to one legal interpretation:

> The land considered as property belonged to its original owners, the Indians, exclusive of a very small area belonging to farmers whose titles had been secured through the channels of the Spanish and French legal systems.[14]

Technically, Native American land ownership first needed to be extinguished before that land could be bought, sold, or granted. Thus, most of the first fully documented settlers to arrive in Charrette Bottoms were caught in a precarious position by settling under either Spanish or French law and later attempting to claim property titles under new American laws. Records soon-to-be revealed will indicate La Charrette Village land claims were not well-managed and most settlers experienced difficulties obtaining complete titles to their farms. Locally, the following factors came into play, resulting in many incomplete titles.

The initial step to adjoin the land claims involved the appointment of a surveyor general who was to obtain all documentation pertaining to each claim for review by the Board of Land Commissioners. Led by Antoine Soulard as surveyor general, this process was underway by November 1804. He soon learned all land documents administered under the Spanish regime had burned in New Orleans in either 1788 or 1794 or were sequestered by the Spanish. By September 1806, Silas Bent replaced Soulard and eventually recovered most of the stolen records— only to discover they were full of "erasures and apparent alterations." [15] Bent found fraud everywhere he looked. On March 2, 1805, a congressional act previously outlined new eligibility laws:

> Any person residing within the territory that had prior to October 1, 1800, obtained from either Spanish or French government any duly registered warrant and on that date had begun actual habitation and cultivation of said tract would have his claim confirmed.

While the October 1, 1800, date referred to either French or Spanish claims, similar requirements were also extended to Spanish claims before December 20, 1803. Finally, failure on the part of the claimant to deliver the proper documents and plats in writing to the recorder of land titles by March 1806 resulted in forfeiture of the claim.[15] Proving one's claim also required the claimant to establish suitable improvements and reside on the property for five years. The typical hearing before the land board reportedly required only about fifteen minutes. Did you clear land and plant crops? Did you build a house? Are you the agent of a land speculator? Have you witnesses? All importantly, did the Spanish governor in New Orleans sign your grant? These events and circumstances clarify the flurry of land claim submissions by La Charrette Village settlers around 1806...but mostly to no avail. Little did they know what might come about when they founded La Charrette Village a few years before. Most of the claims at La Charrette Village, as well as those of their neighbors, would not be granted because one or more of these stipulations were not met. Predictably, such decisions left settlers despondent, forcing them to relinquish their claim to these productive lands once credited as "never requiring fertilizer."[16]

# The Old Village Syndic from St. Charles

Authors frequently state French citizens from St. Charles settled La Charrette Village, even though only Don Carlos Tayon and Joseph Chartran are known to have resided there in the 1790s since departing St. Louis. Dating from 1769, the Missouri River village of St. Charles was approximately fifty miles east of Charrette Creek. Louis Blanchette, a Quebec native who served as its first commandant, founded the village. Don Carlos "Charles" Tayon, a hard-drinking (some accounts also include illiterate because he signed his name as Charletaijon) but zealous and brave army officer, was the second district commandant from 1793 to 1801. Don Santiago (more often John or James) MacKay was his successor.

By 1791, the somewhat triangular-shaped district to the west and north of the confluence of the Missouri and Mississippi Rivers was designated by the same name as the village of St. Charles. The District of St. Charles was the oldest and largest of five districts in Upper Louisiana, but it had the smallest population of approximately 400 Americans in 1804. All the territory north and west of the Missouri River was included—from Prairie du Chien, Wisconsin, to the Pacific Northwest. Undoubtedly, this was the largest district ever in existence in North America. However, the name of St. Charles evolved through a torturous process. First designated as the Village des Cotes (Village of the Hills), it was renamed San Carlos del Missouri, which then became the progenitor of the present-day city known as St. Charles. Thus was the process by which Charrette Creek, Charrette Bottoms, and eventually La Charrette Village became designated as part of the District of St. Charles of Upper Louisiana.

As a syndic without pay, Joseph Chartran led in the formal settlement of La Charrette Village in 1801. His village was limited in size (not subject to expansion) to only seven family homesteads clustered along the north bank of the Missouri River. In 1801, he received a grant for land at Charrette Creek from Lieutenant Governor Zenon Trudeau, authorizing him and his followers to join others already residing in Charrette Bottoms. Before Chartran established La Charrette Village there lived in St. Charles one Josef Chartran, his Osage wife, and their son. Most scholars consider Joseph and Josef as the same person. Chartran once claimed an inventory of 100 bushels of wheat, 150 bushels of corn, and 250 pounds of tobacco. While these events of history document village founding, land claims documents for each Charrette Village settler still needed to be recovered.

## Finding circa 1800 Land Claims

Collaborator Jerome Holtmeyer was confronted with a challenge. Where were the land claim documents for La Charrette Village farms? Local historians had long since discovered Warren County repositories did not hold these documents. Likewise, it was widely known Montgomery County, which previously contained Warren County within its bounds, had two early courthouse fires that destroyed many of its early documents. At this juncture, Holtmeyer reasoned, because the District of St. Charles was the earliest administrative home for the village, he would search the archives in St. Charles.

At the Linnemann Library in St. Charles, Missouri, microfilms of Upper Louisiana land claim records were recovered for village residents. Land claim data were gleaned from these documents plus the *American State Papers* and other resources.[13,17] A number of the farms indicate previous ownership, but those dates and related details are not presented here. The families chronicled subsequently generally represent those seeking to prove their land claims five years after settlement in 1801. However, within a relatively short span of time after seeking their claims, many of these French families sold their land claims to future Marthasville residents named Bryan and Callaway. These French families then reportedly moved upriver to participate in the settlement of Cote sans Dessein. Highlights of these land records and related information for the seven families representing La Charrette Village circa the Lewis and Clark visits in 1804 and 1806 are presented. The reader is directed to Appendix B for an explanation of the French term *arpent* as a unit of land measurement frequently encountered in these and other land records of this time.

## A French Village of Only Seven Families

### Joseph Chartran Family Farm

The syndic's family genealogy, found in the Bordeau file in the St. Charles County Courthouse, reports Chartrand/Chartran was born in

Kashaskia in 1742 and crossed to St. Louis in 1764 shortly after the arrival of Pierre Laclede Liguest. As such, the Chartrans are considered as one of the founding families of St. Louis. The Chartran family was originally from France. However, by 1668, they were in Montreal. During the 1760s, they lived first at Cahokia and then Kaskaskia, both designated as part of the American Bottoms. Joseph, like Jean-Marie Cardinal Sr., had fought in the English-Indian battle of 1780 in St. Louis and moved to St. Charles in the 1790s with his father, Amble Chartran. A probate court file indicates, after leaving La Charrette Village, he lived and farmed forty acres on Dardenne Island near St. Charles, where he died in 1837. Gabriel Marlow, a neighbor at La Charrette Village, verified the appraisal of his Dardenne Island property.

Many of the early 1800 records refer to Chartran as the "Ancient" or "Old" village syndic. He would have been approximately fifty-nine years old when he led in the establishment of La Charrette Village in 1801 and ninety-five at the time of his death. The name of his Osage wife has not been revealed. They had at least one son, Joseph Jr., and four or five unidentified orphan children in their La Charrette Village home. By November 1825, Joseph Jr. had married Francois Sabourin. What influence the orphans had on the land assigned to Chartran at Charrette, if any, is not known. However, a 1798 ordinance of Gayoso's provided fifty additional arpents of land for each child brought with each frontier family. However, typical of the legal confusion of these times, a new American law of 1805 limited each claim to 640 acres, or one section of land.

A survey dated February 1, 1805 supports his land claim of 998 arpents (849 acres) on Charrette Creek in the District of St. Charles. The testimony taken follows:

> On July 31, 1806 Charles Tayon, being duly sworn, testified that when he was commandant of St. Charles the claimant applied to him for permission to settle on vacant lands; that he then submitted the said application to Zenon Trudeau, Lieutenant Governor, who told him he might grant said permission; that the said claimant settled the said tract of land in the year 1801, and did, prior to and on the 20th day of December, 1803, actually inhabit and cultivate the same, and had then four or five orphan children, entirely destitute of the means of subsistence, and looking up to the claimant for the same.

August 7, 1807, John B. Leauzon, being duly sworn, says that he knows the land claimed by the said claimant situated at the village Charrette; that the same was settled by claimant in year 1801, and that he has continued to inhabit and cultivate the same ever since; that the said claimant has generally had four orphan children with him looking up to him for support, and whom he has treated with tenderness, and in every respect as a good father would treat his own; that, in 1803 he had three of them with him. On July 31, 1806 the Land Board granted said claimant two hundred arpents of land, but on December 1, 1809 it was the opinion of the full board that the claim ought not be granted.

The emphasis upon the December 20, 1803, date obviously refers to the newly imposed American law. Chartran's full claim was not granted, purportedly because he had been granted two previous concessions. Chartran attained the granted portion of his La Charrette farm, but he continued seeking a clear title on the remainder as late as June 1833. That year, John Mary (Jean-Marie) Cardinal Jr. testified in St. Charles he knew Chartran, he had settled at Chorette, he had an orchard, and he had cultivated his place for about a dozen years. Charles Reille confirmed Cardinal's testimony, but he thought Chartran had cultivated his land for fourteen years. These testimonies did not sway the land board.

During the time this claim was being administered, Joseph and his family hosted expedition leader Zebulon M. Pike in their home for two nights in July 1806. By 1811, Flanders Callaway, son-in-law of Daniel Boone, owned most of the Chartran farm located at the hub of the village. Daniel and Rebecca Boone frequently visited the Callaway home (see Figure 5). Following Rebecca's death in 1813, Boone stayed in a nearby cabin much of the time. Although logical, it is not known with certainty, as some have claimed, if he stayed in the old Chartran home or another cabin on the farm. Regardless, my maternal grandparents, Karl and Maria Rocklage, lived in the Chartran cabin after their 1887 marriage. Callaway's Fort was constructed nearby, probably early in 1812. None of these structures remain, although the Callaway home has been removed and preserved while the Chartran cabin perished before the Lewis and Clark Bicentennial Committee of Marthasville re-created it in 2004. It resides in nearby Marthasville Park.

Plate 2. The log home of Flanders Callaway. Callaway's Fort was nearby.

## Widow "Vieuve" St. Franceway Family Farm

According to land records, the farm of widow "Vieuve" St. Franceway had previous owners named Mr. Charee and, before then, Mr. Gachaues. The use of Vieuve as her given name may have been more descriptive than factual as *vieux* or *vieille* is the French word for old person or old lady. She was the wife of her deceased husband, Louis St. Franceway. Because the St. Franceway surname freely mutated between Francois and Francoise, even to La Blanc in both American and Canadian records, her family origins proved difficult to follow. She had one child. Her farm was located between the farms of Joseph Chartran and Jean-Baptiste Luzon. Her claim of 850 arpents of land situated on Charrette Creek in the District of St. Charles was presented to the land board as a notice to the recorder dated August 13, 1807. William Russell signed the survey, dated November 4, 1805:

> Joseph Chartran, the syndic of Charrette Village, sworn, says that while syndic of said village he gave permission to claimant to settle on the land claimed; that in pursuance of his permission claimant made a settlement on the land in the year 1800 and has actually inhabited and cultivated the same ever since; she had one child in 1803.

From the above entry, it may be determined that Vieuve's husband died before she settled at Village Charrette because Chartran states he gave her, Mrs. Franceway, permission to settle the property in 1800. Apparently, there were some discrepancies in the appropriate boundary dividing the Chartran, St. Franceway, and Luzon farms, as U.S. Surveys Number 748, 786, and 873 each address that issue. By August 28, 1815, Flanders Callaway also owned her farm.

## Jean-Baptiste Luzon Family Farm

In 1801, another village landholder, Jean-Baptiste Luzon (or Louison, Leauzon, or Leuzon) settled between Charrette Creek and the Missouri River. His August 7, 1807, land claim proceeds as follows:

> Luzon swore that he inhabited his claim five years ago; that he had a wife and child in 1803; he knew Chartran situated at Village Charrette; that the same was settled by claimant in the year 1801, and that he has continued to inhabit and cultivate the same ever since; that the said claimant has generally had four orphan children with them looking up to him for support, and whom he has treated with tenderness, and in every respect as a good father would treat his own; that in 1803 he had three of them with him.

A previously submitted sketch accompanying his land claim indicates that 950 arpents (808 acres) were granted to Luzon. The February 1806 submission included his house and the island created by a slough near the mouth of Charrette Creek when he claimed his family consisted of his wife and three children. The mouth of Charrette Creek shared riverbank frontage with the Chartran, St. Franceway, and Luzon farms, serving as the hub of La Charrette Village. Luzon's neighbors were widow St. Franceway and Jack Amos. An 1812 survey of John McKinney indicated Flanders Callaway now owned the Luzon property.

The possible connection between Jean-Baptiste Luzon and the previously mentioned trapper named Lozie or Lozio comes to light through genealogical research. According to members of the Lauzon Genealogy Association, the names Lozie, Lozio, and Lozo are all casual names derived from Leauzon or Lauzon, both pronounced as Lozo. According to the Web site of the descendants of Nicholas Froget dit Despati, Jean-Baptiste Lauzon married Marie-Louise Froget on October 4, 1773, in Notre Dame, Montreal, Canada. On September 27, 1791, Marie-Louise died in Montreal. Thus, Jean-Baptiste must have left Canada for La Charrette following the death of his first wife. However, he remarried before settling at La Charrette. No other details of his private life have surfaced to verify him further as the same individual living in Montreal.

Like the Chartran family, they had one child as well as several orphans living in their home.

## Jack Amos Farm

Mr. Jack Amos, rendered as Ameys in a February 24, 1805, land transaction of the Louisiana Territory, District of St. Charles, owned the most westerly farm within the village's confines. His only village neighbor, Jean B. Luzon, was to the immediate east. On the above date, Joseph Chartran states Jack Amos sold his farm to Thomas Palmer for seventy-five dollars. Palmer was granted all rights and interest to the land by virtue of improvements made by Amos prior to December 1803:

> Palmer on this day became entitled to any subsequent Acts of Congress that may entitle him to land by virtue of said improvement being situated and lying in the Charrotte Village on the Missouri River lying between and joining to what is called Jack Ameys improvement and Joseph Lavisey improvement-Jack Ameys improvement on the upper side and Laviseys improvement on the lower side. Given by me this day and date above written, his mark (signed) Joseph Shattrans [Chartran].

The reference regarding improvements on the "upper side" and "lower side" indicate those improvements were both upriver from the Amos home as well as downriver. What the implications were regarding the somewhat confusing entry about the Ameys and Lavisey improvements is not clear. Nothing more is revealed of the life or family of Jack Amos.

A subsequent land transaction for this same parcel of land reveals one of the last dated transactions for La Charrette Village. On page 123 in the book of land transactions, Louisiana Territory, District of St. Charles, is the entry: "Charrotte Village February 24th 1825..." This entry verifies the village survived into 1825, possibly longer.

Thomas Palmer, the previous owner of the Don Carlos Tayon farm, and Anthony C. Palmer, the first schoolteacher at La Charrette Village to be introduced later, were probably brothers, according to the Latter-day Saints ancestral file "F" of 1978. Both Palmers were born in Kentucky. Anthony was born circa 1780, and Thomas was born in 1785. Thomas reportedly died in Clinton, Missouri. Anthony married Hester Ayers, daughter of an early St. Charles District justice of the peace, Ebenezer Ayers.

## Charles Tayon Family Farm

The Charles Tayon of La Charrette refers either to "Charles" Don Carlos dit Michel Tayon, who lived in the village of St. Charles as commandant until 1801, or his son, Charles. To avoid possible confusion, the father will be designated as Don Carlos. Charles will be called as his son. These precautionary notes are offered about the Tayon family because no consistent distinction is made between "Charles the father" and "Charles the son" in many of the accounts. Two transactions document Don Carlos owned land at the village while Charles resided there. Supporting this notion, Nathan Boone considered Don Carlos an unpopular man because he did not settle his land grants. An 1805 "Quiet Claim Deed" indicates Don Carlos negotiated for land at La Charrette for "himself and his heirs," further suggesting his plan for his sons to reside there. His sons, Louis and Francis, both settled Charrette Bottom farms that shared western boundaries with the village. Regardless, both Don Carlos and Charles Tayon participated in village settlement activities.

Most other sources support the heritage of Don Carlos, according to descendant John O. Suttle of Lake Charles, Louisiana. Suttle gives Joseph Michel Tailion (Tayon) Sr. and Marie-Louis Basset as the parents of Don Carlos. Joseph Sr. was born in Canada circa 1715. Marie was born in St. Louis, Territory of Quebec, Canada, in 1717. Joseph Sr. and his family lived in the American Bottoms before participating in the founding of St. Louis. He was the first miller of the city, where he also served as a syndic. He was wounded in the 1780 attack on St. Louis. In 1799, he sold sixty arpents of land on the road to Carondelet to future St. Louis fur trader Manuel Lisa for fifty dollars.[18] Joseph Sr. died at the age of ninety-two in 1807. Don Carlos was born at Fort Chartres circa 1760 and married Cecilie Deschamps on November 8, 1780. At least nine children were born during their marriage, but it is not known how many survived into adulthood. One daughter, Cecile Reine, married Jean-Baptiste Roy on June 29, 1807, in St. Charles. Brother Louis married Maria-Louise Barada. Charles and siblings, Cecile and Francis, will all reappear in subsequent events upriver from La Charrette.

Neighbor Joseph Chartran was to the west of the Tayon farm. William T. Lamme resided to the east. The following two 1805 transactions among Larivery, Palmer, and Tayon are not explicit enough to fully clarify how Don Carlos acquired the farm, but some of the former St. Charles commandant's background and reputations may aid the reader in understanding the circumstances.

Like the family of Jean-Marie Cardinal Sr., the Tayon family participated in frontier life with commitment and zest. Don Carlos was second in command of a January 1781 expedition out of St. Louis comprised of sixty-six Spaniards and Frenchmen as well as sixty Native Americans as part of the American Revolutionary War.[19] They marched under orders of Don Francisco Cruzat, commander-in-chief of Illinois on behalf of Charles III, the invincible King of Spain, who declared war on King George III of Great Britain. Because the Mississippi was frozen, most of the 600-mile trip was overland through the snow and ice-laden forest among hostile Native Americans. They eventually arrived in the District of Michilimackinac. After a brief battle, they captured the little British fort of St. Joseph. They returned to St. Louis with the Union Jack. However, by then, Don Carlos ordered his troops to kill five Delaware Indians, earning him the dubious distinction as an "Indian Killer," a charge later dropped upon intervention by his father. He then attained the regular rank of sublieutenant. He was later embroiled in another dispute, this time as a legal witness. His deposition noted he was an Apostolic Roman Catholic and had been trading with the Osage Nation along with Don Benito Vasquez, Don Santiago Chovin, Josef Ortiz, and Luis Chevallier. A lengthy court inquiry involving stolen trade goods on the Arkansas River and some apparent Osage knavery followed. Following his commandant status at St. Charles, he visited the Spanish crown in 1801, seeking favors on behalf of his father and himself. The Spanish employed Don Carlos, but his eleven-dollar monthly salary had been withheld over the past year. While seeking to recover his back pay, King Carlos IV had him arrested and held for three years as an "impudent imposter." Following his return to the District of St. Charles and his land ventures at La Charrette Village, Don Carlos was elected on the first ballot as one of four St. Charles town trustees in 1818. However, his local reputations of being "perpetually strapped for cash" and a "land-grabbing rogue" seeking property on the grounds of "faulty titles" also spoke volumes. In 1802, his son Louis even sought to establish a land claim in Charrette Bottoms based upon "consideration of his father's services." Even his 1807 St. Charles home was purchased, not with money, but with a "500 lien, payable by skins." Local St. Charles historians also reported many other such dealings,[20] earning this natural-born leader the unofficial title of "The Fandango."

Thus, in addition to the two documents shown subsequently, a third document representing a third transaction has probably eluded discovery in clarifying his land dealings at La Charrette. The first document, transacted in the Louisiana Territory, District of St. Charles, involves Joseph Larivery and Thomas Palmer. Palmer is apparently compensating Larivery for improvements on his land claim made before December 1803. However, Larivery sold the farm to Don Carlos on August 8, 1805, as given below:

> Charrette Village, August 17th 1805. Received of Thomas Parmer fifty dollars for all my right title and interest to lands sold and delivered to him this day to do as he may think proper to do with hereafter in this country by virtue of an improvement made by me pryor to December eighteen hundred and three and headright that I may be entitled to acts of congress or any subsequent acts of congress that may entitle me to land by virtue of the said improvement as one of the inhabitants of the Country the said improvements being situated in the Charrette Village on the Missouri River in the District of St. Charles aforesaid lying between and joining of old Joseph Shartrans improvement (or improvements known by that name) and an improvement called Paller Cardinals, Shattrows improvement on the upper side and Cardinals improvement on the lower side of it—the said improvement— I say sold and delivered by me from my heirs—this day and date above written—his mark (signed) Joseph Lavisey.

Common to these times, notice the Chartran surname carries two different spellings within one document, rendered both as Shartrans and Shattrows. Likewise, it is thought Thomas Parmer should be rendered as Thomas Palmer based upon other evidence presented on the genealogy of this village family.

Ralph Gregory, local Marthasville historian, recently translated the second document, a so-called Quiet Claim Deed from its original French:

> This day, August eight one thousand eight hundred and five, appeared Joseph Larive, inhabitant of the District of St. Charles, and Pelagie Cotte, his wife, who by these presents to have effect from this moment, sell, cede, quit, forsake, abandon, now and forever, and promise, guarantee etc. all trouble in dowry, mortgage, debt and other impediments in general whatever to take up without exception. This to proceed according to the government to Mr. Charles Tayon, at this time has agreed to purchase for himself and his heirs a portion

of land at La Charette two arpents wide and forty arpents deep, the landholder at one side is Mr. Paul Cardinal and at the other side is Mr. Jh. Chartrant. The front faces the Missouri river. The rear is a series of indifferent hills. Without things held or reserved by the said sellers, the present sale was made on condition that the price and sum of forty legal silver dollars of the United States be paid. That Mr. Charles Tayon has now paid to Mr. Joseph Larive and Mrs. Pelagie Cotte, his wife, who acknowledge payment hereby and receipt for so much. Signed, sealed and delivered in prescences of Pr. Montardy James Morrison. His mark (signed) Joseph Larive, Her mark (signed) Pelagie Cotte.

Notice Paul Cardinal now resides on the farm of his brother because Jean-Marie Cardinal Jr. had recently departed for Prairie du Chien. The land-grabbing Tayon also attempted other local land claims. In 1802, Don Carlos Tayon submitted one claim for forty-three arpents adjoining La Charrette Village. Syndic Chartran apparently granted Don Carlos permission to settle the property, "provided so much [land] could be found vacant." During testimony on December 28, 1809, it was claimed Charles had resided on the property for seven years—not his father, Don Carlos—and its northern boundary interfered with the William Ramsey claim. In another claim of October 15, 1799, Peter (Pierre) Chouteau and assignee Don Carlos Tayon sought to claim 10,000 arpents of land on the River Renud without any restrictions included in the claim. Such circumstances and disputes, without a doubt, partially led to the land board rendering judgments against all of these claims. The reality that Charles Tayon, not his father, lived on and managed the Tayon family properties at La Charrette was sufficient reason for the land board to deny their claims. James Bryan, Rebecca Boone's brother, later acquired the Tayon La Charrette property. Immediately to the north of this farm, family member David Bryan established a half-acre cemetery on a small knoll overlooking the river bottoms. This later became the "first" resting place for Daniel and Rebecca Boone.

## William T. Lamme-Jean M. Cardinal Jr. Family Farm

The Lamme family eventually owned the two most easterly farms in the village. Their family history, captured in 1876, reveals considerable detail about their lives at La Charrette:[5]

William T. and James Lamme were sons of Robert Lamme, of Bourbon Co., Ky. William T. settled in (now) Warren Co. in 1803. William was a 1st Lieutenant in Nathan Boone's company of Rangers, and was afterwards Major of a regiment. He married Frances Callaway, daughter of Flanders Callaway, and granddaughter of Daniel Boone, by whom he had ten children—Serena, Zarina, Hulda, Cornelia, Missouri, Josephine, Jackson, Leonidas, Achiles, and Napoleon B. Mr. Lamme had a good education, was a fine businessman, and left his family in good circumstances at his death. Zarina Lamme married Willis Bryan, a son of David Bryan, who was the first settler within the present limits of Warren County [sic]. Hulda married John Byran, called "Long Jack," on account of his extraordinary height, who was also a son of David Bryan. Missouri married Jesse Caton. Josephine married Campbell Marshall. All of the above are dead except Hulda, who lives with her son, John C., who is Recorder of Franklin county, and a prominent influential citizen. Achilles Lamme lives in Montana, where he carries on an extensive mercantile business. Napoleon B. lives in California. Serena married Lewis Howell.

In 1821, Lamme also started a tobacco company in Old Franklin, where its production and processing became a major frontier industry, even though he continued paying property taxes at La Charrette as late as 1830. The Chartran, Lamme, and Tayon families were apparently some of the few villagers to continue residing in the region beyond the War of 1812, even though the 1877 *Historical Atlas of Warren County* inappropriately acknowledged the Lamme family as W. T. "Samme."

The Lamme farm, purchased from Jean M. Cardinal Jr., was located between the Tayon farm and the one Joseph Arnow owned. The following entry was transcribed from somewhat-illegible land commissioner notes of the 1806 survey claim:

Wm. T. Lamme assynee Jean-Marie Cardinal claiming plat in the 2(?) Section of the 4th Act of Congress of the 2(?) of March, 1805, 950 arpens of land situate[d] on the River Tuque, promise (?) a certificate of a permission to settle from Charles Tayon, Commandant to the said Jean M. Cardinal dated Feb. 18, 1806, and certificate of survey of said land dated 15th of Feb. 1806, in deed of transfer of the improvements of said land executed by (?) Jean M. Cardinal to the above claimant dated 4th Feb. 1806 and acknowledged before Provenchure (?) of District [of] St. Charles.

The identity of the farm with River Tuque (Tuque Creek) is appropriate as the stream channel was in that location in 1806. Since then, as previously explained, the stream channel has changed considerably. This farm, like all the others, was fronted on the Missouri River. Because no purchase price is mentioned in the above deed of transfer, Lamme may have only negotiated the claim rights from Cardinal. This assumption is further supported by the fact, on June 1, 1811, Lamme applied for a land claim under the name of Cardinal. Like other La Charrette villagers, William T. Lamme apparently preferred hunting, trapping, and exploring to that of farming, as he and Nathan Boone hunted and trapped on the Grand River early in the spring of 1802. We will subsequently encounter both of these gentlemen as they further establish themselves as leaders in this frontier community.

Jean-Marie Cardinal Jr. was reportedly a strong supporter of the United States during the War 1812, no doubt influenced by the reality of his father's death at the hands of the British in 1780. Sometime after his father's death, he returned his mother to Prairie du Chien, where she remarried for a third time to Jo Crelie. Five children were born to Jean-Marie Jr. and Isabel "Elizabeth" Antayat-Peltier. They were baptized in Prairie du Chien between 1808 and 1827 after departing La Charrette Village. He may have married more than once, as the 1806 land transaction with William T. Lamme gives his wife as Maria Jeanne while records in the St. Charles Library record his March 14, 1799, marriage to Jeanne Blin. Captain Thomas G. Anderson reported Cardinal wrote a letter in 1814 on behalf of Prairie du Chien Indian leader Jeune Homme, seeking help from the United States military. Cardinal's concerns seemed well-placed. His mother, stepfather Nicholas Colas, and wife were all Native Americans. Jean-Marie Cardinal Jr., like his father, went by the familiar name of Juan. Paul (Polite, Paller or Pullit) Cardinal was born in 1775. He was a brother of Jean M. Cardinal Jr. and lived at La Charrette Village. Their mother, Angelique Brugiere Cardinal, eventually returned to St. Charles, where she was buried on May 2, 1830, at around ninety-one years of age. Her son, Jean-Marie Jr., may have accompanied her return to Missouri, as he provided testimony on behalf of Joseph Chartran Sr. when he attempted reestablishing an old Charrette land claim in June 1833. The details of events returning Paul and Jean-Marie Cardinal Jr. to Charrette Bottoms after residing in St. Louis for a few years before their father's 1780 death remain obscure.

W. T. Lamme also purchased his other farm in 1806 from Joseph Arnow as presented below.

## Joseph Arnow Farm

Joseph Arnow (Arnois or sometimes Arnoux) owned the village farm farthest to the east. The following document was obtained from St. Charles land commissioner notes of 1806:

> Wm. T. Lamme assignee of Joseph Arnow claims 950 arpens of land situated in the Village of Charrot produces his notice to the Recorder dated Aug. 1, 1807 and a deed of conveyance from said Arnow to claimant dated Feb. 4 1806. Joseph Chartrans being also sworn (?) that he Chartran as Syndic of the village of Charrot gave permission to said Arnow to settle 5 years ago in (?) of orders received of Charles Tayon, Commandant to that effect.

No additional information has come to light on Joseph Arnow. Unlike most villagers, Lamme continued owning both the Arnow and the Cardinal farms for many years. Most of the early village residents apparently sold theirs and moved elsewhere within a few years after their defective land claims. One estimate indicated that ninety-five percent of all such claims during these times were denied because of "incomplete" titles. Other possible reasons for discontent within French communities of this era were centered on new American policies regarding slaveholding, Indian removal practices, and the emphasis upon speaking English. The disregard by Americans for French customs also fostered a sense of intolerance, even though none of these circumstances have been identified with La Charrette. Whatever the reasons for departing, one may correctly assume defective land claims were not part of their original plans when they initiated the settlement.

William T. and Frances Lamme, including some of their children and grandchildren, are buried on the Lamme farm presently owned by family member Margy Miles. Born in 1777, William T. Lamme lived to be sixty-three. Frances lived to be seventy-one.

"They are buried here in my yard...I live on their old farm and have always taken care of the little family cemetery and hope to get people involved to restore it," Margy explained to me.

# Boone, His Family, and Village Neighbors

Rebecca and Daniel Boone figure as prominently in frontier lore as any American pioneers. As such, they were easily the most famous family associated with the village. They arrived with their family and friends in the same time frame as the earliest documented Charrette Bottom settlers. Kentuckians like Boone were mostly of English extraction with roots in the American colonies. Most were more interested in farming than their French and Native American predecessors, but they still treasured the nomadic urge to hunt and explore the wilderness. Colonel Boone traveled overland with his livestock from Kentucky in September 1799 to the District of St. Charles. Boone crossed his livestock at the mouth of the Missouri River in October, while Rebecca and others continued upriver on a barge to Femme Osage where they settled. Some of those traveling with Boone also became associated with La Charrette Village. Among them were Isaac Van Bibber Jr.; George Buchanan; an Irishman, William Hays; his son, William Hays Jr.; and Flanders Callaway. Boone and his friends also brought some of the first black slaves to the region.

In addition to Boone being a legend in his own time, his family exerted a significant, and extended, influence upon the village and community. Not only did the Boones frequently visit family at La Charrette Village, but Daniel eventually lived there, as did one of their daughters, a granddaughter, and numerous great-grandchildren. This influential four-generation presence at La Charrette starts with Rebecca and Daniel and proceeds via daughter Jamima, who married landholder Flanders Callaway. In 1803, their daughter Frances married William T. Lamme, another village landholder. In turn, their ten children all lived at the village in their youth. The presence of the Bryan family of Rebecca's was of near-equal influence upon the local community because they also owned village property and continued intermarrying among their old friends for several generations. After the 1813 death of Rebecca, while living with the Flanders Callaway family, Daniel Boone became most strongly associated with the village. In June 1820, prominent Boston artist Chester Harding renders Boone's most famous portrait at La Charrette.

Like his father-in-law, Flanders Callaway was a product of the frontier. He was born into a family of five brothers in 1752 in Bedford County, Virginia, to James and Sarah Callaway. "He lived his life facing westward."[21] He followed Boone and thirty others into Kentucky over the Wilderness Road to Boonesborough one year after its founding.

Here, he participated in the construction of the new settlement, acquired 400 acres of land on Otter Creek, and aided in the legendary rescue of the Boone and Bryan girls from the Shawnee Indians. The exploits of this handsome frontiersman were not unnoticed. In 1777, he and fifteen-year-old Jamima Boone were married in Boonesborough by Justice Richard Callaway, Flander's favorite uncle. Having visited Upper Louisiana several times since 1795 on extended hunts with Boone family members, Flanders decided to move westward once again with his young family in 1799. By then, he had accumulated considerable wealth from the sale of five parcels of property between 1785 and 1798 before granting 800 arpents of land by Zenon Trudeau at Femme Osage, where they first settled. Between 1811 and 1815, he acquired the La Charrette Village farms of Chartran, Franceway, and Luzon.

Others soon associated with the village were Gabriel Marlow (or Morlowe, Morlot), who purchased his farm with permission from syndic Joseph Chartran in 1802. He sold it to John Busby a year later. The land claim of Marlows states his farm "nearly adjoining Charrette Village" was not a part of the village, reflecting the notion the village was not subject to expansion. Pierre Blanchette, a former St. Charles village resident, acquired a Spanish land grant in 1801 adjacent to La Charrette Village. However, he was likewise not a village resident. He and his twin brother Louis were born in 1759 to Angelique, a Picque Pawnee Indian woman, and Louis Blanchette, the French-Canadian founder of the village St. Charles.

Those even more loosely identified with La Charrette Village included Pierre Burdeaux, his wife, and four children who owned land on Charrette Creek in 1801. James Meek, Adam McCord, John McKinney, and Moses Russell each arrived in the area around 1803. McCord and McKinney were land-trading surveyors who surveyed much of Charrette Township. McKinney reportedly married a Hispanic woman, certainly one of the first of her descent to reside in La Charrette Township. Elijah Bryan recalled yet another La Charrette family when interviewed in 1884.[22] He states John Manley (Manial) and his Osage wife lived there with four or five of their children among ten or twelve other families in the area. Other contemporary neighbors included John-Baptiste Lamarch, John Marlow, Emillian Yosty, Francois Janis, Dabney Burnett, William Ramsey, and David Kincaid. David and Isbel Rogers, his second wife, moved to the forks of Charrette Creek in the spring of 1804 from Femme Osage with their eight children. Their land claim of 1809 was also denied.

Thus, the aggregate heritage of the greater village community around the time of the Lewis and Clark visits spanned three continents as Native Americans, Africans, and Europeans representing the ethnic diversity described earlier by historian John Mack Faragher. French, English, and Indian dialects were spoken as they mingled about in their daily routines, intermarried, and reared their families. This dual process of settlement and amalgamation of cultures allowed this rich, multiethnic society to emerge and become one of the enduring legacies of the village...in a word, Americanization.[23]

These frontier settlers also worked together to develop an infrastructure to serve their collective needs. Their needs were many. Numerous problems and concerns needed to be addressed. What could be done to obtain better prices for the products offered in traded? How could they best protect themselves from Indian raids? How were their children to be educated? What other community needs should be discussed with the syndic and the governor? What were those new taxes being used for? When would they get a post office? The seven village families and their neighbors would address these and other ekistical topics as they attempted to further develop their village community. Immediate needs of great importance to them centered on security, trade, and education.

# Chapter 6:

## Forts and a Trading Post

As suggested previously, many texts are replete with errors regarding the location of two or more forts at Village Charrette. Callaway's Fort was intimately associated with the village, presumably its only fort. Some historians have also associated Fort San Juan del Misuri with the village. Neither fort existed when the Lewis and Clark Expedition stopped there for overnight visits in 1804 and 1806. Likewise, some have claimed a trading post was a part of the village landscape. These topics of long historical standing will be assessed.

## Callaway's Fort

Nathan Boone's company of the 1st U.S. Missouri Mounted Rangers erected Callaway's Fort at La Charrette Village. Shortly before March 1812, Boone's Rangers fortified the village by erecting a frontier fort, perhaps in the form of a blockhouse.[1] Major John Gibson of the regular army relates the following to Dr. Lyman Draper in 1868 about the Rangers:

> In 1811, Nathan Boone raised a company of Rangers for 12 months...We went into building forts in different places to keep the Indians from murdering our helpless women and children. We built Fort Howard, 17 miles from St. Charles...then we came to Pinkney, then we built a fort at Charrette Village; then came Louter Island and built Fort Clemson; then up to Cote sans Dessein, built a fort there...

Some authors have correctly questioned the sequence of these events and whether Major Gibson recalled Nathan or Daniel Morgan Boone some fifty years after they occurred, but they acknowledge the primary facts as correct. The plan of construction for these "family" forts varied from only a palisade surrounding an existing house to more substantial structures, like the one Nathan Boone and his men previously constructed under the direction of General William Clark at Fort Osage in 1808. Clark's two-story military blockhouses were of horizontal log construction. Typically about eighteen feet by eighteen feet below and twenty feet by twenty feet above, they were set off with a wooden shingle roof. The lower level was as a trading post for the Native Americans. The upper level was fitted with loopholes for musketry when under siege. An eleven-foot-high palisade protected the perimeter. Perhaps the best available description of Callaway's Fort is what Reverend Peck recorded when visiting La Charrette on December 18, 1818.[2] He described the fort as "a cluster of cabins" and indicated Daniel Boone lived in one of them as "part of a range of cabins." The first phrase seems to suggest a "family" fort with a palisade surrounding a few structures near the Callaway home. The second phrase is strongly reminiscent of the stream bank layout of Village Charrette itself, as portrayed in Zebulon Pike's sketch of 1806.

# Fort San Juan del Misuri

During the 1760s, the Spanish were previously apprehensive about pending English invasions in Upper Louisiana. For this reason, discussions were underway about the construction of forts. Spanish captain general and Louisiana governor, Antonio de Ulloa, instructed his captain, Don Francisco Rui, to search for suitable locations on the Missouri River to construct fortifications as early as 1767. Rui had his engineers draw up plans for several forts. Two were at the mouth of the Missouri, among others unspecified. Added to these political perspectives was the concern of settlers who had experienced many frightening encounters with Native Americans. The same was true of the new trading companies being formed. All demanded greater protection from Native Americans by the authorities. Subsequently, after Ulloa and Rui had disruptive disputes, lieutenant of the militia, Don Antonio Gautier, was ordered to establish Fort San Juan del Misuri somewhere on the Missouri River above St. Charles as an outpost of Fort San Carlos del Misuri. Several historians have either assumed Fort San Juan del Misuri was constructed very close to or contemporary with La Charrette Village or perhaps near the mouth of St. Johns Creek in Franklin County circa 1793.[3] The earliest known presence of Gautier in St.

Charles was 1796. Nonetheless, the difficulty with these assumptions is that no collaborative evidence has ever surfaced to substantiate the existence of the fort that is consistent with La Charrette Village residents being incapable of recalling Fort San Juan del Misuri when Lewis and Clark inquired of its whereabouts in 1804.

*The Spanish Regime in Missouri* states Gautier's appointment, as well as his orders, came from El Baron de Carondelet, Knight of the Order of San Juan, Brigadier...and so forth...and so forth...and as follows:

> Ascertaining it to be of advantage to the service of His Majesty to form a company of militia at San Carlos del Misouri, and being cognizant likewise of the benefits of appointing to the position of lieutenant of the said company a person of recognized courage, energy, and good conduct, which necessary qualifications are combined in Don Antonio Guatier, I have exercised the authority conferred upon me by the King, and appoint and designate him as lieutenant of the aforesaid company. I therefore direct the officers, sergeants, corporals, and enlisted men to obey him in all the orders which he shall give them orally or in writing touching the royal service, observing and causing to be observed all the honors and privileges which belong and pertain to him without any omission. These presents given at Nueva Orleans, July 9, 1793.

> Your lordship appoints as lieutenant of the militia company at San Carlos del Misoury Don Antonio Gautier

As a footnote to this entry, it is indicated Zenon Trudeau granted Gautier 4,000 arpents of land on Clearwater swamp in 1796 while he commanded Fort San Juan del Misuri. This statement offers the strongest inference regarding the existence of the fort, but nothing regarding its location.

Without providing further documentation on the presence of the fort, the 1988 *Encyclopedia of Historic Forts* offers the following:

> Established about 1796 by the Spanish, it was located on the north side of the Missouri River at old La Charrette ("the cart") between today's Marthasville and Dutzow in Warren County. A small fortification built of logs, it was probably erected by a small party of militia commanded by Lieutenant

Antoine Gautier and intended to safeguard new settlers in the area. The sites of both the town and the fort had disappeared entirely by 1804, washed away by floodwaters.

Assuming this account accurate, one must also accept the presence of a village contemporary with Fort San Juan del Misuri in 1796 and floodwaters destroyed both by 1804. Neither seems plausible from what else is known of events at La Charrette Village. However, there are unpublished claims the fort was constructed across the river from La Charrette at the mouth of St. Johns (San Juan) Creek. If the fort was ever constructed, it was very short-lived and escaped any subsequent documentation. Until more definitive information is revealed, I am inclined to question the existence of Fort San Juan del Misuri with lack of sufficient funding by the Spanish crown being offered as the most plausible reason for its unrealized presence.

## Charrette Trading Post

From the journal entry of William Clark it is revealed:

[I]mmediately below the mouth of this creek five French families reside, who subsist by hunting and a partial trade w[h]ich they mantain with a few detached Kickapoos who hunt in the neighborhood.[4]

Meriwether Lewis noted the villagers had "...settled at this place to be content to hunt and trade with Indians..."[5] Thus, La Charrette Village evidently possessed a modest trading post of some sort long before the construction of Callaway's Fort, probably well before 1800. It is recognized Jean-Baptiste Trudeau operated many small trading posts along the Missouri as early as 1769, which would explain his presence at La Charrette in 1795. Trade would have been conducted with either local Native Americans, those crossing the trail to the Village of the Missouri, and those rowing along the Missouri to include members of the Osage, Missouri, Pottawatomis, Kickapoo, Sac, and Fox tribes.[6]

# Chapter 7:

## Charrette's First School and Post Office

By 1807, the citizens of La Charrette Village in the District of St. Charles, Territory of Louisiana, recognized the need to educate their children so they may become literate. Apparently, the need for literacy could not have been greater. Reports indicate that backwardness among the French inhabitants of colonial Spanish Louisiana in the 1790s was almost unbelievable. The culture was lost. Language was corrupt. Agriculture had degenerated, and people had sunk into an abysmal stupidity.[1] Almost certainly, reading was not a prominent leisure activity and understandably so. The first book and stationary house did not appear in St. Louis until 1820. By way of comparison, Philadelphians boasted of twenty-three printing establishments and seven newspapers by 1776, more than anyplace else in North America. As late as 1840, fifteen percent of white Missourians over twenty years of age could not read or write. It is doubtful if many of the French-Indians at La Charrette could read or write because most signed their names by recording their mark, an "X." The most literate members of society were lawyers, preachers, teachers, and doctors, with whom frontiersmen seldom interacted. Appropriately, the new school was to emphasize reading, writing, and arithmetic, even though lay teachers of the times were noted more for imparting discipline than knowledge.

## School Number 1

A community meeting was called at the residence of one of the concerned parents in order to found a school. The decision to establish La Charrette Village School was formalized on February 25, 1807, as outlined in the following articles of agreement as rendered from the original document discovered in St. Charles County Courthouse records by collaborator Jerome Holtmeyer:

> Articles of agreement made and concluded on by and between the undersigned subscribers of the one part and Anthony C. Palmer of the other part both of the District of St. Charles the territory of Louisiana of the United States, witnesseth that whereas the under named persons having immediate occasion of a Schoolmaster and looking on Anthony Palmer as a person qualified so as to take our children for the space of one year from his commencement that is to say five days in a week Saturday to himself and for his management. We and each of us do promise to pay the sum of nine dollars in trade per scholar that is to say in beef, pork, or beef cattle, or young cattle or country linen at the market place of this country and to be delivered at this village of Charrette or elsewhere as we may hereafter agree and also to furnish with sufficient school house together with firewood when needful, and also to find him in boarding, lodging and washing (such as they have for themselves and families) and said Palmer to go about in his turn to different employees-and also the said Palmer on his part doth promise and agree to teach the above term of twelve months (if the said employers shall continue him so long) the said employers (if it be a majority of them) may discontinue him at the end of any quarter on their paying him for the time he has teach, and the said Palmer doth promise to teach reading, writing, and arithmetic in their true and perfect rules, and also to give due to the school and to take every method in his power for the advantage of the employers in learning their children and also should any disagreement take place between the said employers at least a majority of them, and then the said Palmer then in that case they cannot agree themselves on it—the same to be settled by two disinterested persons chosen by each person, and if they two cannot agree the said parties to agree on a third person or to be chosen by the men then chosen, and they three then chosen shall settle the same, if any there should be-to which performance we of each party do jointly and severally do bind ourselves in the penalty of five hundred dollars to be paid by the party failing to the party complying. The school to commence on the first Monday of February next as witness am besides this 23rd day of January,

1807. William Ramsey 3 scholars, John Marlow ½, Flanders Callaway 3, David Kincaid 2, John Haun 2, Francis Woods ½, David Bryan 4, Dabney Burnet 1. I do assign the within article unto William McConnell it being for value received of him as witness my hand and seal this 25th of February, 1807. (Signed by Dabney Burnett, Anthony C. Parmer)

Presumably, fifteen full-time and two part-time students arrived to study reading, writing, and arithmetic with their "true and perfect rules" sometime Monday morning on February 2, 1807, at the first school in what was to become Warren County. However, children of the original French families of La Charrette Village would not attend. Only close village neighbors, such as John Marlow, David Kincaid, and John Haun as well as new village landholders Bryan and Callaway, enrolled their children.

The model outlined in the contract, whereby parents paid nine dollars directly to the teacher for each student taught, was an old model of European origin referred to as a "subscription" school. Teachers of these times reportedly used the New Testament as their textbook for spelling and reading, although, in St. Louis, Jean-Baptiste Trudeau used an Old French prayer book. Trudeau was also an author.[2] His *Ballad of the Year of the Surprise*, a narrative about the 1780 attack upon St. Louis resulting in the death of Jean-Marie Cardinal Sr., may also have found its way into his classroom. Where Palmer obtained his training to serve as the Village Charrette teacher is not revealed, but *Bryan's History of Pioneer Families of Missouri* indicates "he had a good education" and "was an excellent scribe." His one-room village schoolhouse was most likely furnished with split log benches and little else, just like other schools of the times. Likewise, these frontier schools allegedly remained in session for only three to four winter months out of the year.

How long Anthony C. Palmer taught under this contract is not known. However, by 1813, he was a private in the Missouri Rangers led by Captain James Callaway to protect the frontier while his presumed brother, Thomas Palmer, still owned land at the village as late as February 24, 1825. By 1817, Anthony was the sheriff of the District. On May 9, 1834, both John Davis and Mafes Bigaloe swore to the St. Charles County land clerk they recognized the signature of one Anthony C. Palmer on a deed implying his departure from La Charrette by that time, probably before.

At the time of its founding, La Charrette Village School Number 1 was the westernmost school in existence on the Missouri frontier. It followed the one founded by Jean-Baptiste Trudeau in St. Louis by twenty-three years. School Number 1 must also have served the community as a meeting place for many years because it appears in the 1877 *Historical Atlas of Warren County* north of the village on property previously owned by Jean-Marie Cardinal Jr. and, later, W. T. Lamme. Its location was very close to today's Katy Trail and Boone Monument Cemetery, immediately east of Marthasville. Also shown in the atlas is School Number 2, the Missouri Evangelical College, indicating a continued emphasis upon education by the citizens of Charrette Township. Neither structure has survived to the present. By 1899, there were fifty-eight public schools, sixty-five teachers, and 3,292 students among the 9,900 citizens of Warren County. These statistics emphasize how rapidly the Warren County student population had grown over the previous ninety-two years, functioning with a whopping fifty-one to one student-teacher ratio, not fifteen to one as in the beginning.

## "Charette's" Unrealized Post Office

Mail delivery was first established for the village of St. Charles in 1805, sixteen years after the founding of the United States Postal Service. Postage ranged from twenty-five to seventy-five cents a letter, although most were sent as "collect on delivery." Among the first surviving letters to originate at La Charrette were those of Captain Zebulon Pike in 1806. Both his letters were carried downriver by military dispatch to Fort Bellefontaine, much as a private La Charrette citizen might have solicited someone to carry letters to St. Charles to be mailed. For years, letters from New England to the frontier took as many as three months in route, an obviously slow system. Even so, some at La Charrette were eager to utilize their newly acquired reading and writing skills by participating in the services offered by the United States Postal Service.

Rufus Easton, a delegate to the United States Congress, announced on December 7, 1816, a new post route from St. Charles via St. Johns (directly across the Missouri River from La Charrette where villagers could now transacted their mail) and on to Fort Cooper in Boons Lick was to be established on the Missouri River. Service was to be provided on a weekly schedule. The St. Louis newspapers continued reporting the mails were irregular and often not received. Typical delays were about three to four weeks duration, as indicated by the filed complaints. By now, efforts were underway to connect roads with ferries to further improve delivery of the mails. However, Connecticut traveling preacher Timothy Flint had his doubts, as he went upriver in 1816, noting, "the people here are not yet a reading people."[3]

Nonetheless, applications to acquire territorial post offices both at Marthasville and "Charette" were submitted in 1818.[4] Hugh McDermid was listed as the "Charette" postmaster. By 1819, the United States Postmaster General advertised new routes from St. Charles to elsewhere on the Missouri to assure "speedy" mail delivery without mention of La Charrette Village, Marthasville, or St. Johns. At this time, the Missouri Territory boasted fifteen different weekly or alternate weekly mail routes. Robert Schultz, who researched the United States Postal archives on early Missouri post offices, indicates "Charette" was not shown to be in existence after 1825 and questions if it was ever actually implemented. He postulates nearby Marthasville might have served the village community instead. His suspicion seems well-founded based upon an October 17, 1819 announcement in the *Missouri Gazette:*

> The post-office located at the house of Isaac Murphy, esq. St. Johns, has been discontinued—our subscribers in that quarter are informed that their paper will be sent to Marthasville, until directed otherwise.

Previously, on July 15, 1819, the United States Postal Department announced the October closing of St. Johns post office. Apparently, if Hugh McDermid ever served as the "Charette" postmaster, it was for a very short interval. Most likely, the March 18, 1818, approval of the post office request for nearby Marthasville denied La Charrette its opportunity to acquire postal service. This turn of events may have signaled one of many, eventually leading to the diminished stature of the old village.

Timothy Flint seems to have accurately predicted what the United States Postal Service discovered after operating the post office at St. Johns for two years. According to probate court files, only $31.33 worth of business was conducted there from April 1, 1817, to July 1, 1819. Meanwhile, Marthasville continued prospering with three weekly mail deliveries into the 1840s, probably delivered overland on post route Number 299, not via the river where Isaac Murphy served both as the St. Johns-La Charrette ferrymaster since at least 1815 and the postmaster for St. Johns. Both these enterprises were operated out of the Murphy home at the mouth of St. Johns Creek.

Murphy died in April 1821, leaving his wife, Nancy, with three small children. Nancy continued running the ferry. In 1823, she married Armstrong Hart. They continued the ferry business, at least until his death in 1830. Murphy was a prominent community citizen, an ensign in the 5th Regiment of the territorial militia in the War of 1812 and a clerk of the northern circuit court for a few months during 1819. He was a deputy clerk for the Circuit Court of St. Louis in 1814 when he was assigned the estate of his friend and fellow comrade-in-arms, "Mountain Man" John Colter, who died at La Charrette in 1812.

# Chapter 8:

## Frontier Hostilities

Across a broad spectrum of both society and time, many frontier people exhibited a genuine respect for Native Americans, as illustrated by their intermarriages and other relationships such as trading. In his advanced years, La Charrette Village resident Daniel Boone claimed Native Americans always had been kinder to him than whites. Conversely, there is every reason to believe the Native Americans were not only candid, but also sincere in offering to establish amicable relations with whites. The Native American women who volunteered their services to assist in the construction of St. Louis in 1764 stand out among the many gestures of this nature. Likewise, the compelling journal entries of Jean-Baptiste Trudeau reveal the zeal and commitment expressed by Native Americans, adults, and children alike in order to aid in the rescue of Joseph Chorette when he drowned at Charrette Creek in 1795. Later, Osage Chief Sans Oreille was quoted as saying he was "please[d] with the proof of General Clark's good will toward him, that he was the friend of the Americans."[1] This aside, there were also opportunities for conflict. Perhaps the most deeply held sentiment fostering strife was expressed by a Frenchman named De la Vente. As a trader on the Lower Mississippi, he expressed conventional wisdom for future generations of settlers by saying in 1704, "God wishes that they yield their place to new peoples."[2] Many other interrelated factors were involved in these relationships of acceptance in the face of unreasoned hostilities soon after Village Charrette was founded.

## Distrust, Fear, and International Politics

For years, the British sought dominance in the fur-trading industry. They intimidated the French living along the Mississippi, as elsewhere, and struggled with Napoleonic France since 1793 over trade and related issues. At various times, the British, French, and Americans each chose to infringe upon the territory and rights of the other, especially along the ill-defined Canadian boundary. While Native Americans were always central to success for their fur industries, they were frequently sacrificed as mere pawns on the highly competitive fur industry chessboard. Independent fur traders and Native Americans alike were often possessed with a mixed political allegiance, largely dependent upon their preferred partners in trade at any given moment. Added to these circumstances were numerous intertribal conflicts intertwined with those involving frontier settlers, often instigated by the selfish interest of a third party. John Dunn Hunter poignantly recalls the mood of the Osage after living with them for nineteen years during these troubling times.[3] Hunter observed a "loss of national pride of character" and a most crucial state of affairs among the Osage Indians "...dissipation and vice; disease and poverty...wretchedness and ignominy close the melancholy scene." By now, the Missouri Indians had completely merged with the Osage, who remained in conflict with the Sac, Fox, and other tribes as their traditional hunting territories continued shrinking.

There were still other reasons for discontent. A natural extension of success in the gigantic fur trade was the gradual diminution of game animal populations so central to that industry and the Native American way of life. Certainly, there was legitimacy for concern on behalf of the local Native Americans. They realized settlers had caused abrupt changes in their lives due to overt encroachment upon their tribal lands. The lack of uniform, fair governance and trading policies toward them were all reflections of the desire of settlers to proceed with their characteristically single-minded, westward-looking plans. The United States treaty of 1804 between the Sac and Fox tribes illustrates the point. For a $1,000 annuity plus $2,234.50 as a one-time payment in goods and trinkets, these tribes ceded all claim to lands on both sides of the Mississippi, which also included Charrette Bottoms, to the United States. Article VII of the treaty stated the Native Americans might live and hunt upon these lands "as long as the lands which now ceded to the United States remain their property." This and other ambiguously crafted articles of the treaty set the stage for years of mutual hate and distrust following ratification of the treaty in Washington on January 25, 1805. Tribal populations continued declining. All Native Americans were pushed westward. Many considered themselves independent of territorial law. The only means of retribution in the minds of many was

fighting for their survival. These conflicts and frustrations of long duration eventually cumulated in the deterioration of frontier stability and
contributed, partially, to the War of 1812.

Local events also document why white settlers living among the
Native Americans on the Missouri might have expressed concern. One
account originates from a letter a Kaskaskia resident wrote to his
Kentucky newspaper correspondent. In the letter, the Mr. Van Bibber
mentioned refers to either Isaac or Matthias Van Bibber who came to
Missouri with Daniel Boone. The June 1, 1805, article from *The
Palladium*, a Frankfort, Kentucky, newspaper proceeds to depict condi-
tions at La Charrette Village:

> The Osage are likely to be cut up root and branch, by a con-
> federacy of almost all the nations of the west. Already blood
> has been spilt, and large bodies of men are in motion to attack
> their country. Mr. Van Bibber, with whom you are acquainted,
> has just returned from the Missouri [River]—he states to me,
> that about ten days since, a body of about four hundred of
> Sacks, crossed at a French village, at a place he was, about 50
> miles from the mouth of the river, on their march to attack the
> Osage.[4]

While not mentioned by name, La Charrette Village was most certainly the French village about fifty miles from the mouth of the
Missouri where the warring Sacs crossed to attack the Osage. Episodes
such as this were somewhat common, especially between the acknowledged Osage enemies—the Sac, Fox, and Pottawatomis. The Osage
would soon complain they only served as easy prey for their rivals in
return for being good Native Americans in the eyes of whites. Another
source documents Native Americans "only" slay twelve men in the
District of St. Charles between 1805 and 1809. However, relationships
with local Native Americans would continue deteriorating. Conflicts
over stolen horses on nearby Loutre Island resulted in the death of three
settlers and an unaccounted number of Native Americans in 1810. The
next year, Henry M. Brackenridge experienced robberies and attacks by
the Pottawatomis killing one member of his party. Governor Lewis was
so moved that he ordered whites not to settle on Native American lands,
yet they continued to do so. This ever-increasing population of settlers
became even more fearful, prompting authorities into action.

Further, British courts held in 1805 that American ships could not
carry goods from French colonies to France. In the same year, the British

naval victory at Trafalgar over Napoleon eventually resulted in the barring of British ships from all ports under French control. This entangled international trade fuss continued escalating, including the controversy over Britain's threat to siege American ships at sea and remove seamen alleged to be British subjects. Soon, the British fired upon the *U.S. Chesapeake* and removed four alleged British deserters. During the winter of 1809–1810, frontier farmers saw commodity prices plummet because of these British trade restrictions adding political fuel to the war fires. The "War Hawks" of the Madison Administration, elected mostly from southern and western states in 1810, led the call to arms. Their cause was bolstered after sixty American soldiers, commanded by William Henry Harrison, governor of the Indiana Territory, were killed by Shawnees in an attack led by Tecumseh in November 1811 at Tippecanoe River. Sympathetic British Canadians, eager to entice others to fight their cause, supplied arms to the Shawnees. The War of 1812 was soon engaged between the British and Americans, but, in less than two years, a peace treaty was signed at Ghent, Belgium. While negotiating with John Quincy Adams at Ghent, the English even sought to establish a separate Native American nation to maintain access to the Mississippi River. That concession was obviously never granted. And, while all this may appear somewhat removed from the Missouri frontier, the far-reaching tentacles of these events were soon to be played out around the La Charrette community.[4,5]

# Tecumseh and Black Hawk

In 1808, Tecumseh developed a thesis, leading him to become a sincere evangelist on behalf of Indian Rights. Tecumseh was an exceptional orator, warrior, statesman, and gentleman who believed all the land belonged to the Native Americans and no tribe should sell any part of their common patrimony.[6] At first, he did not urge war on the whites because he believed, if the Native Americans would unite, they could hold their land as well as their heritage. In 1809, for five months, he shared his message with southern tribes as far away as Florida. In 1810, Tecumseh arranged a visit with Harrison asking, "Sell a country! Why not sell air, the clouds, the great sea, as well as the earth?" Harrison responded the United States had always been fair to the Native Americans. Tecumseh sprang to his feet crying, "It is false! He lies!" The governor drew his sword. Troops aimed their guns as warriors raised their guns and tomahawks. The conflict was averted for the moment. The next morning, the two men sat on a bench and talked some more.

Tecumseh continued believing in himself. His party of sixteen continued traveling widely, telling of their plan. They visited with the Osage, according to John Dunn Hunter. The Osage were interested in Tecumseh's message, but they were not aroused. He next proceeded north to visit with the Sac, Fox, and Ioway tribes. These tribes, as well as other neighboring ones, continued claiming hunting grounds on both sides of the Mississippi. Here, he converted Black Hawk of Illinois, a Sac leader, who soon became an ardent supporter, resulting in the battle at Tippecanoe in November 1811. Tecumseh effectively leveraged his cause and immediately attracted the attention of leaders in the fur industry like Manuel Lisa. Lisa worried of alliances being formed between the Native Americans and the British. Even today, some scholars hold Tecumseh as America's greatest Native American thinker and leader of his time. By November 12, 1811, Frederick Bates admitted the extent of the influence of these Native American alliances represented an unknown concern motivating him to reappoint William Clark as brigadier general of the militia in Upper Louisiana.[4]

However, Black Hawk differed from Tecumseh in at least one trait. He detested whites. The influence of Black Hawk largely instigated many of the deadly raids that so concerned those in the District of St. Charles. His warriors were provisioned with arms and supplies from the British, who played upon past emotional disputes and transgressions unique to each opportunity. Years later, during the Black Hawk War, his warriors deserted him in defeat when the Winnebagos surrendered him at Prairie du Chien for a $100 reward as well as twenty horses. While confined in Jefferson Barracks, below St. Louis, President Jackson summoned him to Washington for a talk before it was decided to tour him around eastern American cities in 1837 and 1838, where Black Hawk reportedly drew immense crowds. Charles Latrobe and Washington Irving visited him before touring in the east and described the chief "near his end, and drooped like the bird whose name he bore, when caged and imprisoned."[7] He died in Iowa after the conclusion of the extended eastern tours, only to have white, retribution-seeking ghouls vandalize his grave in order to exhibit his decapitated head at sideshow tents.

# Charrette Village's War of 1812

The interrelated events leading to the War of 1812 also influenced the decision to establish local military fortifications. Two regular American government forts, Fort Madison and Fort Bellefontaine, were established. One was an all-purpose trade/military outpost at Fort Osage and about thirty "family" or "settlement" forts in the region, including Callaway's Fort at La Charrette.[8] The 1st United States Volunteer Mounted Rangers, also known as Boone's Rangers, led by Lieutenant Nathan Boone and Captain James Callaway represented the local United States militia, providing support to the regular forces. Captains like Callaway were paid two dollars a day for their services. Those of other ranks were paid accordingly.

Boone's Mounted Rangers mustered at Callaway's Fort at La Charrette on March 3, 1812, to initiate their military excursions toward the Mississippi. Among the forty-one Rangers, in addition to Lieutenant Boone, was First Lieutenant William T. Lamme, Anthony C. Palmer, and the "Mountain Man" John Colter, all associated with La Charrette. By June 7, 1812, Governor Howard sent another company of Rangers. These were led by Captain James Callaway to support Boone and his men. Apparently, Callaway's Fort was under attack by Native Americans at least once during the War of 1812, but details of the event have not survived.[9]

Assignments experienced by Captain Callaway may be considered as typical of others. His cavalry of thirty-four men were each issued a sword with belt and a pistol on behalf of the United States military. Callaway and his men first served as spies. Next, they patrolled the region northeast of St. Charles. They were later assigned to Lincoln County on the Mississippi. Two months at Peoria, Illinois, followed before they closed out 1812 constructing Fort Clemson on Loutre Island. After a few winter months at home, he again saw similar service on the Mississippi as well as on the western frontier in both 1813 and 1814. Lieutenant Boone maintained an equally demanding schedule throughout the war. Even after the December 1814 conclusion of the war, conflicts between settlers and Native Americans around La Charrette continued. Many settlers still thought the British remained committed to controlling trade on the Mississippi and would maneuver Native Americans sympathetic to the cause into doing their fighting. Regrettably, local documentation of these attacks—before and after the peace treaty—is plentiful enough.

John Busby lived immediately to the east of La Charrette Village in 1802 before selling his farm and moving to the Boonslick region. He was a fifth sergeant under Captain Sarshall Cooper's company at the time of his death. Busby was married to Ruth Hancock, daughter of Stephen Hancock of Hancock Bottoms. During a raging thunderstorm on April 14, 1814, Busby, who lived with his family in one of the corners of Cole's Fort, held his youngest child on his lap. Other children played nearby while Ruth sewed. As one version of this story goes, a lone Native American warrior crept up to the fort and fashioned a hole through the clay chinks between the logs large enough to insert the muzzle of his gun. He aimed, pulled the trigger, and blasted Busby at near point-blank range. The entire pioneer community reportedly became enraged upon hearing of the death of their highly respected friend. Unfortunately, he would not be the last respected citizen to die in this protracted frontier conflict.

Families across the Missouri frontier were now living in constant fear of Native American raids. Even Nancy Howell Callaway, wife of Captain Callaway, decided to move in with her parents-in-law at Callaway's Fort. Captain Callaway usually wrote to Nancy at their home near Crout Run. However, his August 15, 1814, letter to her was addressed to his parents, Mr. Flanders and Jamima Callaway, St. Charles County, "Sharette" Village. The letter originated from Cap au Grisis, a small fort on the Mississippi. Excerpts follow:

Dear wife

I Received your favour of the 13th Inst which gave me great satisfaction to hear that you ware all well. I am sorry that you are reduced to the Necessaty of moving from home, but I am greatly in hopes that your mind will be more at rest than if you ware at home so Lonesome as you must be, and I could almost wish you to let the boys go to School if your Brothers Do but you must be guided by your good judgement

I still hold good sperites and Enjoy Perfect Health no news nor no orders since I wrote you before no Indian sign on this frontier Remember me to my children your mother and all enquireing friends I Remain Dear Wife your Loving Husband Hoping for your Health I am

JA CALLAWAY[8]

A sincere, loving empathy was expressed between frontier parents concerned for the safety and education of their children. Parents were apparently not sending their children to La Charrette Village School during these difficult times. As difficult as times were, Nancy and her children had not yet seen the worst. 1815 would become a dreadful year for Charrette families.

There was soon trouble to the west of Charrette Village. Sac, Fox, and Pottawatomis Indians stole horses in the neighborhood of Fort Clemson on Loutre Island. About fifteen United States Volunteer Mounted Rangers were out scouting when, by accident, they came across a trail of hoofprints they chose to follow on March 7, 1815. Led by Captain Callaway, grandson of Daniel Boone, they arrived at a Native American camp near the head of Loutre River, where they found and retrieved the horses.[8] The shortage of horses was becoming so severe in the region because of Native American raids that oxen and milk cows were placed into service to plow the fields.

On their return, while herding the horses, the Rangers entered an area that forced them to proceed in near single file. Here, a large number of Native Americans laid concealed in ready ambush, according to Major Long. Long describes the battle:

> The assault commenced as the rangers entered a narrow defile near the confluence of the Prairie Fork of the Loutre Creek. Several men were killed at the first fire, and Captain Callaway received in his body a ball that passed through his watch. So furious was the onset that there was no time for reloading their pieces after they had discharged them. Captain Callaway threw his gun into the creek, that it might not add to the booty of the Indians, and though mortally wounded, drew his knife and killed two or three of his assailants; but seeing no prospect of success, ordered a retreat, hoping thereby to save the lives of some of his men. He was the last to leave the ground, and when springing into the creek he received a shot in the head and expired immediately.

Rangers McDermott, Hutchins, McMullen, and Gilmore also lost their lives, instantly transforming Nancy Howell Callaway and the other wives into frontier widows. Nancy would reconstruct what had been a happy domestic life for her for the past ten years. It was not until 1818 that she remarried John Harrison Costlio. She then initiated her lifelong dream to learn to write. Callaway County, a new central Missouri county and home to Cote sans Dessein since 1808, was later named in honor of her late husband.

Plate 3. Indian tomahawk
found by author between McKinney and Ramsey farms.

Perhaps the bloodiest massacre of all involved a Charrette Bottom family. Aleck and Nancy Bryan McKinney decided to stop plowing their young crop of corn because their dogs were barking fiercely and bristling with fear. Aleck and Nancy, married for a little more than a year, were suspicious of warring Native Americans hiding in the adjacent wheat field. Aleck, a surveyor like his father and a successful farmer on the lower reaches of Charrette Creek, had engaged Ranger Housley to stay in his home for protection. The McKinneys and Housley slept lightly that night.

The next morning, May 20, 1815, within a few miles or so across a range of hills from the McKinney farmstead to the northeast, six Native Americans victimized the Ramsey family in a surprise attack. Robert Ramsey, the head of the family, arrived at Charrette Creek in 1798 with his slaves and livestock.[5] Now a one-legged hunter, trapper, and farmer, he lived with his wife and five children. One was an adopted half-Indian boy named Paul. Mrs. Ramsey was milking the cows when Robert heard the commotion. He struggled to attach his artificial leg and then rushed to rescue his mortally wounded and pregnant wife by dragging her to the cabin door. Three scalped children now lay sprawled about the yard.

It was Saturday, and La Charrette Village School was not in session. Neighbor boy Abner Bryan was running an errand to the Ramsey family. At the same time, Jesse Caton Jr. was herding his father's horses in the nearby woods when he came upon this bloody scene after the Native Americans left. He and Abner immediately ran for help, resulting in the sounding of trumpets as a prearranged distress call among the settlers. Instinctively, Daniel Boone, now eighty years old, kept a steady vigilance at Callaway's Fort, pacing back and forth with a gun in his hand. Nathan Boone soon arrived to dress the wounds of the injured.[10] One boy, scalped with dry blood on his face, opened his eyes and told Boone as he knelt by his side, "Daddy, the Indians did scalp me." Though various accounts differ, at least four died, including a sixteen-year-old girl. Later in the day, Daniel Boone traced these warring Native Americans into the woods and concluded they were still in the area. His judgment was well-founded. The next day, they attacked Jonathan Bryan's place, a cousin of Boone's wife, at their cabin near Nathan Boone's place about six miles from Femme Osage.

Paul, another Ramsey child, and Robert survived. Robert lived for two more years. Paul survived and passed middle age as a St. Charles' resident. William Ramsey, Robert's brother, once a soldier of the American Revolution in the Battle of Yorktown and presently commanding a company of local Rangers, had previously signed the Articles of Agreement initiating La Charrette Village School. Charrette children eventually returned to the village school, where they had much to fear and discuss as the community mourned. These and other episodes are now referred to as the "Indian War" era of local history extensively chronicled by Gregg.[4]

Subsequently, seventy-five Native American tribes, including the local tribes, met at Portage des Sioux to establish peace treaties negotiated by presidential commission members August Chouteau, William Clark, and Nina Edwards, which were ratified by the United States Senate and signed by President Madison on December 5, 1815. While these treaties seemed to focus upon peaceful cohabitation with local Native Americans, it would not be the last struggle involving the estimated 200,000 Native Americans living within the Louisiana Purchase.

# Chapter 9:

## Living at the "Last Settlement of Whites…"

Quite naturally, one may wonder about routine life experiences and expectations of the village citizens of some 200 years ago. Were members of the seven village families happy or displeased with life? How did these frontier family members go about their everyday life pursuits and conduct business? What did the villagers do other than household chores, trap for furs, farm, and explore the frontier? What did the children do? What role did slaves play in their lives? How did they manage their health needs and other aspects of personal life? What sort of personalities did they possess? Direct answers to these questions are generally not possible, but it is possible to gain informed insights about these frontier settlers.

Some have described contemporary French villagers as casual and fun-loving. Yet, the demands of daily living at La Charrette gave others reason for pause. Greely offered an unabashed, almost disparaging, assessment of village life:

> An outpost of seven poverty-stricken families existed at La Charrette, the advance guard of civilization.[1]

In nearby St. Charles, another traveler held similar impressions, saying:

> …it would be difficult to find a collection of individuals more ignorant, stupid, ugly and miserable.[2]

Thanks to the interest of an 1811 Missouri Territory traveler and other sources, we can acquire a more balanced, although generic, perspective. Henry M. Brackenridge left his Pittsburgh home as a seven-year-old lad to learn French while living among the families of Ste. Genevieve for two years during the mid-1790s. Later, as a lawyer, statesman, traveler, and author, he documented other French settlements of the era in Missouri, but he did not visit La Charrette Village in 1811 when he sailed past and counted thirty families thereabouts within view along the riverbank.[3] His ambitious host, fur trader Manuel Lisa, was so eager to win the "Missouri Marathon" race upriver that Brackenridge was denied the opportunity to stop and visit.

Few clues exist regarding individual personality traits of the village residents. Aside from what is known in this regard about Don Carlos Tayon and his family, Daniel Boone, the letter of James Callaway, and a will signed by William T. Lamme, little else remains. Of village neighbors, Charles "Indian" Phillips and John Colter, more is known than most others. Conventional wisdom has typically portrayed frontier families with stereotypic character profiles, including independence, bravery, physical endurance, and determination, among other virtues.[4] Convincingly, the exploits of the Cardinal, Tayon, Phillips, Colter, Boone, Chartran, Callaway, and Lamme families fully document this assertion, although precious little is reported in this regard for the children or the women except for Rebecca Boone and Cote sans Dessein heroine Julia Royer Roy. Most were certainly adventurous, freethinking, and creative citizens. Others were predictably unassuming, and at least one family member behaved as a rowdy drunkard. Several had killed another in apparent self-defense. The French were frequently described as mild-mannered, soft-spoken, hospitable, friendly, kind, honest, and peaceable people. Common to these times, most believed in both premonitions and prophecies. Presumably, this mix of traits well served these backcountry pioneers, supporting their desire to survive and prosper largely by personal initiative. Their reward, according to Bryan-Boone-Lamme descendant Charles W. Bryan Jr., "was the thrill of adventure, the confidence that came from continual triumphs over obstacles which are the joys of pioneering."[5]

Likely enough, their beliefs, character traits, and daily experiences gave rise to revealing modes of expression. Living in a society essentially devoid of scholarship, they often created their own lexicon.[4] A prized gun was variously described as a blood-letter, panther cooler, or hair-splitter. Animal traits were often assigned to humans. A greedy individual might be described as a "dog in the meathouse grasping for all and barking for more" while a cautious person "refused to be hooked." One could compliment a friend by calling him a "horse" or "a real panther." "Singing songs to a dead horse" was a metaphor for a poorly received speaker. An inebriated frontiersman might be designated as being "chocked full of liquor" while a belligerent one might cry "Hell's afloat and the river's risin'!" "Swimming water" was a witty means of warning of a deep subject under discussion. It is into this unfamiliar world of forgotten phrases of self-sufficient frontier families that we now cautiously probe.

Plate 4. How La Charrette Village may have once appeared. From a model by the author.

## Homes, Farming, Food, and Health

La Charrette Village, like other French villages, was distinctively different from most frontier settlements. Public streets between platted city lots were not sold to prospective buyers. They did not exist. Instead, it was a cluster of haphazardly arranged stream bank structures restricted to only seven independent families. Most French villages had a single street or, more correctly, a corduroy cart path worn into the packed earth. It was dusty when dry, and muddy when wet. But it was seldom ideal. This path connected farmhouses farther apart than in a typical village, but it was much less dispersed than those of their neighboring American farmers. This cart path at La Charrette paralleled the Missouri River, providing citizens access to one another as well as to Charrette Landing and other points of interest along "Rue de Charette," as it was known in Cape Girardeau.[3]

All activities centered on the village. Henry Brackenridge was deeply moved by his boyhood remembrances of Ste. Genevieve, where he described the men coming and going—morning and evening—to and from the fields with their oxen or horses pulling carts and old-fashioned, wooden wheel plows. To him, it was a pleasing sight to behold. Common fields were adjacent to the village, even though land claims, surveys, and other documents offer no indication of any such shared community property for La Charrette villagers. Instead, each homestead was situated on a long sliver of land connected to the much larger portions of each farm. This panhandle arrangement provided each farm with approximately 500 feet of either river or creek frontage, spread out somewhat like the spokes of a cartwheel from syndic Chartran's farm, the hub of La Charrette Village (Figures 4 and 5).

Indications are that fur trader Jean Baptiste Trudeau, squatter Jean-Marie Cardinal Sr., and possibly his associate, Jose Tebeau Sr., were among the first to erect structures there, sometimes referenced as camps.[6] Most likely, they either erected tents, the so-called hoop cabins or Indian bark huts while conducting business there. Later, "cabin raising" by Chartran and his followers gave rise to permanent structures of hewn timbers set upright in the ground, just as in other French and Indian homes of this era. The irregular spaces between the logs of these bousillage cabins were "chinked" and "daubed" with a mixture of mud and straw called "cat and clay." Most were long, narrow one-story structures with porches on one or more sides. A window with sash and glass was a rarity. Artist Ramsay Peale, while traveling with the Long Expedition of 1819, did not see any glass windows in any of the Cote sans Dessein homes former La Charrette family members constructed. Routinely, the tiny windows were either covered with hides or left open to the elements. The single cabin door swung on leather hinges fastened with an old-fashioned wooden latch. If one desired greater security, the latch would be fashioned with cleverly designed hardwood tumblers serving as a lock. Upon the ridge of a house or over the yard gate, a wooden cross might be seen. Six or more individuals routinely occupied these cramped, little cabins of one to three rooms. Picket fences enclosed a yard and garden-like area interconnecting the cabin with other outdoor structures. A separate shelter used for housing of slaves may have doubled as a detached kitchen/dining area for some. Storage shacks and a shed for chickens and geese represented less permanent structures. Nothing suggests any of these structures were well-maintained or impressive like the horizontal log home that Flanders Callaway later constructed there.

The aroma of smoke habitually held heavy in the humid Missouri River atmosphere, alerting travelers they were approaching a camp or settlement. Woodpiles, stacked near the cabins, always needed replenishment to maintain the fires. The inside of a typical village cabin appeared more medieval than modern. An open fireplace provided the needs of cooking, heating, and a modest amount of lighting, similar to the Native American lodges. Wood was more than the universal frontier fuel. Wooden floors were constructed from split logs with the flat side up, known as a puncheon floor. Dirt floors were also common. Wooden beds were of the one-legged variety. A small sapling was cut to the desired length of the bed. Holes were then bored into the sapling and the logs of corresponding height in a corner along the cabin wall. Sticks were fitted into these holes, and clapboards were woven in between them. A single leg was fashioned to support the fourth corner of the bed. A straw mattress supported bedding placed upon this structure. Bear hides were heavy quilts. Somewhat similar constructed beds were sometimes located in an overhead loft. Likewise, the sparse furnishings serving as tables, chairs, and benches were all of homemade, wooden construction, as were many cooking and eating utensils. Metal utensils such as cups, pots, kettles, and skillets were considered expensive and required judicious usage. Strings of rawhide suspending onions, gourds, peppers, dried meats, and sausages might be attached to the rafters.

Homemade clothing was simple. It was functional, but ill-fitting. Men and women might wear a coat with oversized sleeves and an attached hood known as a capeau made from blanket material. Some men wore homespun hunting shirts and linen trousers, but most probably wore deerskin leggings and shirts, like those Ramsay Peale purchased in 1819 in nearby Cote sans Dessein. He paid $2.50 for a pair of leggings and $4 for the shirt. A leather belt typically held a scabbard with a hunting knife and tobacco pouch. Women sometimes wore long dresses made from the best "country linens" or calico, but leather deerskin garments were most common at La Charrette, especially their ever-present aprons. Other necessities such as ready-made shoes and boots were not available for purchase, forcing these frontier villages to have their own boot and shoemaker, even as a part-time pursuit. Therefore, most La Charrette villagers preferred Indian deerskin moccasins. During colder weather, deer hair was stuffed inside for insulation. Reportedly, men often tied a cotton handkerchief about their head or wore the French stocking-like cap called toques. They habitually smoked pipes as they went about their chores with a gun nearby.

La Charrette villagers did not acquire their daily life essentials through extensive trade with outsiders. Instead, their goods were obtained through local production and barter. Most chores were sharply divided. The women, children, and slaves tended to the needs of gardening, clothing, and food preparation. Soiled garments were washed outdoors, either in the creek or a great wooden pot with homemade lye soap. Either way, they were scrubbed by hand on a wooden pallet. After wringing dry by hand, the women hung the laundry on nearby bushes and vines to dry. Lye soap was made from a mixture of ashes and animal fats cooked over an open fire and allowed to cool before slicing into small bars. Other chores expected of women included mending of clothes, knitting, gathering the eggs, stoking the fire, dipping candles, instructing the children, tending the sick and injured, and every other affair during their husbands' long absences when they hunted and trapped. Their hands were always busy.

French housewives at La Charrette, those like widow St. Franceway, were universally appreciated for the exceptional dishes they prepared.[6] Their gumbo, omelets, preserves, and pastries excelled over the diet of dried meat, cornbread, and milk, which was customary among American pioneers. Native Americans wives like Elizabeth Cardinal, Mrs. Joseph Chartran, and Sarah Colter predictably offered an even wider variety of cuisine, adding Indian elements to the meals. Even their garden plantings reflected this same dual French-Native American origin. Wild grapes, blackberries, and cherries complemented the beans, squash, and corn from the gardens. Syndic Chartran's orchard offered domestic fruit, including peaches, apples, and plums. Men, boys, and slaves were most often responsible for the small tobacco plots. Likewise, farming and procuring meat and milk products from the appropriate wild or domestic animals was mostly their responsibility. Butter was churned by shaking cream in a bottle or gourd or by trotting around while mounted upon a horse until it was sufficiently transformed.

To satisfy the desire for sugar and wax, everyone remained on ready alert for bee trees. Smoking of the hive was part of the typical harvest technique. Syrups also provided a source of sweet food for settlers. Sugar camps were active, especially during late winter when the sap rose in the trees. Cooking the maple sap over an open fire would render it into thick, sticky syrup. Daniel and Rebecca Boone took several weeks to obtain 400 pounds of syrup at their Missouri sugar camp, a three-sided structure open to the south. During this favored family activity, Rebecca, who so often played the role of community doctor and midwife, complained of feeling poorly. Within a week, on March 18, 1813, she died. She was buried in the Bryan Cemetery, also known as Boone Monument, located immediately north of La Charrette Village.

Salt, an essential daily staple, was a commodity provided through local trade as early as 1805. Approximately seventy-five miles upriver from Charrette was Boonslick, where Nathan and Morgan Boone paid men fifteen dollars a month to boil large volumes of water and chop wood. The water was obtained from a salt spring to obtain this mineral needed to cure meat, season food, and preserve pelts. Fifty pounds of the resulting salt was sold all along the river for $2.50. Hand-hollowed sycamore log segments were modified to serve as kegs. The Boone brothers reportedly boiled 300 gallons of water over an open fire to acquire fifty pounds of salt. The venture was so successful that they greatly expanded it in 1807. Loutre Lick, which also provided salt, was on the east bank of Loutre River, relatively close to the village.

Wheat and Indian corn were the two primary crops for these reluctant farmers. They stored these grains in large hand-hollowed cottonwood longs set upright as a silo. Wheat reportedly yielded from five to eight fold (more than the seed planted), while corn would yield a hundred fold. Father Vivier of Ste. Genevieve noted corn was good food for cattle, slaves, and the natives, who considered it a treat. Mr. Duquette built the first regional windmill for grinding grain in St. Charles in 1798. Horses often powered other village mills. More commonly, hand mills were employed. This apparatus consisted of two stones, the upper one with a hole in the center. Through which, a child might drop grain as this stone was rotated over a larger, flat one beneath. Others even reverted to the still more primitive technique of placing grain in a hollowed stump while fraying it with a pestle.

Grain was ground for baking and brewing. Starting commercially around 1800 in St. Louis, whiskey production was an important industry. Charrette families brewed their own whisky and brandy, as evidenced by the two gallons of whiskey they sold for eight dollars to celebrating members of the Corps of Discovery in 1806. The men, women, and children drank it freely, as it was considered pure, healthy, and pleasant to the taste. However, Flint, a traveling minister in the area, disagreed upon seeing "murder everywhere, and in which the drunkenness, brutality and violence were mutual."[7] These spirits would have certainly been a welcome alternative to the turbid waters obtained from either the river or the creek for drinking and culinary purposes. To compensate, most families collected their water in earthen jugs before its use, allowing impurities to settle to the bottom of the container before consuming it. Springs offered the purest source of water on the frontier, but few were near Charrette Bottoms. Sometime during the late nineteenth century, Father Pierre-Jean De Smet proudly proclaimed, "I have drunk the limpid waters of its sources and the muddy waters at its mouth,"[8] indicating the consumption of impure Missouri River waters continued decades into the future. These waters predictably served as the origin of many deadly diseases.

Indications are that farming was a secondary enterprise to that of trading in furs at La Charrette. Many village guests imply their crops were not well-tended. Those who owned slaves, like the Lammes, Tayons, and Callaways, often assigned farming-related tasks to them. Livestock in many French villages were allowed to graze by tethered ropes or by carrying cut grass to them in a stall.[3] However, around the time of the Lewis and Clark Expedition, indications are that livestock were free-ranging near the village. In all likelihood, livestock had access to the open range throughout the year with split rail fences protecting field crops, as was the case in New Madrid. Adding support to this practice was one observation noting that cattle and horses were forced to consume tree bark and reeds during the winter. Others, such as a workhorse or milk cow, might well have been tethered or restrained in a stall, depending upon immediate needs and circumstances. A few horned cattle and hogs as well as some yard chickens and geese comprised a typical livestock inventory. Most would have been smallish, scrub stock compared to the standards of today. While living in the village of St. Charles, Don Carlos Tayon reportedly hitched his team of oxen to the plow with rawhide strips tied to their horns. His son Charles presumably employed this same crude, albeit effective, technique while farming at La Charrette Village.

An extraordinary abundance of barking, tail-wagging dogs would have greeted anyone arriving at La Charrette. Dogs were everywhere, occupying a highly symbiotic role with the settlers. These hounds served many essential needs. As well as being twenty-four-hour sentinels, they were much prized for their abilities to assist in the hunt. On occasion, they were credited with protecting individuals from a raging bear or other wild animal. They remained on constant alert for any unwanted wildlife entering the village, such as snakes, coons, foxes, bears, wolves, and skunks. Children and dogs always shared a special companionship, as they played and roamed the region in unison. Cats also served highly useful roles, both as pets and as ratters to reduce mouse and rat infestation in granaries and other structures.

Wooden carts the French used were a curiosity to outsiders. These carts, called *charettes*, often credited as the village's namesake, were constructed entirely of wood. Americans referred to them as "barefoot" carts because they did not have iron rims on the wheels. They were constructed from two pieces of scantling approximately ten feet long framed together by two or more cross pieces. Upon this structure, a rounded front of wickerwork served as sideboards to help secure the cargo. This assembly was mounted on an axletree with solid, wooded wheels. Riding in a *charette* hitched with twisted rawhide traces to either oxen or horses harnessed in tandem was neither easy, nor pleasant, especially because reins were not used to guide these draft animals. A combination of verbal commands and a whip, administered by someone walking alongside the cart, directed the animals. In addition to the *charette* and the cumbersome wheel plow, other common implements included axes, saws, wedges, sledgehammers, hoes, grubbing hoes, spades, and rakes. All were designed as they had been in previous centuries, incorporating as little expensive iron as possible. These implements were shared in many community activities, such as harvesting of timber; construction of buildings, fences, and skiffs; as well as the construction and maintenance of docks. Such community activities were often social events as the wives provided food and beverages to support whatever project was underway.

Log canoes, which were anchored at La Charrette Village Landing when not in use, were also important to local travel needs. Most often, these wooden, dugout canoes navigated streams such as Tuque Creek, Charrette Creek, or its first north bank tributary, the Fallen Timber Branch. These sturdy vessels, buoyant and relatively easy to construct, were fifteen to twenty feet in length and were tapered at both ends. The pirogue differed from a log canoe, as it possessed a square stern. Either was fashioned from a cottonwood log, hollowed by use of woodworking tools and fire to within one to two inches in thickness. It reportedly took four men four days to complete a single craft. Wooden oars guided and propelled them through the waters. Sometimes, two pirogues were secured in tandem with the small deck between them loaded with furs or other cargo. These dugouts were unlike the five sleek trading craft of Canadians James Reed and his partner Ramsey Crooks, the future chief executive of John Astor's vast American Fur Company, who were docked at La Charrette Landing on September 20, 1806. These flatbottom boats loaded with trade goods for the Osage and Otoe Indians were thirty feet long and eight feet wide. Significantly, they could successfully navigate over shallow waterways with only six oars. Envious Captain Clark observed these craft upon his return to La Charrette Village that September evening and pronounced them as the best "for the navigation of this river of any which I have seen." That evening, La Charrette Village was host to more than sixty oarsmen, furriers, and expedition members, undoubtedly among the largest aggregates of overnight guest ever to gather there.

Neither health insurance nor universal health care was provided at La Charrette. The cause and effect relationships of many illnesses were poorly understood at best. At La Charrette, superstition freely mingled with the emerging medical sciences. Without ready access to physicians, women assumed the primary responsibility to nurse sick and injured family members as well as their neighbors. The advice of the village expert, such as an experienced woman like Rebecca Boone, was often sought whenever the need presented itself. Patients were bled, purged, and sweated, in accordance with accepted medical practices of the day. In a 1791 letter to his wife's parents, Dr. O'Fallon, a native of Ireland and brother-in-law to William Clark, offered numerous treatments and remedies to attain good health.[9] O'Fallon was previously a surgeon in the Connecticut and Pennsylvania lines in the American Revolution. He advised the senior Clarks to use pokeberry tincture for rheumatic pains and to induce perspiration. His doctor's pills were formulated to cure many other ailments. The pills contained saccharin, aloes, castile soap, calomel, and opium. Mrs. Clark was to take foetida pills, an equal mixture of three tinctures—foetida, soot, and castor—to be administered with five grains of gum of asafoetida and two grains of castoreum. These multipurpose pills apparently worked best when accompanied with the bitters, a mixture of tea, chamomile flowers, gentian root, orange peel, and the lesser seeds of the cardoman. As a bitters substitute, "blessed thistle" was recommended. To expel wind and promote digestion, O'Fallon recommended his drops be taken several times a day. Three or four drops of a 50:50 lavender and peppermint oil mixture with a lump of sugar represented one dose. Both Clarks were advised to exercise frequently by riding horseback. Thirteen years later, the Lewis and Clark Expedition coleaders took $90.69 of medical supplies with them.[10] As well as lancets, forceps, and other medical equipment were fifty dozen of Rush's pills and thirty drugs such as Peruvian bark, jalap, opium, Glauber salts, saltpeter, and mercurial ointment. Once these drugs and folk remedies had been exhausted, about all that could be done was comfort the patient until the illness ran its course or the patient expired.

Contagious diseases were particularly threatening to local citizens. Carlos Dehault Delassus of St. Louis recognized this fact when a smallpox outbreak was reported among the Native American tribes in the District of St. Charles during the late winter of 1801. In April, he sent a letter to Casa Calvo, requesting Don Carlos Tayon of St. Charles and Don Francisco Saussier of Portage des Souix take appropriate precautions for the residents of their villages. By May, Calvo had agreed to implement the request. None who traded with the Native Americans were allowed to return home until subjected to a designated quarantine procedure, including an airing of their peltries by passing them, one at a time, through smoke. The Isla a Cabaret was the designated quarantine site.

The most common afflictions of the day were sore throats, whooping cough, scarlet fever, pneumonia, and malaria. The most usual accidents were associated with hunting, falling from one's horse, swimming, and routine tasks of conducting household and farm chores. Large families were typical, as a new child arrived approximately every two-and-a-half years. A midwife's services were most commonly engaged for these events; however, many women died in childbirth. A large percentage of children never survived past their fifth birthday. Older daughters of a family routinely cared for infants and small children, greatly easing that burden upon their mother, while simultaneously preparing the daughter for motherhood. Surgeons reportedly traveled with Spanish forces exploring and protecting the territory as early as 1767. One such surgeon was Don Juan Baptiste Valleau, while Drs. Antoine Saugrain and Bernard G. Farrar were among the first physicians to reside in St. Louis, arriving between 1804 and 1807. By 1817, nearby Marthasville would be blessed with two physicians, setting into motion the process of improved health care for Charrette citizens. Average life expectancy at birth approached forty years in the early 1800s on the Missouri frontier, a statistic that would improve to forty-seven years by 1900.

## Spiritual and Leisure Activities

Some have suggested the expression of spiritual matters and leisure activities were essentially one and the same in a spiritually desolate area like La Charrette. Even so, some speculate either Father Peter Didier, or his successors named Lusson or Dunand at St. Charles Borromeo, may have administered to the spiritual needs of frontier residents at Charrette Creek. It is not known whether these priests traveled to their flock at the village or if they came to the humble vertical log church in St. Charles. However, it was not until 1816 that the Missionary Society of Connecticut appropriated $615 to support the work of Salmon Giddings and Timothy Flint in and around St. Louis.[11,12] Later that year, Flint moved his family to St. Charles stating his intention to preach "at several other settlements in that vicinity." When his family was taken ill for forty days, "they took us in," Flint recalls, proclaiming his days there among his happiest. Regardless, it was not until 1818 that the first village congregation was formed at La Charrette. Contrary to the fact that most of the French landholders like Don Carlos Tayon claimed to be strict, exemplary Catholics, the first church at La Charrette was of the Baptist persuasion. Reverend James E. Welch organized the Friendship Baptist Church, the first church of Warren County, in the home of Flanders Callaway, where twelve parishioners, mostly members of the Boone family, met.

A year later, Reverend John Mason Peck, a Connecticut native of Puritan ancestry, preached in the Callaway home.[13,14] Peck engaged Daniel Boone as a hearer and described him as "slightly bald, his silvered locks were combed smooth; his countenance ruddy and fair...His voice soft and melodious." Peck thought Boone to be "intelligent—not moody and unsociable as if desirous of shunning society and civilization." However, the abundance of Missourians' blasphemous behavior appalled Peck. As a typical traveling preacher, he stayed overnight in the Callaway home and recalls:

> On Thursday morning, the 17th of December, I rode along a blind trail, or bridle-path, over hills and through ravines, fifteen miles to the cabin of Mr. James Stevenson. My route lay along the bluffs that bordered on the Missouri River, the country thinly settled, and wagon-tracks seldom seen. I had sent on an appointment at Mr. McDermid's, but it failed in being circulated.

This westbound route would have taken Peck across Charrette Creek near West Point crossing, currently associated with the Katy Trail metal truss bridge, an ideal site to view the stream a bit more than two miles west of modern-day Marthasville. By December 22, he would arrive at the rapidly growing town of Cote sans Dessein to continue serving his far-flung congregation.

Such were the experiences of an underpaid traveling frontier preacher. Nevertheless, Peck had the opportunity to observe much of human nature and perhaps report upon it more objectively than most. While passing a tavern stand in Missouri, possibly the one owned by Nicholas Coontz west of St. Charles,[15] he observed "the landlord with a company of gentlemen busily employed at the card table."[14] However, things were different at La Charrette Village.

> In a French village there was no tavern, for it was not needed, the stranger always finding a welcome in the house of these friendly, hospitable people.[6]

Red wines, cider, and peach brandy were among the favorite beverages served as they played a game of craps in their homes. Peck further expressed his concern over how these French villagers observed the Sabbath as a "day of hilarity" with mass in the morning and social amusement in the afternoon. Still others claimed honesty and punctuality characterized all dealings of a French settler. They never locked their homes as well as reportedly spoke the truth and scrupulously carried out their bargains and those of their fathers. Almost universally, strangers were received with generous hospitality in either the village or the wilderness countryside surrounding La Charrette. Numerous travelers, including members of several expeditions, recall food, entertainment, and accommodations at all hours of the day or night.

In a culture where horses and horsemanship reigned supreme, horse races and pride of one's mount was second nature to any self-respecting village citizen.[4] Likewise, shooting matches, boat races, and whose capacity was most nearly bottomless were all favorite amusement events. These activities each contributed to the telling of tall tales, allowing additional incentive for wagers placed upon almost any upcoming contest. In fact, most leisure and amusement activities represented an extension of everyday activities. Idle time for contemplating the world—alone or in conversation with another—might be passed with knife in hand, whittling on a stick while chewing a quid of tobacco under a shade tree or when sitting on the cabin porch. Women socialized and gossiped while mending clothes, harvesting blackberries, curing meats, or attending to any other of their shared chores. Undoubtedly, the village children played with their Native American cousins, just as Henry Brackenridge did in his youth. The boys might practice bow and arrow marksmanship with their Kickapoo neighbors while the girls shared their corn cob with husk dolls. Later, as the local presence of Native Americans diminished, these multicultural interactions included the black children of slaves when they were not in their separate school for a few winters' months of the year.

In spite of the rigorous lifestyle sometimes portrayed at La Charrette Village, Brackenridge considered the French on the Mississippi to have acquired the art of happy living, something he thought most Americans had not yet achieved. Prophetically, he may still be correct. He stated his hostess, Madame Beauvais

> was a large fat lady, with an open cheerful countenance, and an expression of kindness and affection to her numerous offspring, and to all others, excepting her colored domestics toward whom she was rigid and severe.[3]

Others claimed there was a fiddle in every house with a dance every night. Meriwether Lewis penned his impressions of French-Canadians residing at nearby St. Charles, offering further insights concerning their character:

> In their manners they unite all the careless gaiety and ample hospitality of the best times of France; yet, like most of their countrymen in America, they are ill qualified for the rude life of the frontier. Not that they are without talent, for they possess much natural genius and vivacity; not that they are destitute of enterprise, for their hunting excursions are long and laborious and hazardous; but their exertions are desultory, their industry is without system and without perseverance.

Indisputably, the status of near self-sufficiency combined with the freedoms associated with frontier life helped La Charrette villagers offset what observers have frequently described as various degrees of poverty. Further, they undoubtedly found satisfaction in devoting their lives to what they enjoyed, the spirit of frontier development, exploration, and opportunities so unique to their times. Even though others looked upon them as poor compared with those residing in St. Louis and elsewhere in the east, nature blessed them with the essentials for a rewarding frontier life.

# Fur Trade Economy

The fur-trading industry was central to economic life on the Missouri frontier. In fact, of all the motivations influencing trade, Indian policies, trade routes, politics, peace treaties, explorations, and settlement activities west of the Mississippi River, the single most compelling force was that of fur trading. For nearly three centuries, fur trading had been one of the largest and most important commercial industries in North America, having a potent influence upon the history of the West. Furs, syrup, beeswax, and other commodities of the Missouri frontier served as currency, just as tobacco did in colonial Virginia. Typical deals recorded in barter trade include ten pounds of peltry for a bushel of ear corn or thirty pounds of peltry for 100 pounds of flour.

St. Louis was established in 1764 to trade furs with Native Americans. However, it was not long before the Native Americans were delivering insufficient quantities of furs to "Chouteau Town" to satisfy the growing international demand. First, the Chouteaus and others sent their traders up the Missouri, but it was not until after 1789 did significant trading extend beyond the Osage Indians on the Missouri. Subsequently, Native American tribes farther upriver in eastern Kansas and beyond participated. At the same time, more independent trappers continued to infiltrate the region.

Next, Auguste Chouteau sought greater control of the Osage fur trade by coming to their aid in time of need, while simultaneously astutely positioning himself with the authorities. A coalition of Indian tribes—the Ioway, Sac, Fox, and others as far away as Mexico—were prepared to attack the Osage in 1793, largely at the behest of secret orders from Spanish representatives. Warring parties had suffered minor losses on both sides, but this feud was largely over trading privileges. This year, the raid was postponed, with Osage extermination plans now set for 1794. By then, eight more tribes along the St. Francis River joined the coalition. Like the year before, these plans never materialized, even though the Osage continued suffering some losses, even after all trade with them was terminated. Chouteau then went to New Orleans with several Osage chiefs to visit the governor-general with a plan to subjugate the Osage by the construction of a fort offering them protection. The Osage next attacked settlers at Ste. Genevieve, killing one man, which sufficiently moved the governor-general to authorize the construction of Fort Cardondelet to secure peace. For his role in this peacekeeping trade mission, Chouteau sought—and was offered—sole trading privileges with the Osage for the next six years.

Fur trade between Auguste Chouteau and the Grand and Little Osage Indians during 1800 represented $20,000 in merchandise, including the twenty-five percent markup, which was traded for $30,000 worth of fur.[16] Similarly, Regis Loisel traded farther up the Missouri with $60,000 of goods for $100,000 of furs bartered from members of the Sioux tribe. In 1802, the upstart fur trader, Manuel Lisa, outmaneuvered the Chouteaus. He rightfully pleaded to authorities that the Chouteaus ran a monopoly in the trade. The outcome of his clever, determined lobbying left the Chouteaus to trade exclusively with the Osage on the Arkansas River, that is, the Osage of the Oaks. The furrier trade was indeed a big competitive business. Nevertheless, not everyone associated with the Missouri fur trade shared equally in its wealth. At least that is what Corps of Discovery members concluded on May 25, 1804, about the Village Charrette economy, "The people at this village is pore, houses Small, they sent us milk & eggs to eat."

However, a glance into local fur trapping and trading activities would not fully support the conclusion offered by Corps members. For example, Jean-Marie Cardinal Sr. had traded for 2,000 livres worth of deerskins in 1777, while Daniel Boone, with his faithful twenty-two-year old black servant named Derry, harvested about forty beaver pelts on the Bourbeuse Creek in 1800. Twice in 1802, his son Nathan trapped beaver with William T. Lamme. They reported a good hunt that spring and caught an additional 900 beaver in the fall. Hatters from Kentucky came to Missouri to purchase the spring pelts, but Boone and Lamme sold the fall-harvested pelts in Lexington, Kentucky, for $2.50 each. Later that year, Osage Indians robbed Derry while trapping with members of the Boone family on the Niango River. In another episode on this same trip, the Native Americans stole Daniel Boone's capeau coat, the gunpowder in his horn, and all of his furs. They even forced Derry to cook a meal for them before departing. Nathan Boone, William Hays Jr. as well as Flanders and James Callaway returned home while Derry and Daniel Boone continued hunting until they eventually acquired about 200 beaver skins. Again in 1803 and 1804, Osage and Sac Indians robbed Nathan Boone of horses, blankets, coats, and hides while he was hunting with family members. The latter encounter left Boone and Matthias Van Bibber in shirtsleeves in a November snowstorm before arriving home days later. Alone, in the spring of 1805, Nathan attempted recovering his stolen horses, equipment, and furs. However, after seventeen days of haranguing by the Native Americans, he only came away with two of his stolen traps. These reports suggest fur trading around La Charrette was sometimes highly profitable, but it was always a high-risk, highly variable enterprise. Others have chosen to describe it, perhaps most accurately, as either a feast or famine venture.

Fur-trading companies quickly exploited every resource available to increase the harvest of furs. Central to their mode of operation was reliance upon cheap labor provided by Native Americans and young American hunters and trappers. They contracted with single young men to procure furs by roaming the countryside. Fur company representatives motivated these youthful trappers to wander along the Missouri River and other streams to seek their fortune and participate in the excitement of wilderness exploration. Their ambition was to obtain as many bison, bear, deer, beaver, mink, fox, coon, and muskrat hides as possible, either through bartering with Native Americans, trapping, or hunting. These itinerant young men frequently took a Native American wife, causing Spanish officials worry and frustration over these social outcasts.

A typical annual contract provisioned each trapper with five traps, a horse, ten pounds of powder, twenty pounds of lead, four knives, hatchets, awls, a kettle, and related tack in exchange for their commitment to return, whereupon the furs would be purchased. Later contracts became more formal and extensive. General Thomas James was inspired to explore the west based upon the favorable comments of Meriwether Lewis. In 1806, Lewis validated in St. Louis what others had already boasted about on the Upper Missouri, declaring it to have more beaver than any place on earth. James signed on as one of 350 members of the newly formed Missouri Fur Company trapping expedition headed up the Missouri to the Rocky Mountains. Andrew Henry, a field captain for Lisa, was responsible for this party traveling on thirteen barges and keelboats. They left St. Louis after signing a two-page formal contract stipulating all expectations and contingencies:

Articles of Contract and Agreements, this day entered into between Benjamin Wilkinson for the St. Louis Missouri Fur Company of the one part and Thomas James of the St. Louis District of the other part, Witnesseth...etc., etc.

> The contract concludes...all which the contracting Parties aforesaid promise to do and perform under penalty of Five Hundred Dollars, if either party shall break this Contract.

St. Louis March 29, 1809 (signed and witnessed) [17]

John Colter, a Lewis and Clark Expedition member and La Charrette neighbor, had previously assisted Lisa and Henry in 1807. He now led James and the others upriver to their trapping grounds near the forks of the Missouri River. Here, James was assigned four men to supervise for the next three years. They were each provisioned with the six beaver traps, a rifle, ammunition, and other essentials. The contract provided for James and his crew to share in one-fourth of the assumed profits upon their return to St. Louis. The expedition members suffered from ill treatment, hard labor, bad food, and numerous personal conflicts, resulting in many deserters. James complained of fair promises made in St. Louis that were later broken in Indian country. One can only imagine the headaches associated with managing the contracts of such a far-flung frontier enterprise. Yet, the motivation for wealth as well as the opportunity to travel combined with the thrill of adventure was strong incentives to attract participants.

Local independent La Charrette trappers like Luzon, Cardinal, Boone, Phillips, Colter, and Callaway all preferred beaver pelts because they were twice as valuable as a single deer hide. In the fall of 1810, they met two old friends from Kentucky who went trapping up the Missouri, perhaps as far as the Yellowstone. These old friends, Michael Stoner and Jim Bridger, returned to La Charrette the following spring with boats laden with furs. Trappers held much pride in accomplishments such as these because every means of cunning and skill was required in securing these crafty animals. These, like other trappers, carried a wooden canister filled with secretions from the musk gland mixed with urine of previously killed beaver to bait the area where traps were set along the edge of a waterway. The scent attracted beaver, causing them to explore within the area of the trap, trip it, and secure a fore foot. Attempting to escape, the beaver swam to deeper water and eventually drowned from the weight of the trap. However, not all traps set for beaver were successful. Frequently, the trappers caught animals of lesser value. Or worse, animals would trip the trap without success. Even worse still, both the beaver and the trap were occasionally lost. Not only was fur trapping risky and of varied economic outcome, but it was always hard and often disappointing work. John Colter, to avoid notice by inhospitable Native Americans, even set his trapline at dusk and ran it before daybreak.

William T. Lamme was typical of other village men who "never ceased rowing from morning to night" as they navigated local streams, just like at Ste. Genevieve.[3] With a supply of venison jerky stuffed in his pouch slung over his shoulder on a rawhide strip, he ran his trapline in hopes of securing pelts. Trapping activities were intense during the winter season when furs were most luxuriant and valuable. Hunting larger game with firearms accompanied this activity, but it was somewhat less seasonal than trapping. All pelts were cleaned, and everyone knew the proper procedures to follow. Larger ones were staked out on the ground for cleaning and stretching before being hung on wooden racks to dry. The trappers turned smaller ones inside out before fitting them over a willow or grapevine hoop or onto a wooden pallet to cure. Then they packed the furs into ninety-pound bundles. A horse could easily pack two bundles, each representing about seventy beaver pelts. Preparing furs in this manner could earn a lad ten cents a day. Several times each year, these products were sold: either to traders coming to the village or by transporting them downriver to St. Louis markets. Nathan Boone considered anything over 200 beaver or 400 deerskins a fair season's hunt. Such expectations would soon become more difficult to achieve.

As is common to all industries, the interrelated roles of competition, changing economic conditions, and politics were involved in the fur trade. Before the United States Congress passed acts in 1804 to establish trading houses and regulate the fur trade with the Native Americans, Auguste Chouteau sought interviews with Jefferson and Gallatin in Washington, representing a special committee of five prominent St. Louis businessmen. President Jefferson considered Chouteau to be well-disposed, but motivated by power and money, just as lobbyists of today. Yet, the industry prospered. Following each of the expeditions—Lewis and Clark, Pike, and others—trading interests were spurred. However, following the War of 1812, a considerable decline in the trading of furs ensued as the so-called government factory system (subsidized federal trading post) began failing. Some forts eventually closed due to a scarcity of trade goods and declining fur prices. Although it fared better than other forts of the time, Fort Osage also eventually closed.

The Missouri Fur Company headed by Manuel Lisa chose to improve its fortunes with an eye toward expansion to gain a competitive edge within the industry. They invested $11,000 (and lost fifteen men) in an 1812–1813 expedition to establish new trade liaisons with various Indian tribes. According to John C. Luttig, Lisa's clerk, the expedition failed because of hostilities with the Native Americans they attempted to contact.[18] Luttig, who lived at St. Charles, maintained a daily journal in his handmade, fifty-page book, thirteen inches long by eight inches wide. He was one of some eighty-five employees Lisa hired that year but chose to record nothing of La Charrette Village as he passed there in May 1812 or on the return trip in 1813. However, by June 5, 1813, the *Missouri Gazette* reported more details on this failed expedition:

> Mr. Lisa of the Missouri Fur Company arrived in St. Louis a few days ago from the Mandan villages on the Missouri; the Aricaras, Chyans, Grosventre, Crows and Aropahayas are or may be considered at war with the Americans. The British Northwest Company, having a number of trading-houses within a short distance of the Missouri, are enabled to embroil our people with the savages, who are constantly urged to cut them off.

Canadian traders continued offering stiff competition, but independent American traders had soon become powerful enough to serve all the Native Americans' needs. By 1816, the British were no longer allowed to operate on American soil. Once again, following favorable reports of the Long Expeditions in the early 1820s, the fur industry experienced a respite. However, it was not long until the United States Congress ceased to fund its bankrupt, ineffective factory system. By 1822, it abolished American trade with all Indian tribes, effectively placing the fur trade in the hands of private, but licensed, traders. By 1834, while in London, John Jacob Astor stated, "It appears that they make hats of silk in place of beaver," signaling a major decline in the fur trade.[19] Even before then, in 1822, the defunct estate of once-prominent St. Louis fur mogul Manuel Lisa could not pay Forrest Hancock of neighboring Hancock Bottoms the $99.10 due him. Lisa sensed the onset of the decline, but he invested and extended credit unwisely toward the end of his career. In the face of a declining beaver population and competition from silk, the frontier fur trade soon saw Ramsey Crooks, Auguste Chouteau, and other prominent furriers retire from the business, although other members of the Chouteau family continued in related trading businesses until about 1866. This dying industry contributed much to the development of North America. Even the term "multimillionaire" was first popularized to describe the $25 million (or more) accumulated by German-born John Jacob Astor before his 1848 death.

# Black and Indian Slaves

The incentive to clear more land was evident on the frontier, just as in the colonies. The demand for more wheat and other preferred crops was rapidly growing. Not only were these crops important as food for humans and the export trade, but they were also "fuel" for the nations growing population of draft animals and other livestock. All work related to clearing of new lands for crop production was of the hard, backbreaking variety. Likewise, seasonal land preparation, planting, cultivation, and harvesting of crops were all labor-intensive activities fostering the use of slaves. In addition to their roles in agriculture, slaves were useful in much of the pre-industrial revolution frontier society, including wet-nursing and domestic servants. Some citizens clearly opposed slavery, but most frontier preachers of the day continued advancing the popular notion that slavery had approval from "Above."

Slavery also fit within the accepted social hierarchy of La Charrette families. The top to bottom rank in the social hierarchy of the times progressed from the missionaries, to military officers on to merchant-traders down to common soldiers, boatman, hunters, and trappers followed by permanent settlers. Slaves ranked below all others—men, women, and children—Indian or black.[20] French settlers on the Mississippi River in the 1700s bought and sold Native American slaves just as black slaves. The lower reaches of the Missouri River provided many of the Native Americans to support this trade. From the American Bottoms, it was claimed "they get as many savage slaves as they wish, on the river of the Missouris, whom they use to cultivate the land; and they sell these to the English of Carolina, with whom they trade." Most Native American slaves were purchased with liquor from other Native Americans who had captured them in battle.

Certainly, Native Americans were captured and traded within the region surrounding La Charrette. At least one is documented as working there. Nicholas Colas, the Native American slave owned by Jean-Marie Cardinal Sr., remained associated with the Cardinal family both in Wisconsin and Missouri. He was reportedly an Osage Indian, whom Angelique Cardinal married after the death of Jean-Marie in 1780. La Charrette landholders Don Carlos Tayon owned five slaves, one a French-Indian named Joseph. William T. Lamme held at least five black slaves. O'Reilly's Spanish regime expressly forbid trafficking in Native American slaves, but not blacks. Black slaves, thought to represent about fifteen percent of society, predominated at the village after the arrival of Southerners like Flanders and Jamima Callaway. Thus, York, Clark's black servant assigned to the Corps of Discovery, was likely among the first black slaves to witness La Charrette Village.

In 1770, Pedro Piernas, lieutenant governor of Ylinueses, published a decree requiring all citizens to justify and declare their "red" slaves.[21] Joseph Tayon Sr. of St. Louis, father of La Charrette landholder Don Carlos Tayon, declared he had purchased Marie Louise, a "savage" women for 1,500 livres of silver and Marie Rose, a "savage" girl of about eleven years that cost him 400 livres. Marie Louise had two teenage sons. All were baptized according to an affidavit signed with his cross because Joseph did not know how to write.

Joseph also owned Marie Jean Scypion. Marie Jean was an Afro-Indian woman. At this time, most female slaves were Native Americans, and most male slaves were black, resulting in many slave children possessing mixed heritage. Separate laws governed black and Indian slaves, causing legal confusion for descendants of those of mixed heritage like Marie Jean. She attempted to press her claims for freedom before the local Spanish magistrate in 1780 with two of the Tayon daughters providing assistance. She claimed, because Spanish ordinances now prohibited Indian enslavement, by law, she was a free citizen. Her case was divisive to both the Tayon family and the community of St. Louis. At one point in this dispute, Auguste Chouteau advised Madame Marie Louise Tayon Chauvin, Joseph's daughter, the matter should be kept out of public view to avoid "great injury" to owners of Indian slaves. Undaunted, Madame Chauvin testified she had seen Chouteau tie and whip some of his Indian slaves who also sought their freedom. Marie Scypion died a slave in 1802, but her daughters eventually persuaded Missouri courts to free them in 1834.

William Clark of the Lewis and Clark Expedition also owned slaves. York, his African-American slave, greatly contributed to the success of the Corps of Discovery, where he so often served as a curiosity to many Native American men and women alike. He was married before joining the expedition in Louisville in October 1803. By 1808, Clark and his bride, Julia Hancock, were moving to St. Louis to take on new territorial duties there. York and a few other slaves traveled by land from the Cumberland River to Kaskaskia with Clark's horses, carriage, and cart.[22] Clark and his manservant were now at odds because York and his wife, owned by another slaveholder, were separated. They, naturally enough, desired to be together. Irritated by York's attitude, Clark threatened to sell him. By November 9, 1808, Clark was motivated to write, if conditions do not improve, "I wish him Sent to New Orleans and Sold, or hired out to Some Sevare Master until he thinks better of such conduct." Another letter of July 1809 reveals York had been in jail, "taken York out of the Caleboos and he for two or three weeks been the finest Negrow I ever had." Details of his infraction are not revealed, except York had been "insolent and Sultry." This abhorrent aspect of slavery played out over the next six years, to include, shortly before his unexpected 1808 death, the intercession of Meriwether Lewis seeking leniency on behalf of York. A slaveholder in Louisville eventually hired York out. Later still, Clark granted York his freedom and even set him up in the drayage business. Sometime after 1832, York died in Tennessee of cholera. Indications are that he and his wife eventually reunited sometime before his death.

At La Charrette Village, slaves were considered valuable property. Flanders Callaway sold Venus, a black slave woman and two Negro boys, Daniel and Westly, to his eldest son James Callaway for $450. This January 17, 1815, account reported in the Maher Collection by the Missouri Historical Society explains the alertness of Venus saved members of the Callaway family from a pending Indian attack at Fort Howell on Howell's Prairie near St. Charles. Slaves like Daniel and Westly did not acquire their surname as a birthright. Instead, the surname of their master was assigned to them. Records indicate the priests at St. Charles Borromeo church married a few black couples, but the baptism of fatherless babies called mulattos was more common.

Even after La Charrette Village faded from existence, Flanders Callaway managed black slaves on his farms there as chattel property. His last will and testament, recorded in the Warrenton Office of Circuit Clerk, 1833–1837, stipulates Jemima Callaway should exercise her right of dower:

> [T]hat is to say the Negro girls Kipley, Lucinda, Dorcas, and Lavina and at the death or marriage of my said wife the said four above Negro girls and their increase if any to descend to my youngest son, Daniel Boone Callaway and his heirs.

Son Larkin and his heirs were to receive "forever one Negro boy named Jeff." Nonetheless, all Missouri slaves gained their freedom on January 1, 1863, but they did not gain full liberty until the passage of Civil Rights legislation a century later when the use of degrading words like "girl" or "boy" to describe mature adults finally became unacceptable.

# New Laws

While the first prison in St. Louis was a fifteen-by-twenty-foot stone structure constructed by the Spanish regime in 1774 at a cost of $165, La Charrette Village citizens managed their need for law and order without anything more than the authority to proceed. Most La Charrette settlers carried firearms. Several like Cardinal, Colter, Phillips, and Boone purportedly killed an adversary. Even duels were reported as relatively common in settling personal disputes, even though none were ever reported at La Charrette. Traditionally, the appointed syndic of a French village was charged in hearing legal conflicts. At La Charrette, syndic Chartran served as a trustee—judge, jury, and sheriff—all in one. Around the first day of each year, he was required to schedule a public assembly in the presence of the lieutenant governor. Fines were collected and set aside as a public improvement fund. Disputes were routinely heard immediately, and appeals were not common. After a hearing of both parties at La Charrette Village, the decree of "ancient" syndic Chartran was promulgated. With rare exceptions, both parties typically agreed to the terms. Unfortunately, none of the proceedings of this uncomplicated legal system have survived.

However, as soon to be revealed, village law became a complicated legal maze involving multiple cultures and administrations. Logically French, Spanish, and American legal systems were each implemented during their respective administrations, but it did not transpire that way. One author explains "a dual system of procedure" caused more than a "little perplexity to the judges and lawyers" attempting to administer the law.[23] Most village citizens realized, as French control shifted to the United States, they would have new responsibilities. They needed to work the roads and render up to six months of militia service, furnishing their own rifles, powder, balls, and knapsacks. In 1804, Congress established new laws for the District of Louisiana that Governor William H. Harrison was to administer. The law book of fifty-five pages introduced the public whipping post, pillory, and imprisonment for debts. All were unknown provisions to previous civil laws in the territory, although whipping was abolished in 1826. Additionally, the status of territorial citizenship provided cause for consternation when an 1804 congressional act extended citizenship to the residents as soon as possible:

> The inhabitants of the ceded territory shall be incorporated in the Union of the United States, and admitted as soon as possible, according to the principles of the Federal Constitution, to

the enjoyment of all rights, advantages and immunities of the citizens of the United States.

Of course, there were taxes. On October 1, 1804, the first law establishing public revenue in the district was enacted to regulate county rates and levies. Under this act, all houses in towns, town lots, outlots, and mansions in the country valued at $200 and upwards; water and windmills; ferries; all horses, mules and cattle more than three years old; and slaves, with various notable exceptions, were now assessed for local revenue. The first property taxes collected at La Charrette Village in 1805 ranged from less than a dollar to as much as twelve dollars for landowners (See Appendix A). This new law spawned yet other laws, along with more confusion and disputes regarding their administration. Moreover, these new laws were yet to be superseded by others associated with development of the territory, statehood in 1821, and when Warren County was formed in 1833. However, the actual transition from French to Spanish, then back to the French, and finally to American administrations was an exceptionally uneven process.

In reality, the influence of Spanish law prevailed far longer than might have been reasonably expected, resulting in what must have been an exasperating reality for local citizens as well as the legal profession. When Count O'Reilly took administrative control of the region from France in August 1769, he abolished the authority of all French laws, substituting those of Spain instead. Any land titles in Missouri under the previous administration became invalid as of November 26, 1769. Only land titles granted after May 23, 1772, carried the proper authority according to the Spanish. Legal scholars explain how the next transfers of power proceeded.[23] The return of Louisiana under the dominion of France and its subsequent transfer to the United States did not weaken the Spanish laws in the province for a moment. The French, during the short continuation of their power, from November 30 to December 20, 1803, did not make any alteration in the jurisprudence of the territory:

> According to the law of nations, and the treaty between the United States and France, of April 30th, 1803, and the acts of Congress of March 26th, 1804, March 3rd, 1805 and June 4th, 1812, the Spanish laws of Upper Louisiana were expressly continued in full force, until altered or repealed by the proper legislative authority. There was no legislation on the subject, until the 19th of January, 1816, when the territorial legislature of Missouri declared that the common law of

England, and the statutes of the British Parliament, made prior to the fourth year of James the First, to apply its defects, should be the rule of decision, so far as the same were not repugnant to, or inconsistent with, the *laws* [omitting to say *statute* laws] of the territory.

Even the litigation of *Lindell v. MaNair* claimed the January 1816 legislation applied only to common law. The older judges in the territory were inclined to agree, as did many citizens. These and other uncertainties and delays allowed Spanish codes and legal precedence to continue almost up to the time when Missouri acquired her statehood.[24] In actuality, local territorial law represented a dual system of Spanish and American laws and customs both functioning at once, but to various degrees at different locations within the territory. As previously noted all too vividly, circumstances such as these proved disastrous to La Charrette Village settlers when seeking complete titles to their land claims during the formative years of the Louisiana Purchase.

At this same time, unwritten, but equally, legitimate legal codes were honored within frontier society. This reality caught the attention of lawyer/scholar H. M. Brackenridge while visiting St. Louis during this period of legal confusion.[25] In an old ruined barracks where court was sometimes held, he came upon an imprisoned Mascontin Indian who had lived nearby with his wife among the Kickapoos. His Kickapoo wife had left him for another man. While visiting St. Louis, the husband and wife had a chance encounter. They argued and fought, resulting in the death of his wife. He was arrested. After eighteen months in prison, Brackenridge offered his pro bono legal services to the Indian soon facing trial for first-degree murder. Brackenridge did his best to represent his client, but he noted he did not have any concept of the pending trial, only the fear he was to be "hung like a dog." The Pittsburgh lawyer offered a brilliant defense based largely upon the notion that common English law recently adopted by the territory provided for the extradition of aliens to their home jurisdiction for trial and punishment. However, it was the Americans, not the Indians, who were aliens. Brackenridge asked during the oral defense, "Is the Indian an alien?"

He proceeded to answer his own question:

It cannot be contended for a moment that he answers the description of an alien in a single particular. He is a native of the soil; he was here when we first set foot on it—he and his forefathers time immemorial. As respects him, we are the aliens.

He is neither a citizen nor a denizen. By our acts of Congress, he is expressly excluded from the tax list, militia roll, from the census, and of course from all the duties, as well as privileges, of citizenship.

We found the Indians existing in societies, in their tribes, and villages, under their rude but well-established laws and usages; we have permitted them to remain in the midst of us, and within the limits of our local jurisdictions. Never until now have they been told that their intercourse with each other must be regulated by the same laws that the white men have established for themselves, and with which the poor Indian has no possible means of becoming acquainted.

The verdict was not guilty. The Indian was held in jail for a few days after the verdict was promulgated to assure his safe release. However, not all Native Americans were represented so well. Much to the consternation of many Missourians, their entangled frontier legal systems were becoming too complex—verging on dysfunctional—since the days when "ancient" syndic Chartran offered his decrees at La Charrette Village.

# Chapter 10:

## The Village Guestbook

Were it not for the journals faithfully maintained by various expedition members and travelers, our knowledge of western frontier events would be much diminished from what they are. Many who took the time at the end of an exhaustive day's work were not greatly disposed to write. Their journal entries often lacked in some essential detail, including confusion over dates. Many journals clearly reflect one's best efforts to spell both familiar and new words phonetically. However, we should not judge them too harshly. They did their best under adverse conditions—perhaps around a campfire or by moonlight, in a rain-soaked tent filled with hungry mosquitoes, on an empty stomach, in fear of the unknown, or among hundreds of other such adversities. There were ample excuses not to write.

However, there were pragmatic reasons for recording these daily events. Regardless of whether private or public monies funded an expedition, someone in St. Louis, Washington DC, or elsewhere expected to see a complete, accurate report upon their return. Some of the traveling scholars and preachers had other motives. Their desire just to learn and explore often motivated them. Others combined these attributes with the hope of publishing a book about their travels, thereby becoming experts on the world's most exciting topic of the day—the great American West. Regardless of motivation and circumstances, what they wrote soon became established as fact around the world. Without the faithful determination of these men and women, much of what is known about La Charrette Village would be impossible to reconstruct. They recorded many things. Most would record what impressed or amused them. Some were under strict military command to record specific facts, while others recorded aspects of their ventures for a perceived readership. Few offered flattering observations as they passed La Charrette Village.

# Lewis and Clark's Arrival

Lewis and Clark made final preparations for their epic voyage during the winter of 1803–1804 while camped at Wood River, a small stream across the Mississippi from the mouth of the Missouri River, eighteen miles above St. Louis. Here, they assembled and trained their men, established winter quarters, secured provisions in anticipation of every need conceivable to them, and overcame obstacles and disappointments while simultaneously participating in events in St. Louis.

Their dream of charting a trade route to the "Sea of the West" had its origin in the minds of many previous explorers—Cartier, Champlain, Groseilliers, Radisson, and Trudeau—dating from at least 1665 and, from there, to Thomas Jefferson. James Maury, an early teacher of the future president, and his father both helped shape this ongoing dream. Even before the United States acquired the Louisiana Purchase and before being elected president, Jefferson was eager to explore west of the Mississippi. In a 1783 letter, he propositioned the older brother of William Clark, George Rogers Clark, asking if he would like to lead such a party. The next year, when serving as minister to France, he offered John Ledyard a similar opportunity, but neither of these offers materialized. In 1790, the 300-pound General Knox, United States secretary of war, was prompted to engage Captain John Armstrong to cross the continent by way of the Missouri.[1] Armstrong proceeded up the Missouri with one servant, apparently to achieve secrecy, without military escort until "turned back a short distance above St. Louis by disturbances among Indians." Jefferson, Washington, and Hamilton funded in part a fourth attempt of 1792, which included Andre Michaux in their plans. This venture was abruptly canceled after learning Michaux was a secret agent of the French. The fifth attempt involved more careful preparation and attained full success.

This time, on January 18, 1803, before the Louisiana Purchase, President Jefferson submitted a confidential letter to members of congress. He sought—and received—$2,500 to fund a dozen or so army regulars to explore Upper Louisiana. His foresight was further evidenced as he continued seeking all available information about this wilderness. Even documents from the Missouri Trading Company's expedition led by Jean-Baptiste Trudeau that had traded at "Chorette's Creek" in 1795 found their way to Monticello. Trudeau's journals listed the objectives of his expedition. He was to trade with the Native Americans, discover new Indian nations, reach the Pacific Ocean, and eventually establish forts along the entire route. All became consistent with the long-term ambitions of the Lewis and Clark Expedition.[2, 3] However, at this time, the most important need for the expedition leaders at Wood River was obtaining information to accomplish a safe, efficient passage up the Missouri. In all reality, they seem to have pushed off upriver on May 14, 1804, without having received supportive assistance from the most informed authority on the upper reaches of the Missouri River. Manuel Lisa, previously introduced, apparently possessed all the essential traits of a successful river tycoon fur trader, but none of a diplomat.

Lisa arrived in St. Louis in September 1798 as a young man, and he soon won the enmity of the Chouteau family and other fur traders for years to come. Lisa, an exceptionally industrious and competitive hardline fur trader, was born to Spanish parents in New Orleans. His attempts to muscle into the Missouri fur trade were soon rewarded. By 1802, Lisa and three others formed Manuel Lisa, Benoit, and Company to trade in furs. It has been stated Lisa knew and understood the Upper Missouri and western Indians as well as—or better than—anyone. He made at least twelve trips upriver during his life, later earning him the title as the "Father of Missouri River navigation."

Undoubtedly, the river conditions, the Native Americans, the trading post, and the squatters along the route were all discussed when Lewis dined in the Lisa home. Lisa even offered Clark a crew for the expedition.[4] Lewis wrote Clark, "Engage them immediately, if you think from their appearance and character they will answer our purpose." However, to the disappointment of both Lewis and Clark, this deal was never consummated.

Ensuing encounters led this once-developing relationship between Lisa and the captains to deteriorate. Lisa only spoke Spanish fluently. He never acquired a fluent or correct command of either French or English.[5] Most importantly, Lewis reportedly "had difficulties with Lisa in St. Louis during the winter of 1803–04 and disliked him intensely, as did many others." Lewis suspected Lisa had circulated a petition critical of him. As a result, he preferred consulting with others.[6] This feeling of uneasiness between Lisa and the expedition leaders restricted the flow of much-needed information. A few weeks before the expedition departed Wood River, on May 6, 1804, the relationship worsened as Lewis wrote Clark about an incident involving storage kegs. Lisa had purchased the entire St. Louis inventory of kegs to demonstrate his displeasure over not getting more of the expedition's business. Lewis was furious.[3] He penned, "Damm Manuel, and triply Damm Mr. B. [Lisa's partner Francois Benoit]. They give me more vexation and trouble than their lives are worth." More excerpts from the letter to Clark reveal even greater frustration. "Those gentlemen," he wrote. He then stopped and crossed it out before continuing, "These puppies, are not unacquainted with my opinions...strange indeed, that men to appearance in their senses, will manifest such strong symptoms of insanity, as to be wheting knives to cut their own throats." Predictably, Lisa held his opinions too, later describing Lewis as "...a very headstrong, & in many instances an imprudent man."[3] More in jest than earnest, present-day authors have since described Lisa as, "Half French, half Spanish, and half grinning alligator." More balanced views on the life of this dynamic, fur-trading icon are available.[7]

Only fur trader and explorer James MacKay, a Scotchman residing in Saskatchewan by 1776 and in St. Louis by 1793 before serving as commandant of St. Charles, was considered a near equal to Lisa in his knowledge of the Upper Missouri. Like Trudeau before him, MacKay maintained extensive journals of his trip up the Missouri during the fall of 1795 for the Missouri Trading Company. Lewis had profitable talks with MacKay on January 10, 1804, at Wood River. He provided Clark with his "Mandan" map, other documents, and much oral information. Likewise, Auguste Chouteau had been instrumental in advising and outfitting this historic mission. Both captains had spent many hours in the Chouteau home, but he was not an authority on the far reaches of the Upper Missouri. Lewis and Clark had done their best fact-finding under the prevailing circumstances in St. Louis. Besides, they had many other details to oversee to properly provision and prepare the expedition before pushing off. Each detail was important. Nearly 300 different items were on the list of provisions; Lewis weighed and inventoried them all. Rowing and target practice for crewmembers, disciplining rowdy troops, acquiring every provision, rearranging bales and kegs on the keelboat, as well as understanding the current status of Native American tribes along the route all required attention. The bitter news over the belittling appointment of Clark as a second lieutenant only added to an already demanding situation.

Further, Lewis would have preferred to prepare and train upriver on the Missouri. "Their original intention was to pass the winter at La Charrette, the highest settlement on the Missouri." [8, 9, 10] That was not to happen. On December 7, 1803, Lewis and his interpreter Nicholas Jarrot, a fur trader from Cahokia, crossed the Mississippi at St. Louis to visit with French colonel Carlos Dehault Delassus, lieutenant governor of Upper Louisiana, to gain permission to enter the territory before the transfer of sovereignty took place. Lewis wanted to avoid the distractions associated with the Wood River location next to St. Louis. Instead, Delassus demanded they stay where they were until after March 10,

1804, when he would no longer administer the region following the Spanish-French-American transfer. Lewis and Clark obliged. They wintered with their forty-one men at Camp Wood until 4:00 PM on May 14.

By now, the expedition was progressing slowly up the Missouri River when it struck three huge, saturated logs hidden beneath the murky waters on the first day of their voyage. Lewis and Clark hastily altered protocol. They positioned two sergeants over the bow, others elsewhere, in search of these oversized, unsuspected torpedoes charging down the river. On May 20 at St. Charles, cargo was shifted forward to better accommodate these hazardous river conditions. Both Lewis and Clark entered near-identical journal notes that evening, indicating they had "suped this evening with Monsr. Charles Tayong (Village Charrette landholder Don Carlos Tayon) a Spanish Ensign & late Commandant of St. Charles."[6] While here, Lewis added two half-breed privates to his roster, Peter Cruzatte and Francis Labiche, both experienced river voyagers to assist as interrupters. Cruzatte, of Omaha and French heritage, had only one eye, but he was an accomplished fiddle player who often entertained the crew. By May 24, the Corps of Discovery had advanced upriver to Boone's Settlement with their overloaded flotilla of one large keelboat, two pirogues outfitted with sails, a handful of smaller craft, and two mounted horsemen on shore announcing the arrival of the expedition, now expanded to forty-five members. That evening, they visited as well as "bought corn and butter."

Plate 5. Lewis and Clark Discovery Expedition of 1996. Keelboat reproduction in foreground. Appearing in the background, farthest upriver on the north bank, is where extinct La Charrette Village was located. Picture taken by Jerome Holtmeyer from Renneck Riverfront Park, Washington, Missouri.

"To a Small french Village called La Charatt of seven homes only. This is the last settlements of whites in the bend to the Starbord," is part of the Friday, May 25, 1804, journal entry of Captain William Clark as the Corps of Discovery arrived at La Charrette Village. Here, the Corps met with the villagers and camped for the night a quarter-mile or more above the village at the mouth of Charrette Creek (Figure 5). While there, Lewis held a fortuitous encounter with fur trader Francois Regis Loisel. Loisel had just completed investigating activities of British insurgents on his 1,200-mile upriver trip to Cedar Island, where he had built Fort aux Cedres a few seasons previous.[11] There is no indication this meeting was planned, although Lewis Labeaume in St. Louis advised Lewis to seek out Loisel whenever possible. The journal entry of Corps of Discovery member Joseph Whitehouse indicates the Loisel boat arrived loaded with deerskins from their trading voyage with Native Americans far up the Missouri. Loisel later became a partner in the Missouri Fur Company headed by Manuel Lisa, but he was now a partner with Hugh Heney. That evening, Loisel shared much valuable and detailed information with Lewis about current Missouri River conditions as far up as Cedar Island and beyond. Clark recorded the following in his journal while at Village Charrette:

> Camped at mouth of a Creek called River a Chouritte, [La Charrette], above a Small french Village of 7 houses and as many families, settled at this place to be conv. to hunt, & trade with Indians, here we met with M. Louisell, imedeately down from Seeder [Cedar] Isl. Situated in the Country of the Sciox [Sioux] 400 Leagues up he gave us good Deel of information [and] Some letters he informed us that he Saw no Indians on the river below the Poncrars [Poncaras]. Some hard rain this evening.

Loisel was considered among the most knowledgeable with regard to the geography of the Northwest as far upstream as the mouth of the Teton River. One opinion revealed:

> A meeting with Loisel would be one of great importance to the explorers, for next to MacKay, this man should have been in a position to give more detailed information [sic, and more current] than any other person.[5]

At 7:00 AM on Saturday, May 26, the Corps of Discovery bid farewell to Regis Loisel and La Charrette villagers before confidently proceeding with their flotilla and two horsemen. They had just departed the current, though transient, Missouri gateway to the American West as portrayed by nationally renowned artist and Warren County native Billyo O'Donnell on the front cover. Lewis recorded he was pleased with recent expedition progress. Other Loisel employees soon provided the explorers with updates on upriver conditions as reflected in another of Clark's journal entries.

> Mr. Labaum [Labeaume] informs that a Mr. Tebaux (probably Jose Tebeau Sr. or Jr.) who is at present with Louasell [Loisel] up the Missouri can give us much information in relation to that country.

By June 12, Dorion was encountered on his return to St. Louis with two rafts loaded with furs and buffalo tallow. In October 1804, Jean Valle, another Loisel associate, intercepted the Corps of Discovery north of Cedar Island near the Cheyenne River. Valle specifically advised them of stream conditions as they approached the Black Mountains. Dorion was employed on-the-spot as another expedition interpreter. Thus, the extensive experience and fortuitous contacts with Loisel and his men helped the Corps of Discovery overcome any information gaps left by Lisa, MacKay, the Chouteaus, and others while in St. Louis.

On day twelve of the expedition, Sergeant Patrick Gass and three others recorded in their journals what would become for historians an often-discussed mystery regarding the name of the village they had only recently departed. He and Sergeants Floyd, Whitehouse, and Ordway recorded, perhaps inadvertently, the name of La Charrette Village as "St. Johns" in their almost-identical journal entries. It has been proposed one of the four sergeants made the error, copied later by the other three. Regardless, St. Johns was a stream across the Missouri River from La Charrette near present-day Washington. The possibility these Corps members had contact with someone from St. Johns while at La Charrette Village seems the likely source of this error. By June 1, they passed the Osage River, where the two men on horseback rejoined the expedition. They reported the land they had passed through was "the best they had ever seen."

One of the prime objectives of the Corps of Discovery, as stated by President Jefferson, was establishing friendly relations with the Native Americans. However, the Corps of Discovery members engaged very few Native Americans along the lower Missouri.[12] After a little more than two weeks of travel, they had only traded four deer for two quarts of whisky with a small band of Kickapoo. At the mouth of the Osage River, they encountered two bands of Osage Indians. They reported their warrior populations at 500 Grand Osage and 250 for the Little Osage. Upstream, beyond the mouth of the Kansas River, they encountered a small hunting party of Native Americans identified by the same name as the river. They later went up the Platte River, seeking the Otoe and the Pawnee Indians, but they found none. Finally, in late July, George Drouillard, one of the expedition's valued hunters and half-Indian interpreter, came upon a lone Missouri Indian. They went to his village and returned to the expedition with a few chiefs, including some Otoes, resulting in daylong activities named by Clark as "Council Bluff." Such encounters would continue establishing friendly relationships with the Omaha, Yankton, Lakota, Shoshone, Mandan, Flathead, and numerous other tribes along their long route.

While among the Zoto Indians on August 19, Sergeant Floyd was first reported as very ill with colic. On August 20, Sergeant Charles Floyd expired immediately after landing late that afternoon. He was buried with full military honors atop a hill named in his honor as Stg. Floyd's Bluff. Today, this case of "colic" purportedly represents a ruptured appendix. A solid masonry, 100-foot-tall obelisk now marks the grave of this first American soldier to die west of the Mississippi.

Later, while seeking the Columbia River on October 12, 1804, Sergeant Gass wrote:

> Most of our people having been accustomed to meat, do not relish fish, but prefer dog meat, which, when cooked, tastes very well. The country on both sides is high dry prairie without a stick of timber. There is no wood of any kind to be seen except a few small willows along the shore; so that it is with difficulty we can get enough to cook with.

The 190 dogs consumed during the course of the expedition were obtained through barter with Native Americans along the route. But Seaman, also known as Scannon, the Newfoundland dog owned by Meriwether Lewis, was spared. The 1,001 deer, 375 elk, 227 bison, 43 grizzly bears, and 12 horses provided the bulk of the meat consumed by the hardworking crewmembers.

The ensuing interval, in excess of two years and four months away from La Charrette Village, became one of the most inspiring quests of natural history ever accomplished. Some have rightfully equated it with the space age travels of today. The eight Corps of Discovery journals chronicled a drama of human perseverance seldom equaled. "We proceeded on" was the most frequently recorded phrase in the journals, reflecting the expedition members' sheer, dogged determination. The expedition navigated to the headwaters of the Missouri River, winter at Fort Mandan, cross the Continental Divide, proceed down the Columbia River, and thereby chart the Northwest Passage to the Pacific Ocean before returning. Not only did this epic journey chart new routes, rivers, and land formations as well as record weather and life among Native Americans, but they also discovered and documented hundreds of species of plants, aquatic life, reptiles, mammals, and birds never before known to exist. Numerous specimens of skin, bone, horn, petrified remains—even live birds and prairie dogs—were collected, preserved, and sent downriver. As a result, this western wilderness was soon poised to join the rest of the developing world as a part of the United States of America.

Unsurprisingly, some did not favor this outcome for the United States. Pedro Vial, a native of Lyons, France, was an experienced explorer of the southwest and the Lower Missouri River, as previously noted. He was now under orders from the governor of New Spain, Joaquin Alencaster, to march his soldiers north from Santa Fe to entice the Native Americans to disrupt the Corps of Discovery activities in 1805. This subversive action obviously failed. In 1806, an even larger force was sent out on the same mission. This time, Vial's troops deserted him, aborting that plan as well. Vial even led a third attempt plus a fourth undertaken by Facundo Melgares.[6] All failed, but two came within days of disrupting the expedition's progress. Ironically, by September 14, 1808, alliances had shifted when Meriwether Lewis, now governor of Upper Louisiana, issued a license to Vial to hunt on the Missouri River, where he had explored during the late 1700s.

The Corps members did encounter numerous trappers and traders as they began meandering their way downstream in 1806. Four trappers returning from Texas brought exciting news telling of Captain Zebulon Pike departing Fort Bellefontaine to explore the Red and Arkansas Rivers. By September 16, they met Mr. Robidoux, a trader from St. Louis, traveling on a large boat propelled by six oars and accompanied by two canoes on his way to trade with the Kansas Indians. It was now they began anticipating their return to civilization with confidence.

# A Joyful Return to La Charrette

Plate 6. Warren County farmland on the north bank of the Missouri (as seen coming downriver at Charrette Bend). Hereabouts "the sight of cows" inspired Corps of Discovery members to shout for joy. Picture taken from across the river in Franklin County from Chitwood Bluff, May 2001.

As the late summer of 1806 concluded, the Corps of Discovery was still making excellent progress, fully anticipating La Charrette Village. This time, they would arrive from the west. The crew plied their oars with enthusiasm. It was hot and sultry. They were almost out of provisions. On September 17, they passed the Island of the Little Osage Village. The next day, they rose early from camp four miles above the Grand River. Still, the hunters were unsuccessful, so they chose instead to subsist upon the few remaining biscuits and eat many of the sweet-tasting papaws, a member of the custard-apple family of fruit in abundance along the shoreline. While vigorously rowing in the oppressive heat of late summer, sweat crept into their eyes. It was hastily rubbed away as they continued rushing downstream. It was now Friday, September 19, as they sought La Charrette the next day. Several crewmembers now began complaining of an extremely painful burning sensation in and about their eyes upon approaching the Osage River. Their eyes were inflamed, and many eyelids appeared as if they were sunburned. Chalk-like substance on the skin of the papaws caused infectious conjunctivitis. Handling them and then brushing their eyes to remove sweat had infected the men.[6] The next morning, the eyes of three crewmembers were so severely swollen that they could not see to row their canoes. The two canoes Clark had lashed together on the Upper Yellowstone were set adrift with their loads shifted to accommodate this latest obstacle. By noon of the next day, Saturday, September 20, they passed the Gasconade River. They were now only forty miles from civilization. Late that evening, they negotiated Charrette Bend as a familiar, tiny French village slowly flickered into view, highlighted by the approaching sunset shimmering upon the waters of the Missouri:

> That afternoon, the sight of cows on the bank near La Charette brought enthusiastic shouts! As the voyagers landed at the village, three rounds of small arms were returned by nearby trading boats. In the evening, the citizens, whose homes many of the men visited, provided food and entertainment. Dancing with or watching the ladies, the first nonnative women the party had seen in more than 2 years, was a favorite pastime. Departure time in the morning, Sunday, was 7:30 a.m.[8]

A more informative chronicling of this September 20 and 21, 1806, event is offered from Clark's notes:

> The party, being extremely anxious to get down, ply their oars very well. We saw some cows on the bank, which was a joyful sight to the party and caused a shout to be raised for joy. At [blank in MS.] p.m., we came in sight of the little French village called Charrette. The men raised a shout and sprang upon their oars, and we soon landed opposite to the village.
>
> Our party requested to be permitted to fire off their guns, which was allowed, and they discharged three rounds with a hearty cheer, which was returned from five trading boats which lay opposite the village. We landed and were very politely received by two young Scotsmen from Canada—one in the employ of Mr. Arid, a Mr. [blank in MS.], and the other, Mr. Reed. Two other boats, the property of Mr. Lacomb and Mr. [blank in MS.]. All of those boats were bound to the Osage and Otos.
>
> Those two young Scotch gentlemen furnished us beef, flour, and some pork for our men, and gave us a very agreeable supper. As it was like to rain, we accepted of a bed in one of their tents. We purchased of a citizen two gallons of whiskey for our party, for which we were obliged to give eight dollars in cash, an imposition on the part of the citizen.

Every person, both French and Americans, seemed to express great pleasure at our return, and acknowledged themselves much astonishment in seeing us return. They informed us that we were supposed to have been lost long since, and were entirely given out by every person, &c.

Rose early this morning [September 21]. Collected our men. Several of them had accepted of the invitation of the citizens and visited their families. At half after 7 a.m. we set out. Passed 12 canoes of Kickapoos ascending on a hunting expedition. Saw several persons, also stock of different kinds on the bank, which revived the party very much. At 3 p.m. we met two large boats ascending. At 4 p.m. we arrived in sight of St. Charles...[13]

Certainly, this must have been one of the finest hours of Missouri hospitality for everyone present. Imagine the conversations in the village that eventful evening! The Corps members learned most Americans had considered their party forever lost to the wilderness. The exciting stories they told of unimaginable discoveries and experiences as well as what they had endured and conquered. Where were Charles Floyd and John Colter? Corps members also had questions. Was the nation at war? Why had Jean-Marie Cardinal Jr. and his family left La Charrette? Who won the presidential election? Had they seen Pike? Whose boats were docked over there on Luzon Island? One may contemplate if those present that eventful evening fully grasped the significance of what they had accomplished and what they were experiencing. Corps members had actually returned to this humble settlement on this magnificent river that had so consumed and tested the energies and commitments of these brave men for the past 848 days. What a struggle for knowledge! Joyful in the extreme!

Even the National Geographic Society chose to re-create this scene of arrival in its 1970 booklet, *In the Footsteps of Lewis and Clark*, with an oversized sketch. Without any cows depicted on the riverbank, the fifteen Corps of Discovery members are shown in their small canoes approaching La Charrette Village landing. Some villagers are onshore with their Canadian guest as an international welcoming committee. Several women and children waving their greetings from the shoreline accompany men standing on the dock with guns in hand. Between them and their returning heroes were two villagers maneuvering into position to assist the explorers in docking. In the background, onshore, are two, single-story French houses, one with the typical low front porch. Even in this sketch, all evidence the excitement reflected in facial expressions and body postures.

An historic moment of grand proportions had unfolded at La Charrette Village. The Lewis and Clark Expedition had returned to the place of its last rendezvous with "the advance guard of civilization!" Imagine...over 8,000 wilderness miles! Even in those times, their efforts were recognized as exceptional, especially for those with an interest in proceeding westward with their lives. La Charrette villagers were last to wish members of the Corps of Discovery "good luck" on their outbound journey, and they were the first to welcome them back to civilization. They did what others in St. Charles, St. Louis, and Washington DC could only do in the days and weeks ahead. They celebrated. It is frequently reported that crewmembers danced with or watched the women on that joyful evening, the first white women seen in more than two years, even though several Village Charrette wives were actually Native Americans. With two gallons of much-desired whiskey in their possession, spirits undoubtedly flowed freely and ran high that night! It would not be until January 1807 when the explorers would celebrate in the nation's capital with the president and other dignitaries. Later still, word of their success spread about the globe. But Thomas Jefferson, who so desired to travel west and see his Louisiana Purchase, never ventured farther than sixty miles west of Staunton, Virginia.

Another sketch re-creating an incredulous moment of arrival happened in St. Louis at 10:00 AM on September 23, 1806, after an absence of two years, four months, and ten days. This time, it featured, perhaps with deliberate nostalgia, Seaman the dog.[12] "Our dog" was how Clark once recorded the expedition's faithful companion. But Seaman may not have celebrated upon his return by frolicking after squirrels as he once had. July 15, 1806, was the last journal entry on his behalf. Mosquitoes were so excessive at that time, compelling Lewis to record, "my dog even howls with the torture he experiences."

The Chouteau brothers hosted an elaborate gala dinner and ball the very next evening at Christy's Inn in honor of Lewis and Clark. Eighteen toasts were proposed during the course of the celebration. One pledged, "To The Missouri—Under the auspices of America, may it prove a vehicle of wealth to all the nations of the world."[14] Once again, speculation about the animated conversations surfaced. Political as always, Auguste Chouteau was preparing to outfit, and escort, his second delegation of Osage chiefs to Washington, including the talkative Mandan Chief Shahaka, who, a few days before, had arrived with the expedition at La Charrette Village on his way to St. Louis. Chouteau's first such delegation of Indian chiefs had only recently been returned to their lodges by members of the Pike Expedition. Subsequent explorations, peace treaties, and development of the American West were soon to proceed, thanks to the committed men of the Corps of Discovery, one woman, her infant son, and one dog.

## Clark's Osage Treaty

Two years and one day after celebrating at La Charrette, newly appointed Indian agent, Brigadier General William Clark again returned to the village. This distinguished, redheaded leader now sat confidently in the saddle of his mount, commanding a company of eighty St. Charles Dragoons. Nathan Boone took the lead over this westward route familiar to him, an ensign of the Sixth Company of the militia for the District of St. Charles since 1806. Others, including Lieutenant James Callaway, rode two abreast. They mustered, according to the law, at eleven o'clock on Thursday, August 25, 1808, to depart from St. Charles. Boone set a demanding pace for the Dragoons, marching nearly twenty miles each day. Their mission was to construct Fort Osage, the first American fort west of the Mississippi, and negotiate yet another treaty with the Osage Indians conceding their hunting grounds both north and south of the Missouri. Their overland route more or less followed old U.S. Highway 40, now U.S. Interstate 70 for a little more than a day.[15] By Saturday, Clark recorded the headwaters of Charrette Creek in his journal, "Set out at half past 6 oClock, and entered a butifull level plain reaching to the N. E. & Passed through this butifull open Plain for 4 miles, head of Charret or its heads to S..."

Over the ensuing month, Clark and his men constructed the fort, once known as Fort Clark, upon a seventy-foot bluff of the Osage River and concluded the treaty before returning to St. Charles. Clark was "unwell" and proceeded downriver to St. Louis by boat with a few other men. This time, as they passed La Charrette Village on Thursday, September 22, Clark wrote in his journal:

> Set out early passed the Chirotte village at 7 oClock wind high put out 2 men at this village, Saw great number of pelicans—killed one arived at the Landing oppost [opposite]...

The name of the two men delivered to La Charrette Village is not disclosed. The reader is however encouraged to study Clark's journal where he describes the local Missouri countryside with a uniqueness of pride and feeling befitting his highly colorful style of prose.

However, the treaty Indian Agent Clark attempted to dutifully consummate soon took on a new omnipotent-like complexion. Treaty negotiations angered Chief White Hair and other tribal leaders, who threatened Clark by reminding him of the frontier people their braves had killed in 1805. Even so, Clark thought the discussions went well. At the time the treaty was signed, seventy-four Osage men, under the leadership of Chief Big Soldier, son of White Hair, were still in St. Louis, returning stolen government horses. Chief Big Soldier and his men now considered the treaty invalid because they had not participated in its signing. Clark took note of the circumstances and agreed to reconsider. He later consulted with Governor Lewis and Pierre Chouteau.

To explain events associated with this diversion, several periods will be visited each with new characters, before returning the reader to Clark's treaty. These revelations were obtained from the notes of Thomas Say and others of the Long Expeditions (1818–1819) and consolidated later by Dr. Edwin James.[16] James, the first man to climb Pike's Peak to its summit, and his party were traveling overland and had just crossed into the southern range of the Osage tribe when they encountered a lone Indian scout. The American flag was waved as a peace gesture. The friendly Indian soon shared some "fine ripe blue plumbs" with his guest and later arranged for five or six other warriors to provision the party with fresh venison for the evening meal. James does not record if these were wild Osage plums or some of those they cultivated. They were now about twelve miles south of the Osage Village. The Native Americans had just located a herd of bison and were eager to return to their lodge to prepare for the fall hunt. Later the next day, September 2, 1820, they all arrived at the Osage lodges.

Extensive portions of the James narrative contains details on the ethnological nature of the Native Americans they visited, including their desire to trade, manner of dress, grooming, adornment, hunting skills, child rearing, eating habits, and behavior. Even the "beautiful symmetry" of Osage stature was recorded. Each contrasted to other tribes encountered. James continues by recording the reputation of the Osage tribe as peaceful, never influenced by the British. This nonmalevolent behavior was exhibited despite repeated land concessions to the United States concurrent with their neighboring tribes experiencing similar constraints and restrictions.

The James narrative next reverts to their stay at Fort Osage "last season" when Mr. Sibley had "politely furnished" them with a copy of a report he had submitted to the government. Sibley, after listing the strength and whereabouts of the Osage of the Oaks, Grand Osage, and Little Osage tribes, reported on their present conditions:

> These tribes are at war with all their neighbours, except the Konzas, and a part of the Sauks and Foxes; with the Konzas they are and long have been on the most intimate and friendly terms; with the Sauks and Foxes they are at present barely at peace. All the chiefs (except Clermont) are very weak and unpopular.

The Sibley report continues for some seven pages. The next two paragraphs recount history, whereupon we are returned to the 1808 treaty negotiated by Indian Agent Clark and Pierre Chouteau:

> In the year 1804 the President of the United States gave his promise to a number of Osage chiefs, then on a visit to Washington, to establish for them a trading-house on the plan authorized by a law of [110] congress. In 1806 the President repeated the same promise to another deputation of Osage chiefs then there. In 1808 the President ordered the establishment to be made, and accordingly in October of that year it was made. So far this was a gratuitous act of the government; but in the following month it assumed a very different character. On the 8th November 1808 Peter Chouteau (the U.S. agent for the Osage), arrived at Fort Clark. On the 10th he assembled the chiefs and the warriors of the Great and Little Osages in council, and proceeded to state to them the substance of a treaty, which he said Governor Lewis had deputed him to offer the Osages, and to execute with them. Having briefly explained to them the purport of a treaty, he addressed them to this effect (in my hearing) and very nearly in the following words: 'You have heard this treaty explained to you; those who now come forward and sign it shall be considered the friends of the United States, and treated accordingly; those who refuse to come forward and sign it shall be considered enemies of the United States, and treated accordingly. The Osages replied in substance, 'that if their Great American Father wanted a part of their land, he must have it; that he was strong and powerful, they were poor and pitiful. What could they do? He had demanded their land, and had thought proper to offer them something in return for it. They had no choice; they must either sign the treaty, or be declared the enemies of the United States.

The treaty was accordingly signed on the same day; and so much were the Osage awed by the threat of Mr. Chouteau, that a very unusual number of them touched the pen; many of whom knew no more the purport of the act than if they had been an hundred miles off; and I here assert it to be a fact, that to this day the treaty is not fairly understood by a single Osage.

Pierre Chouteau was commissioned to complete negotiations on the Clark treaty because he had been the Indian Affairs agent for Upper Louisiana since 1804, but he currently had jurisdiction over only the Osages while William Clark served as the general superintendent of all other Indian tribes in the territory. Following this meeting with Chouteau, about thirty Osage chiefs lodged complaints with the territorial governor, but their pleas fell upon deaf ears. The current treaty obligated them to further relinquish to the United States an immense tract of land, nearly 50,000 acres, generally described as that between the Missouri and Arkansas rivers. They had traded virtually half of Missouri and much of Arkansas for an annuity of $1,500 plus access to one little blacksmith shop with smithy, a mill, some plows, and other considerations. Once operating in almost all of Missouri, many Osage now chose instead to live in eastern Kansas with their Missouri cousins, even though Congress did not ratify the treaty until April 28, 1810.

However, not all had left Missouri. (They would be dealt with later.) For now, the hunting lands surrounding La Charrette Village continued to be held in contention between the Fox, Sacs, and Pottawatomis, but the territorial governor effectively played one tribe off against another as they also gradually relinquished their heritage. It is widely accepted the Osages had been as peaceful and accommodating as any tribe in support of white settlement activities, including previous land concessions to the east. Only during the Spanish regime, plus a few frontier skirmishes with whites, were the Osage implicated in a 1720 massacre of the first military expedition out of Santa Fe to Missouri.[17] Apparently, they were still willing to abide by the wishes of those now administering the territory. The Chouteau family, Clark, and many others considered the Native Americans to be child-like savages compared to whites. Their view toward Native Americans was paternalistic. They respected the Native Americans, but it was always conditional, requiring their approval and support based upon the tribe's continued loyalty and obedience. How husbands to Osage women—those associated with La Charrette like Joseph Chartran, Jean-Marie Cardinal Jr., Jose Tebeau Jr., and John Colter—reconciled these views goes unanswered.

# America's First "Mountain Man"

The presence of the Lewis and Clark Expedition upon Village Charrette had not yet run its full course. During the return trip down the Missouri River, four Corps of Discovery members chose to remain in the wilderness. Early in the summer of 1806, Corps members said their good-byes to Charbonneau, seventeen-year-old Sacagawea, and their son "Little" Baptiste near the Mandan villages in present-day South Dakota. Here, Private John Colter, introduced previously, sought permission to be relieved of his duties. He wanted to continue living in the wilderness to begin a new life of hunting, trapping, and exploring. After discussing his request, Lewis and Clark permitted Colter to leave the expedition with the proviso that no one else ask for a similar discharge. None did. Colter, who joined the Corps of Discovery as a hunter and its third member, indicated he thought he would be "lonely" in St. Louis. The following sentiments about Colter are preserved in the Lewis and Clark journals:

> The example of this man shows us how easily men may be weaned from the habits of civilized life to the ruder but scarcely less fascinating manners of the woods. This hunter has now been absent for many years from the frontiers, and might naturally be presumed to have some anxiety, or some curiosity at least, to return to his friends and his country; yet just at the moment when he is approaching the frontiers, he is tempted by a hunting scheme to give up those delightful prospects, and go back without the least reluctance to the solitude of the woods.[18]

Everyone wished Colter, one of the Corps' youngest members, "every suckess" as they parted. On August 14, 1806, Colter joined two independent American trappers, the first white men Corps members had seen since leaving the Mandan villages in April 1805. Only a short while ago, Forrest Hancock and Joseph Dickson intercepted other Corps of Discovery members farther downstream. Provisioned with two years worth of ammunition and supplies, Colter hunted, trapped, and explored with Dickson and Hancock as an adventuresome trio on their way to the Yellowstone. These three men may have reportedly crossed paths previous to the expedition, possibly around La Charrette. Hancock, brother to Stephen and son of William, was from Hancock Bottoms neighboring La Charrette Village, although some authors claim he and Dickson were both Illinois traders. Actually, Dickson had moved to Cahokia, Illinois, from Tennessee in 1802. While hunting, trapping, and cutting timber on the

Gasconade River in Missouri, he met Hancock. By August 1804, the two men were headed up the Missouri in their cottonwood pirogue. They spent the first winter near Sioux City, Iowa, and then worked for Charles Courtin in Teton Sioux country the next year.

Within six weeks, a dispute erupted between this trio of fiercely independent men, the first to trap on the Yellowstone, dissolving their casual partnership. Dickson stayed alone on the Yellowstone, but he endured great hardship while Colter and Hancock continued working among the Mandans. A little later, they also went their separate ways.

Later in 1807, Colter consented to work for Lisa while continuing to add to his wilderness mental data bank. Some speculated Colter was even engaged to map a transmontane trade route to Santa Fe for Lisa.[19] He traveled alone for over 500 miles, often on snowshoes, with his rifle and a thirty-pound pack while contacting Native Americans on behalf of the Missouri Fur Company. He continued to prevail over wilderness adversities of extreme cold, a leg injury, and illnesses. These and other travels allowed him to discover the now-famous Jackson's Hole Valley, the headwaters of the Colorado and Snake Rivers, the valley of the Big Horn River, plus Yellowstone and Grand Teton National Parks. His only known stone head appears at Pierre's Hole inscribed "John Colter 1808."[19] When Colter later reported seeing boiling mud, burning lakes, and steaming geysers in (or near) Yellowstone, everyone ridiculed and derided him. The embellished retelling of his experiences was soon exaggerated into "Colter's Hell." It would not be until 1870 when William Henry Jackson's photographs set the record straight for the rest of the world to appreciate what John Colter had discovered.

Soon Colter encountered yet another old friend, this one a former Corps of Discovery crewmember. When they met, John Potts was ascending the Jefferson River, accompanying the Andrew Henry outfit in the spring of 1808. Later that year, some 500 Blackfeet Indians captured them in a surprise assault. Potts was killed, disemboweled, and dismembered after recklessly shooting a brave. His slaughtered body parts were flung into the face of Colter. By now, Colter was naked, barefoot, and disarmed before he was given the opportunity to run for his life over a rocky prairie besieged with thorny brush and prickly pear. It was five or six miles of miraculous running...running from death! Blood streamed from his mouth and nostrils with a lone Blackfeet brave still in dogged pursuit of Colter. His body was cut, pricked, bruised, and exhausted. Abruptly, the powerfully endowed Colter halted and turned upon his astounded assailant who stumbled, allowing Colter to overwhelm and kill him with his own spear. A few slower braves were still charging on over the horizon. Next, Colter's escape continued underwater in the Madison River by playing like a beaver beneath a pile of driftwood. Spared almost certain death at the hands of Blackfeet Indians, he was now confronted with a slower death at the hands of starvation and exposure. Prodigiously, after traveling more than 250 miles, day and night, in the cold of early winter with only the brave's spear and blanket, Colter arrived at Fort Raymond on the mouth of the Bighorn eleven days later. Thomas James records "the company at the fort did not recognize him in his dismal plight until he made himself known." The emaciated Colter recuperated from infected and swollen limbs, contemplated his future, and chose once again to remain in the wilderness he so deeply loved. For most of this time, he apparently remained employed by Lisa in hunting, trapping, and other assignments.[19]

Colter would not return to "civilization" until arriving in St. Louis in May 1810. Alone, he traveled 3,000 miles from the Missouri headwaters to its mouth in a small canoe in only thirty days. In haste, he glimpsed Cote sans Dessein for the first time and doubtlessly dreamed of owning a La Charrette farm as he sped by. Having remained continuously—and longer—in the wilderness of the Upper Missouri and Rocky Mountains than any other man of European extraction of his day, he earned the title as the first "Mountain Man" of the American West. His wilderness experiences became an exceptional mental data bank unique to John Colter. He sometimes drank too much, but he asked forgiveness and was later recognized as an excellent hunter and a highly dependable member of the Corps. Upon his return to St. Louis, he and George Drouillard, fellow Corps of Discovery member and interpreter, shared information from their mental data banks with William Clark to construct government maps. For decades, these maps were virtual blueprints for expansion into the American West.

John Colter fell in love and married Indian Sarah Loucy upon his return to civilization. They became La Charrette Village neighbors while living near Dundee in Franklin County, immediately across the Missouri from La Charrette where children Hiram and Evelina would later join their family. Some uncertainty surrounds these aspects of his private life, including a previous wife, other children, and his gravesite. Another Corps of Discovery member and friend, Robert Frazer also resided nearby. Colter died of hepatitis two years later near Charrette, Missouri.[21] His was a somewhat "better off" than average estate of $233.76-1/2 after full payment of debts, according to estate administrator Daniel Richardson on December 10, 1813. His present-day grave marker is positioned east of New Haven, Missouri, on the very edge of a majestic south bluff of the Missouri River overlooking the memory of La Charrette Village to the immediate northeast. Sadly, his original grave contents may have served as part of the fill for the track bed of the Missouri Pacific Railroad when double tracks were added at Tunnel Hill in 1926. His present-day tombstone inscription reads: John Colter Member of U.S. Volunteer Mounted Rangers Nathan Boone's CO. Mar. 3, 1812 to May 6, 1812. Died May 7, 1812.

Apparently, this stretch of the Missouri River was a favorite location for this exceptionally private family man—a naturalist, trapper, expedition guide, farmer, explorer, ranger, and hero figure. Or perhaps the neighbors—Boone, Lamme, Frazer, Tayon, and Phillips—attracted him. All of John Colter's exploits were recorded in the journals of his comrades traveling with Lewis and Clark, John Bradbury, or Thomas James. None were recorded by the "Mountain Man," John Colter. James relates he "wore an open, ingenious and pleasing countenance of the Daniel Boone stamp." Over the years, his heroic exploits have appeared in numerous publications, including the works of Washington Irving.[21] Without a doubt, he inspired others like Mathew Kinkead to take up his trade as a "Mountain Man" when western migration begun in earnest. Kinkead, a native of Kentucky, lived on a failed 1804 land claim on the forks of Charrette Creek before moving to Boonslick in 1809. He later crossed the Santa Fe Trail and sipped whiskey with Kit Carson. He became a naturalized citizen of Mexico while exploring the greater Southwest, where he and Teresita Sandoval, his common-law wife, eventually established themselves as founders of Fort Pueblo to become known as Colorado's first cattlemen.

As the first mountain man of the American West, before Jim Bridger, Louis Vasquez, Jed Smith, and all the rest, unassuming John Colter, about five foot ten, perhaps introverted, was most disposed to chat with his friends like Daniel Boone and Indian Phillips as others have speculated. None were inclined to write. They detested lies and liars, and they had learned to distrust others embellishing their tales. When these exceptional men shared their experiences somewhere around what would soon become Charrette Township of Warren County, Missouri, they spoke with authority concerning the breadth of the North America wilderness. Indeed, their wilderness conversations represented an unprecedented mingling of the minds between the greatest of American frontiersmen—heroes, wilderness men, and famous hunters. None of these conversations have survived, but Nathan and Olive Van Bibber

Boone, Daniel's son and daughter-in-law, at least held John Colter in the highest of esteem and expressed that sentiment by naming their son, born May 13, 1816, John Colter Boone. Nevertheless, the most exalted and enduring compliment paid John Colter was to be bestowed 150 years later by Professor Goetzmann. In the epilogue of his 1966 Pulitzer Prize-winning volume on the giants of western exploration, he ranked the leaders among the giants starting with "Lewis and Clark, Zebulon Pike, John Colter..."[19]

Today, the John Colter Memorial and Visitors Center in New Haven, Missouri, honors this unique American hero.

Plate 7. John Colter's present-day tombstone. Located on the edge of the Missouri River bluff near Little Boeuf Creek in Franklin County. From this vantage point New Haven Reach looms westward into a broad and majestic expanse of the river he so loved, and mastered.

# The Missouri Marathon

Shortly after John Colter settled across from La Charrette, a distinguished English scholar visiting the village called upon him. John Bradbury, F.L.S. London, a corresponding member of the Liverpool Philosophical Society and honorary member of the Literary and Philosophical Societies of New York, was sent to America as a naturalist to collect plant specimens for the Liverpool Botanic Gardens. His travels took him as far upriver as the Oregon Territory into what was to become South Dakota with members of John Jacob Astor's American Fur Company. There, lawyer/author H. M. Brackenridge, who had traveled the river with Lisa's Missouri Fur Company, joined him. Both Brackenridge and Bradbury maintained extensive journals of their travels, which were subsequently published. Bradbury alone documented specimens of 1,500 plants and other life forms. Each contributed greatly to our present-day understanding of the frontier. Brackenridge did not visit La Charrette Village, as did Bradbury, but he was traveling with two guests important to the Corps of Discovery—Toussaint Charbonneau and his wife Sacagawea who had only recently left their son, Baptiste, and his future in the hands of William Clark in St. Louis. Clark later adopted Baptiste and maintained his promise to see to his educational needs as well as his little sister Lisette. Brackenridge records his impressions of his travel companions of 1811:[22]

> We had on board a Frenchman named Charbon, with his wife, an Indian woman of the Snake nation, both of whom had accompanied Lewis and Clark to the Pacific, and were of good service. The woman, a good creature, of mild and gentle disposition is greatly attached to whites, whose manner and dress she tries to imitate, but she had become sickly and longed to revisit her native country; her husband, also, who had spent many years among the Indians, was become weary of the civilized life.

As always, competition was fierce between fur industry giants Astor and Lisa. Their race upriver, now referred to by historians as the Missouri Marathon, was one of great importance for these fur industry leaders to maintain contacts with their field captains, forts, and trappers. Lisa set a new record traveling 1,200 miles in just sixty-one days—without stopping at La Charrette—as he tried joining his partners upriver. His creditors in St. Louis delayed his departure, adding to his anxiety. However, only days before, Lisa tried delaying the departure of the Astor crew by having Pierre Dorion entrapped for an old whiskey debt. Pierre was the son of Dorion, an expedition interpreter for Lewis and Clark. Fortunately for Bradbury, Astor's crew established a considerable lead over Lisa and ascended the Missouri River at a more leisurely pace. Their crew of French-Canadians reportedly sang and rowed their boats in mutual harmony. Astorians, Bradbury, and his host, Wilson P. Hunt, camped one evening at St. Johns Creek, across the Missouri from Village Charrette.

On the morning of March 17, 1811, Hunt and Bradbury were strolling along the south banks of the Missouri River where they were "much struck" by the "vast size" of the cottonwood trees.[23] Many exceeded seven feet in diameter and continued upward "with a thickness very little diminished" to an estimated height of eighty feet or so. After breakfast, they crossed the river and, by afternoon, landed at a little French village, "name Charette." Bradbury observed a "striking instance of the indolence of the inhabitants." He continued:

> The rushes in the neighborhood had been already destroyed by the cattle, and from the neglect of the owners to provide winter food for their horses, they had been reduced to the necessity of gnawing the bark off the trees, some hundreds of which were stripped as far as these animals could reach.

Bradbury was indeed correct in his observations regarding animal husbandry. If the livestock were reduced to consuming bark and rushes as he described, there was obviously little else for them to consume. However, his comment about indolent villagers may be partially redeemed by their ulterior motives. Girdled trees stripped of their bark generally die, rendering them dry and easier to burn. It was a crude but effective technique to aid in the clearing of land for cultivation.

Upon departing La Charrette Village, Mr. Hunt pointed to an old man with white hair standing on the riverbank. He indicated he was the discoverer of Kentucky, none other than the renowned Daniel Boone. As Bradbury had a letter of introduction from Colonel Grant, Boone's nephew, he returned to shore to speak with this famous woodsman and emerging international hero. Bradbury waved for the boat to proceed upriver after introducing himself to Boone. The two of them spent much of the afternoon visiting. Daniel Boone told him he was eighty-four years of age, had spent a considerable time in the backwoods, and had lately returned from his spring hunt with nearly sixty beaver pelts. Washington Irving later wrote of this encounter in *Astoria*, indicating, "The old man was still erect in form, strong of limb, and unflinching in spirit..."[24]

After Bradbury bid Boone farewell, he proceeded north for a mile or so before swimming across Charrette Creek and the Missouri River to catch up with his party. Rain had been Bradbury's almost constant companion, filling Charrette Creek's banks that March afternoon. He tied his clothes together in his deerskin hunting coat, pushing the bundle before him as he intermittently swam or waded across the broad, shallow river. About three hours later, he caught up with his boat at Little Boeuf Creek near the homestead of Mr. Sullens. Bradbury inquired about John Colter's whereabouts. From General Clark, he learned of a supposed forty-foot-long petrified fish skeleton John Colter could locate for him. Colter lived about a mile from the Sullens. Sullens sent his son to fetch Colter, who arrived the next morning, March 18. The petrified fish skeleton was never found, but the shy, blue-eyed Colter indicated his inclination to join the party and once again proceed up the Missouri River with Hunt and Bradbury. However, he reluctantly declined the offer, explaining he had only recently married.

These nineteenth-century conversations between the scholar John Bradbury, the first professional scientist to enter the vast western frontier of America, and the self-styled wilderness hero, John Colter, should have represented the very epitome of discussions on natural history. The contrast in the background of these two men brought together at the height of their respective careers, each as naturalist, could not have been greater. Their common love of nature with all its diversity should have been the only adhesive needed to bind these two giants of their trade. To the contrary, Colter was reluctant to speak freely to Bradbury with his "foreign" ways.[25] Reciprocating, Bradbury probably chose to record less than he might have of their conversations. Regardless, this conversation that became the primary account of Colter's incredulous escape from the Blackfeet Indians. All subsequent retellings of this event, thrilling in the extreme, hold their origin in Bradbury's account and a lesser one by Thomas James. During the morning of March 18, 1811, Bradbury preserved this jewel of frontier history somewhere around Charrette Bend near the mouth of Little Boeuf Creek.

## Zebulon Pike and the President's Guests

Interspersed between the visits to La Charrette by the Corps of Discovery members and those of Missouri Marathon fame appeared a twenty-seven-year-old explorer, military leader, and national hero figure by the imposing name of Zebulon Montgomery Pike. Captain Pike started working his way up the Missouri from Fort Bellefontaine, four miles above the mouth of the river, on July 15, 1806. He had more on his mind than learning about an old trade route to Santa Fe from some of the villagers. His plans also included intercepting the mysterious Dr. John H. Robinson, the expedition's private citizen and volunteer medical officer, adding an interpreter to his ranks, and joining with fifty-one Osage, Otoe, and Pawnee Indians—all while at La Charrette Village.[19, 26] One of several instructions from General James Wilkinson to Pike and his twenty-two crewmembers was transmitted in his letter of June 24, 1806:

> You are to proceed without further delay to the Cantonment on the Missouri, where you are to embark the late Osage captives and the deputation recently returned from Washington, with their presents and baggage, and are to transport the whole up the Missouri and Osage rivers to the town of the Grand Osage.

Pike's primary responsibility for the expedition was the safe return of these Native Americans to their lodges to help establish lasting peace. Of the nearly sixty Osage recently captured by the Pottawatomis, the United States had ransomed the surviving forty-three. The United States Indian Department ordered them immediately returned to their homes. They had been held near St. Louis for several months to recover from a kind of influenza-like infection and became restless awaiting their escort home. Some had even been handed over to the Sacs in the area, forcing Wilkinson to buy them back. President Thomas Jefferson wrote on January 16, 1806, to William Henry Harrison, governor of the District of Louisiana

> that the Potawatomis must be strongly reprimanded to make satisfaction for those killed, that they must understand that the river is now ours, and that it is not to be a river of blood.

In addition to the forty-three Osage survivors were eight chiefs, one Otoe, two Pawnee, and five Osage, who had just returned to St. Louis from a visit with President Thomas Jefferson, "The Great White Chief," in Washington DC. The safe return of the president's guests to their lodges was of the utmost concern to American political and military leaders.

Pike's expedition was now proceeding westward up the Missouri. Two boats were each fitted with a square sail and mast, but the river currents were too treacherous for sailing. They were soon taken down. Instead, they pushed with long poles because the waters frequently became too shallow for efficient rowing. In nearly constant rain in the sultriest days of Missouri summertime, they traveled ten to fifteen miles each day. The fifty-one Native Americans (men, women, and children) trudged along the riverbank. They were led by Lieutenant James B. Wilkinson, the general's son, and Dr. Robinson as they headed for La Charrette Village. By Wednesday morning, on July 16, Pike indicates in his journal they rejoined their "red" brethren for breakfast near St. Charles.

The Native Americans led by Lieutenant Wilkinson and Dr. Robinson arrived at La Charrette before Pike and his crew, perhaps on July 20. Torrential rainstorms roamed the area for four days before Pike's arrival. Some of Pike's crew became ill as they proceeded in fear of the nearby warring Pottawatomis. General Wilkinson starts his July 19 letter to Pike, "I send after you the Circumferenter and Bark left by Dr. Robinson. I expect the Bearer may find you at Charette." Pike's journal entries for three consecutive days reveal activities associated with his rendezvous at La Charrette:

21st July, Monday.—It commenced raining near day, and continued until four o'clock in the afternoon: the rain immensely heavy, with thunder and lightning remarkably severe. This obliged me to lay by; for, if we proceeded with our boats, it necessarily exposed our baggage much more than when at rest; for the tarpaulin could then cover all. We set sail at a quarter past four o'clock, and arrived at the village of La Charette a little after dusk of the evening, here we found Lieutenant Wilkinson and Dr. Robinson with the Indians—also Barney (our interpreter) with letters from the general and our friends. The weather continued cloudy, with rain. We were received into the house of Mr. Chartron [Joseph Chartran], and every accommodation in his power offered us. Distance 6 miles.

22d July, Tuesday.—We arranged our boats, dried our loading, and wrote letters for Belle Fontaine.

23d July, Wednesday.—I dispatched an express to the general, with advertisements relative to Kennermann, the soldier who deserted. We embarked after breakfast, and made good progress: Lieutenant Wilkinson steered one boat and I the other, in order to detach all the men on shore, with the Indians, that we could spare. We crossed to the south side, a little below Shepherd River. Dr. Robinson killed a deer, which was the first killed by the party. Distance 13 miles.

Both of the July 22 letters to Fort Bellefontaine composed by Pike carried "Village De Choreete" in the letterhead. He outlined his plan to reach Santa Fe, undoubtedly encouraged after sketching the first map of the Santa Fe Trail, aided by the travel experiences of Jose Tebeau Jr. and brothers Paul and Jean-Marie Cardinal Jr. At Eckert's Tavern in St. Charles, Pike discussed his idea of traveling to Santa Fe a few days before with George C. Sibley and Thomas Mathers, who later became Santa Fe Trail commissioners. While there, Manuel Lisa once again tried thwarting an expedition. This time, interpreter Vasquez was maliciously arrested and detained over a disputed debt, just as these explorers were about to depart St. Charles.[28] For now, the half-French, half-Spanish, and half-grinning alligator only desired to frustrate the expedition, but to no apparent extent.

Pike depicts "Village De Choreete" as four little houses at the mouth of Charrette Creek while visiting (Figure 4). A few days before, he sketched six little houses to illustrate St. Charles. Perhaps appropriately, this humble sketch is the lone, surviving visual representation of La Charrette Village.[27] Note Louter Creek was still designated as Otter River on his map, just as had Bourgmond in 1714. He also recorded this as the seventh encampment of the yearlong expedition.

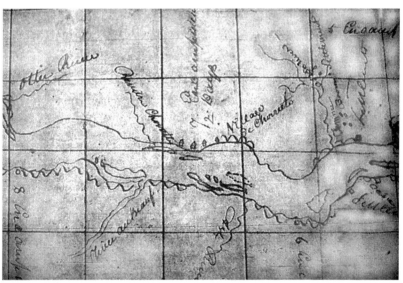

Figure 4. Village "De Choreete," as rendered by Zebulon M. Pike in 1806.

While a guest in the syndic's home, Chartran surely became impressed, as were other Charrette villagers, upon inspecting Pike's

Model 1803 Army rifle with its thirty-three-inch barrel capable of firing a fifty-four-caliber bullet, acknowledged as the most modern military weapon of its times. To reciprocate, villagers shared hospitality, upriver conditions, the status of local Native Americans, as well as their knowledge of overland routes soon to be known as the Santa Fe Trail. After one day and two nights of rest, Pike and his crew continued upriver to the Grand Osage village and eventually onward to explore the greater Southwest via the Osage, Arkansas, Red, and Rio Grande Rivers.

Now included in his party were Dr. John Robinson; St. Louis resident, A. F. "Baroney" Vasquez, the expedition interpreter; and the fifty-one Native Americans. Pike's rendezvous at La Charrette must have swelled the local population by at least seventy-five people, rivaling statistics attained later that year when members of the Corps of Discovery and the American Fur Company stayed overnight on September 20, 1806. As they traveled west from Village Charrette, Pike considered the country a hunter's paradise—"one of the most beautiful the eye ever beheld"—and predicted the grass- and flower-covered prairies would one day support a profitable ranching enterprise. Deer, buffalo, turkey, geese, and fish where in such abundance that the crew constantly gorged themselves, according to the expedition leader. Within days of returning the Osage to their lodges, Pike laments the loss of his dog acquired on his Mississippi River Expedition. "This was the dog Fisher presented to me at Prairie des Chien."[28] Just as with Lewis and Clark, dogs were considered vital to the success of expeditions. Fisher was noted for his ability to retrieve anything out of the water.

Upon reaching the Osage lodges in mid-August, for another brief moment, Captain Pike again became insightful. "The reunion," he notes, "was such as to make a polished society blush, when compared with those savages, in whom the passions of mind, whether joy, grief, fear, anger, or revenge, have their full scope."[29] Having safely returned the fifty-one Osage Native Americans to their families, Pike and his men began forging westward. Before they departed, an express from General Wilkinson arrived on August 18. A letter from Pike's wife, Clara, was enclosed. She related she and their children had been ill. A few days later, one of the Pike children died, but Pike would not learn of his loss until a year later. Also transmitted was a letter from Wilkinson with some curious remarks:

> In regard to your approximation to the Spanish settlements, should your route lead you near them, or should you fall in with any of their parties, your conduct must be marked by

such circumspection and direction as may prevent alarm or conflict, as you will be held responsible for consequences. On this subject I refer you to orders.

Three days later at his camp near Grand Osage, Pike held a meeting with the Osage leaders, explaining their new status as part of the United States. He distributed medals and gifts and requested horses in return to support the overland trip. The Osage chose to dicker. Fifteen horses were eventually "purchased." Thirty chiefs and warriors to accompany the expedition came with the deal. The fifteen newly acquired horses, plus seven Lieutenant Wilkinson had conscripted, would furnish their needs for now as they struck out across the Great American Desert. We will later learn how Wilkinson's assertive behavior proved costly to two La Charrette hunters.

By January 27, 1807, after spending a miserable early winter in the Rocky Mountains and coming within days of perishing, Pike claims to have located the Red River. Within ten days, he sent Dr. Robinson, alone, to Santa Fe. He confronted the first, albeit unsuccessful, commercial trader of Santa Fe Trail, Jean-Baptiste La Lande, son of Etienne and Francoise La Lande of Kaskaskia of the American Bottoms. Jean La Lande had gone west with trade goods on behalf of Kaskaskia, Illinois, merchant William Morrison in 1804. He was offered many favors and opportunities upon arrival in the old city of Santa Fe. The charms and opportunities were so tempting that La Lande experienced a change of heart and chose to reside there rather than return to Illinois and render an account of the mission. Unbeknown to La Lande, Morrison had arranged in St. Louis with Pike to recover payment for his stolen goods. While approaching Santa Fe with its 5,000 residents, Spanish troops arrested Dr. Robinson. It was later revealed Robinson not only knew of the plan to collect this bad debt before joining the expedition, but he was also aware of the plan to go to Santa Fe to study trade opportunities—not seek out the Red River as officially claimed.[19] Vigorous diplomatic discussions between the Spanish Governor Joaquin Alencaster and Robinson ensued, resulting in the worthless promise from the governor to arrange repayment of the international La Lande debt at some future time. William Morrison was never compensated for his losses. La Lande remained a wealthy, well-connected Santa Fe citizen.

Meanwhile, Pike apparently remained confused over which river he was actually following. He had mistaken, as would others for years to come, the upper Rio Grande for the Red River. Nevertheless, he pleaded his innocence when Spanish authorities later confronted him on the Conejos River, a western affluent of the Rio Grande. By now, Alencaster had dispatched his calvary to intercept the rest of the expedition. Pike had been unaware of Spanish spies lurking about St. Louis, who had forewarned Governor Alencaster of his pending arrival. The confusion of Pike over the Red and the Rio Grande Rivers only served to diminish his claim that he was not unlawfully wandering into Spanish Mexico. In Santa Fe, Pike met Governor Alencaster and continued his pleas of innocence. On March 3, 1807, while headed south under Spanish escort, Pike's party was surprised to see Dr. Robinson in Albuquerque. These circumstances took Pike and his men to El Paso del Norte and eventually landed them in Chihuahua, Mexico, charged with illegal entry into northern New Spain. His little map from La Charrette Village raised some serious questions. Spanish authorities thought it represented a future military route of attack. After numerous discussions, often interlaced with bluffs, humor, lavish dining, and entertainment, the Spanish released Pike to continue homeward with his expedition.

However, his chest filled with twenty-one expedition documents, including his little map of the future Santa Fe Trail drafted with the help of La Charrette villagers, remained in Mexico for years before being rediscovered. Lieutenant Melgares now served as their escort as they crossed the Rio Grande below Eagle Pass, Texas on June 1, 1807. From there they went to San Antonio. They later paid a four-dollar ferriage to cross the Sabine River, arriving at Natchitoches, Louisiana, at 4:00 PM on July 1, 1807, concluding the expedition. While in today's Texas, Pike noted what was soon to entice others to the region. "It has one of the most delightful temperatures in the world."

Previously in late March, while in Carrizal, Mexico, Pike was shocked when he read a newspaper account informing him of a conspiracy of highly placed Americans seeking to form a new country out of lands in the Southwest he was now attempting to explore. Aaron Burr, former vice president of the United States, was implicated, as was Pike's childhood mentor, General James Wilkinson. Pike was forever guilty by association as leader of the expedition, even though the full truth of the Burr-Wilkinson conspiracy to dismember the Union was never established during an 1811 court of inquiry. Today, historians know Wilkinson worked with the Spanish for years and, as such, was the likely perpetrator. Regardless, once completed, the expedition was hailed a success. Even so, author/historian W. E. Hollon was prompted to bestow the undisguised title of *The Lost Pathfinder* upon his book about Pike's misadventure.[29]

Because Pike's ventures were published four years before those of Lewis and Clark, his renderings gave the American public its best description then available of the Southwest. Pike was soon a world figure, sparking the desire for adventure and settlement in the American West. His expedition is credited as a major influence on opening trade over the famous Santa Fe Trail and fostering the expansionist movement into Texas. His exploits also earned him the honor of Pike's Peak, a Colorado mountain he saw, but never climbed, to its summit. Today, Professor Goetzmann ranks Pike as one of the three "leaders among the giants" stopping by La Charrette Village before proceeding on to explore the American West.

As for the individual, Pike was a prominent young army officer of limited formal training whose flamboyant and sometimes questionable career ended when a magazine exploded and killed him, along with several of his men in 1813. His only surviving daughter would later marry Symmes Harrison, son of President William H. Harrison.

## Bereaved Osage Disrupt Charrette Hunters

Back on the Osage River in Missouri Territory, where Pike had left the fifty-one Osage Indians, they and their families continued struggling to find life with dignity. Only a few months before, they had been La Charrette Village guests for three or more nights before Pike and his crew returned them to their lodges. They continued to be besieged with severe depression caused by their emotions of grief. However, the reason for their grief soon took on a vast, new dimension. While traveling along the Missouri with Pike, for an hour during sunrise, they mourned the loss of their loved ones suffered at the hands of the warring Pottawatomis. They chanted while sobbing bitterly as tears streaked their cheeks. According to expedition interpreter Vasquez, their song of grief generally ran:

> My dear father exists no longer; have pity on me, O Great Spirit!
> You see I cry forever; dry my tears and give me comfort.[26]

Pike's crew observed this ritual every morning since departing Fort Bellefontaine. It continued after they had been safely delivered with their possessions to the Grand Osage villages. At the very least, these observations should have further aided William Clark in resolving one of his questions about Native Americans. To learn more about Indian behavior and religion, Clark made a list of some ninety questions before heading west in 1804. One asked, "Do they Mourn for their disceased friends and what [is] their cerimony on such occasions."[3]

Upon being reunited with family and friends at their lodges on August 15, 1806, the Osage fell into mutual embraces of love. Lieutenant James B. Wilkinson recorded their behavior:

> Wives throwing themselves into the arms of their husbands, parents embracing their children, and children their parents, brothers and sisters meeting, one from captivity, the other from the towns—they, at the same time, returning thanks to the Good God for having brought them once more together.[26]

Their rejoicing, however, was to be short-lived...literally. More was being exchanged between Osage tribal members than sincere, tender affection. Foreign, unseen influenza viruses lurked about and were unwittingly transmitted to loved ones.

A short time later, sometime in September 1806, William T. Lamme of La Charrette Village and his neighbor, William Hays Jr., Daniel Boone's grandson, arrived at the Grand Osage village for their fall hunt. They immediately obtained permission to hunt on the Grand River from White Hair, the Osage Chief, in the presence of Pierre Chouteau. A little later, Lamme and Hays were robbed of their horses and hunting equipment valued at $1,335.15. The Osage were seeking retribution for the "evil fever" Pike and his entourage imposed upon them. Nor had they forgotten the horse trading deal involving Lieutenant Wilkinson one month before. The Lamme deposition of January 17, 1807, to Joseph Browne, Esquire, secretary of the Territory of Louisiana and ex officio governor thereof in the absence of the governor proceeds:

> When Captain Zebulon Pike passed up the Osage River with his party some short time previous to the arrival of your Petitioner, he had taken a Census of the number of this Nation of Indians [the Osages], since which time and during the last autumn an uncommon mortality prevailed throughout the nation. They had lost to the number of 200 grown persons, besides a large number of children.
>
> This misfortune the indians believe was visited upon them by Captain Pike, whom they are superstitious enough to believe endowed with the power of dispersing both good & evil.

Shortly after his departure an uncommon & to them unknown fever made its appearance in the nation, from which, few who were affected with it escaped with their lives. They were generally taken violently ill suddenly often delerious and frequently fell a sacrafice to its rage in the space of half a day.

For this evil which they felt so severely and which they believe was drawn upon them by Capt. Pike, they entertain an emnity toward the Americans and are supposed to have robbed your Petitioner for sake of revenge.

Believing therefore that his case will be found to merit redress as he went regularly to hunt and trade with a nation of indians between whom and the U. States, there exists an entercourse, Your Petitioner trust that you will exercise the power with which you may [be] vested to obtain for him that redress for his losses which he was not able to obtain from the Indians. Very respectfully your petitioner subscribes himself Sir Your Excellencys Most Obt. Humble Servant.

(Signed) William T. Lamme

Presumably, the tribal members at the Grand Osage village who became ill and died had been exposed to viruses similar to those that had infected the six chiefs who died during their trip to Washington DC. Their party originally consisted of fourteen chiefs. Perhaps the surviving eight chiefs, upon their return from visiting President Jefferson, were vectors, infecting the others. This process of social assimilation cost them dearly. They were not habituated to European diseases, as Native Americans first experienced during an epidemic in Hispaniola in 1493. In 1804, Lewis and Clark estimated the Grand Osage population at 500 warriors that, by now, had been reduced to approximately half that number. It is not known if Lamme ever recovered any of his $1,335.15 lost to the exasperated heart-broken Osage. However, for his partner, William Hays Jr., it represented the second hunting-related theft at the hands of local Native Americans within four years.

# Artists, Scientists, and Major Long

Many other expeditions and individuals also passed La Charrette Village. While some would record its presence, others would not. Trappers and traders named Thomas Ashe, Christian Schultz, and Nathaniel Pryor each went upriver in 1806, 1807, and 1808, respectively. None of their records mentions specific events about the village. Neither did two Santa Fe Trail traders, James Baird in 1812 or those with Jules de Mun in 1815, record the village. The de Mun travelers instead chose to spend the night nearby on DuBois Creek, across the Missouri River from La Charrette. Later, a certain Colonel Farnum, a John Jacob Astor associate, left St. Louis for the Pacific around 1814 to deliver messages all along his route.[29] His extensive journal entries reputedly noted events, places, and people everywhere on the Missouri. However, after his manuscript was submitted for publication, it became lost following the death of his New York publisher. General William H. Ashley, a forty-four-year-old Missouri senator, led in the planning and financing of several attempts to reach the Yellowstone to trap beaver. Only crewmember Louis Bompart maintained a cursive record of the 1822 Ashley-Smith trip on the lower Missouri indicating "We camped at the Isle of Loutre" on May, 20.[31] Nonetheless, still others were yet to record their experiences at La Charrette.

Following the War of 1812, many politicians and other American leaders considered the Trans-Mississippi West as an area of strategic importance for a variety of reasons, mostly related to settlement and trade. As a result, Secretary of War John C. Calhoun was authorized to plan several expeditions, all under the leadership of Major Stephen Harrison Long. Long, a Phi Beta Kappa graduate of Dartmouth, and his crews passed the village numerous times, both land and the river. His first expedition not only failed to visit the "advance guard of civilization," but it also failed to accomplish its primary goals. However, La Charrette was visited at least once, as a crewmember participating in another of Long's highly ambitious, but ill-fated, expeditions recorded.[32]

Calhoun envisioned a cordon of forts west of the Great Lakes and up the Missouri to Montana to prevent the British from further infiltrating the northern reaches of the United States. Designated as the Missouri Expedition, another military venture, it represented a four-part troop movement up the river. During the summer of 1818, one battalion of the Rifle Regiment only traveled as far as an island above Leavenworth, Kansas, to establish a temporary winter camp. Two other regiments of approximately 1,100 men joined these forces later in the year. This larger contingency only got as far as Council Bluffs at present-day Fort Calhoun, Nebraska, when the Panic of 1819 started, a time of "dishonored credits, declining commerce, and exhausted coffers."[32] Additionally, claims of expedition mismanagement by the press and eroding political support all resulted in the United States Congress voting to literally discontinue funding of the Missouri Expedition in midstream. The expedition was abruptly concluded. The troops, now afflicted with scurvy, began unloading their boats and returning downriver. Surgeon John Gale was one of a very few to record these events.

During his 1818 upriver voyage of the calamitous Missouri Expedition, Gale recorded La Charrette Village, even though his journal contains an entry on the inside front cover stating, "Kept in the main by Lieut. Thomas Kavanaugh of the Forsyth." Subsequent handwriting analyses, along with other factors, suggest it was actually John Gale's work. Regardless, the Sunday September 6, 1818, entry reveals:

> Passed Wood River on the North, and halted at 1 Oclock at a village on the same side Called La Charrette. Originally settled by the French, who have since removed to Osage River, it is now occupied by Americans. During our stay here, we had a fine Shower, after which the Wind Sprang up fair, and continued so until we had passed a very difficult pass immediately above the Village. In 1804 this was the highest White settlement on this River. Made this day 10 miles. Encamped at evening on the South side.

Gale's entry confirms village history and Charrette Bend, of which we will learn more about later, was a difficult turn to negotiate on this river. It also supports the contention that some of the French settlers of La Charrette had by now moved upriver to live across from the mouth of the Osage River at Cote sans Dessein.

Major Long was next ordered to explore the so-called Middle West, essentially the lands between the routes traveled by the Corps of Discovery and Zebulon Pike.[16] This 1819–1820 expedition was known as the Scientific Expedition. It left Pittsburgh on a stern wheeler steamboat named the *Western Engineer*, headed for St. Louis via the Ohio and Mississippi Rivers before advancing up the Missouri in June 1819. Among the twenty-four crewmembers now headed upriver were America's first artists to venture westward, Titian Ramsay Peale and Samuel Seymour.[33] Each was prepared to capture the visible grandeur of nature with their sketchpads and palettes in hand. Seymour, a noted landscape painter, passed the mouth of Charette Creek and the village sometime in late June or early July, but he did not choose to capture any local scenes. Peale was a less famous member of the Charles Willson Peale family of artists/scientists, drawing and painting many natural history subjects during the voyage with great accuracy. When in St. Charles, Major Long divided his crew into two groups, one to continue up the Missouri with him while five others, led by zoologist Thomas Say and artist Ramsay Peale, would simultaneously plod overland immediately to the north of Village Charette. While walking, they described the countryside in revealing detail.

Consistent with other expeditions under Major Long's command, a comedy of errors and misfortunes besieged this eight-day overland journey. When in St. Charles, Peale arranged to purchase a French mare with an old Indian packsaddle to carry their gear. The beast escaped twice. Once retrieved, it only again became lost to the wilderness on the third day out of St. Charles. To the amusement of horse traders of the day, critters such as these with their pigeonlike homing instincts were often resold to subsequent unsuspecting travelers. Nonetheless, the men continued overland on what they described as a hot, treeless plain without water or game. Somewhere northeast of La Charette, they encountered two settlers. Mr. Nailor refused to give or sell them either food or water until they finally wheedled him into giving them some water. That evening, they dined on a few biscuits, one hawk, and water. The second settler was thankfully more gracious, offering them water and selling them a few provisions. "For the ham we paid 10 cents per pound, and 25c for all the bread, milk, and corn for our horse."[32] By breakfast the next morning, the crafty pack animal had escaped for the last time.

Parakeets were heard screeching. Many turkeys, larks, Bartram's sandpiper, and partridges were also noted as they trudged around the headwaters of Charette Creek. Say, a founding member of the Philadelphia Academy of Natural Science and later known as the father of American descriptive entomology, first described heel flies in Missouri. He depicted them vividly as "a species of green headed fly which torments horses and cattle so much that crossing the prairies in the day is next to impossible."[32]

As the five men approached Loutre Island above Charette Creek, Peale expressed their displeasure, "much fatigued and our feet very sore...the longest 21 miles I ever traveled."[33] While awaiting the arrival of the boat, they hunted and explored in the river bottoms for the next few days. They continued recording every unfamiliar form of plant and animal life, including equisetum, otherwise known as scouring rushes or horsetails, described in 1811 by John Bradbury at La Charrette. They also noted the fertile land, many corncribs, smokehouses, and dog-run dwellings.[34] On July 2, they joined the other expedition members on the *Western Engineer* before proceeding upriver to the rapidly growing town of Cote sans Dessein, where some of the original La Charrette villagers now lived. "Must have been upwards of a hundred" spectators staring at the boat, wrote Peale as they arrived at Franklin in mid-July. While there, expedition members inspected Boonslick to learn about local salt production techniques. However, of all of the contributions associated with any of the military expeditions Long led, except for cartographic materials, the works of Say, Peale, and Seymour have become most enduring.

# The Duke from Wurttemberg

The great westward American migration was gaining momentum by now. The American West was attracting worldwide attention as exploration gave way to settlement activities. It was as if everyone desired to learn more about the mysteries of this vast wilderness expanse. Most were interested in settling with their families. Others traveled more as curious tourist, perhaps desirous to publish a book or advance their social standing back home. Prince Paul, Duke of Wurttemberg, and his royal entourage fell within these later categories. This German duke would record the last known journal entry on La Charrette Village as he came upriver in May 1822 while traveling with the French Missouri Company. According to the Duke, their seven days of river travel before arriving at the village had been vexing. Excerpts from his journal provide a unique insight into his impressions and experiences on the Lower Missouri:

> On the morning of the eighteenth we left our camp very early. Only with great difficulty, by strenuous pushing and pulling, our boat advanced among the many sandbars, shallows, and entangled clusters of tree trunks. Noticing many head of cattle running wild in these parts, and fresh meat being a necessity, I bought a two-year old steer in the settlement for four dollars.

> We left our ship's camp at four o'clock in the morning on May 19, but we had hardly covered two miles when a violent gust of wind from the south compelled us to lay by. The danger was

great. Tall timber standing close to the bank was being drawn into the water close to the boat. We could have been submerged without being rescued had they fallen on us. In the afternoon we had a short but violent thunderstorm, after which I sent my hunter out to hunt. During the night several heavy thunderstorms followed one another and again drenched our boat.

The morning of the twentieth promised neither favorable nor clear weather, but the wind turned to the east. I entertained the hope that we might continue our journey more speedily than before. In this expectation I found myself disappointed however. We had scarcely advanced four miles when a quarrel broke out anew, and despite my admonitions an open and furious attack against the boat leader, Dutremble, followed. During the night it stormed severely and the Missouri suddenly rose several feet, continuing to rise all of the twenty-first. About ten o'clock in the morning the sky cleared and we had a fine, though windy, day, but this was most welcome.

On the same day (the twenty-second) a cloud of insects descended upon us toward evening and we were horribly tormented.

When I went hunting very early the next morning (the twenty-third) I was surprised by quite miserable weather. I was thoroughly drenched, even though I had taken refuge under a densely foialaged cottonwood. Since my gun had become useless, I had to return without accomplishment. I decided to take a few men with me and visit a dwelling six miles away to purchase some provisions. At the first house we found no livestock. At the second house we found some very uncivil people, especially a ninety-year-old fellow whose whole aim was to overcharge me and make fun of our distress. Very much disgruntled I went my way, leaving the impolite old man with his swine.

On the evening of the twenty-fourth Dutremble came, bringing five men with him. Among these were three Negroes and one mulatto, all slaves owned by the partners of the French Missouri Company.

During the night we were visited again by several loud thunderstorms and a heavy downpour. Yet in the morning it cleared and we looked forward to a fine day. Going ahead on foot along the river bank to a place which the Creoles call Chaurette, named after the creek which flows here into the Missouri, I shot two head of game. Left on the edge of the water with a marker, they were happily found by the crew and taken on board.[35]

The Duke continued to Boeuf Island and into the Far West for the next two years, continuing to record his experiences for posterity, reminiscent of McMurtry's *Sin Killer* novel of today. His remembrances were often recorded without much sympathy or understanding of western society, but not all of his local impressions was negative while approaching La Charrette Village. He was impressed with the "aromatic fragrance" of grapevines in blossom, marveled at the "picturesque" limestone cliffs on the right bank, and acclaimed two species of tanagers as "the most beautiful birds of North America." He also saw a few "extraordinarily fine sycamores" and "some very beautiful butterflies," but he did not record anything about the Creoles or their village.

Later in the mid-1820s, wilderness explorers like Zenas Leonard and William Ashley did not even start their journal entries until upstream from Village Charrette. Nor were settlers, investors, land speculators, artists, dignitaries, or royalty dissuaded from progressing westward as they passed a succession of riverbank ghost villages like La Charrette. By the time Pierre Louis Vasquez, discoverer of the Great Salt Lake; the famous Pennsylvania lawyer/artist George Catlin; or Phillip Maximilian, Prince of Wied-Neuwied, the Napoleonic War major general and sportsman, came upriver on April 12, 1833, little apparently remained of La Charrette Village except lost memories and forgotten dreams.[36] By then, newly designated Marthasville Landing marked the old village site as the prince proceeded to visit Joseph Roubedoux III of Cote sans Dessein. On his return trip in 1834, he spent the night below Berger Creek near Washington. In his *Voyage en l'Amerique du Nord*, he tells of visiting Washington "of only a few isolated dwellings; the inhabitants were very courteous and obliging."

Certainly, many others passed La Charrette Village during its near quarter-century life span. Undoubtedly, some stayed overnight, traded, or chose just to visit, even though no further recorded evidence has crossed this distance in time, telling of those events to assist us in interpreting village history. If only the ancient syndic had the vision to maintain a guestbook. But that, of course, is fantasizing. Perhaps that is as it should have been. His memories were sufficiently endowed without formalizing such minutiae. Besides, he and his followers were busily constructing yet another chapter of the American dream. Nevertheless, Missouri frontier society would continue advancing its agenda without a village named La Charrette.

# Chapter 11:

## Beginning of the End

Just as alternatives overwhelm the founding date of La Charrette, its date of demise abounds in a void. No published reports offer a specific date— or proof of the cause—for the village's disappearance. Most simply indicate it was short-lived, succumbing to the fate of floodwaters of this mighty river, known to be too thick to drink but too thin to plow. One source erroneously concluded the village had disappeared by 1811.[1] This conclusion was based upon the travel log of Henry M. Brackenridge, who did not visit the village. To the contrary, Brackenridge recorded about thirty families residing along the riverbank at Charrette Creek as he sailed upriver at 10:00 AM on Monday, April 8, 1811.

Various local records, including early tax records, were scrutinized for clues of a failing village. Rather than designating landholders by village affiliation for tax purposes, those records reflect either watershed regions (Tuque or Charrette Creeks) or numbered tax districts (See Appendix A), providing no leads on a possible date of its demise. As noted previously, the last known event recorded at La Charrette Village was a land transaction dated February 25, 1825, for Thomas Palmer, although other such documentation may have escaped the author's attention. Because La Charrette Village was within Montgomery County between 1818 and 1833, one would logically seek out those county records for clarification. Once more, fate intervened. Two Montgomery County Courthouse fires, one during the Civil War and another in 1901, destroyed those potentially useful records. The most conclusive fact could have been the discontinuance of "Charette" post office after 1825, but that is also flawed in the face of its uncertain realization. Once again, without either a certain date or reason for its disappearance, the loss of the village opens itself to speculation.

One or more of several 1820 events on the Missouri River might have been responsible for its decline. Gerber relates the "Old Woman," as he referred to the river, swept away a forest island of a thousand trees in a single night in 1823, the county seat of Gasconade County in 1825, and left only the graveyard at Old Franklin the next year.[2] By 1828, the situation apparently worsened, convincing Old Franklin residents to move to higher ground two miles away, whereupon New Franklin was established.[3] Perhaps one of these events destroyed the village by the excesses of the "Old Woman." An early Sioux City, Iowa, newspaper stated, "Of all the variable things in creation, the most uncertain of all are the action of a jury, the state of a woman's mind, and the condition of the Missouri River." Certainly, it is not beyond the realm of possibilities that the village suffered incremental losses due to one of these or other floods. However, the statement by a Missouri riverboat captain to twelve Catholic families arriving from Germany in 1833 that "there is no house close by" upon approaching Marthasville Landing forever dispelled the presence of the village. Thus, sometime between 1825 and 1833, La Charrette Village became another of many Missouri River villages to fade from existence, perhaps ravished by her floodwaters. The fact that William Clark, territorial governor of Missouri since 1813, did not record any severe Missouri River floods between 1826 and 1831 offers only indirect support for the contention it might have been an 1825 flood that consumed all—or a portion—of the village.

The renowned ornithologist, dual genius of art and science, John James Audubon, succinctly captured the drama of a Missouri River flood destroying property and lives along this stretch of the river as he practiced his passions of sketching and articulating nature. On Sunday April 30, 1843, one day removed from St. Charles while traveling with Captain Joseph La Barge, he recorded the following from his river steamer as a haunting memory of what La Charrette villagers might have encountered only a few years before:

> At one place we passed a couple of houses, with women and children, perfectly surrounded by the flood; these houses stood apparently on the margin of a river coming from the eastward. The whole farm was under water, and all around was the very perfection of disaster and misfortune. It appeared to us as if the men had gone to procure assistance, and I was grieved that we could not offer them any. We saw several trees falling in, and beautiful, though painful, was the sight. As they fell, the spray which rose along their whole length was exquisite; but alas! These magnificent trees had reached the day of oblivion.[4]

However, it might not have been any one cataclysmic event, as described by Audubon, that dismantled La Charrette Village because an equally compelling argument may be advanced that floodwaters did not destroy the village. The fact the land at the riverbank location of the village has experienced accretion to the present time argues to the contrary (Figure 5). Ralph Gregory, a local Marthasville historian, among others, suggested the 1817 founding of Marthasville eventually overwhelmed the little village. In the November 22, 2001, issue of *The Marthasville Record*, he reported a few old houses and barns still remained when he was a boy some nine decades ago. A third alternative involving all of these factors can neither be ignored. In this scenario, the village may well have lost a few of its riverbank structures to rampaging floodwaters, rendering some houses uninhabitable, as excessive quantities of sediment accumulated around them. Under these conditions, it seems reasonable to speculate that village residents would be eager to move to higher ground, perhaps choosing to reside in Marthasville, Cote sans Dessein, or elsewhere. By 1815, members of the Boone and Bryan families owned most of the farmland once associated with the village, suggesting that slaves or guests like Daniel Boone may have resided in the remaining structures. Subsequent land transfers may have further added to the diminished stature of village, especially in the presence of the more appealing town of Marthasville with its shops, mills, and physicians. Perhaps Ralph Gregory said it best while visiting with me, "The beginning of the end of Charrette Village was the founding of Marthasville in 1817." Regardless, the village was not recognized as such after the mid-1820s, even though its river landing would service the Marthasville community for at least the remainder of the century. These uncertainties will remain until more conclusive evidence is uncovered. Conducting properly managed archaeological digs, as suggested in a *St. Louis Post Dispatch* article on August 18, 1997, is one alternative. For now, we may only assume La Charrette Village life was gradually extinguished by a series of incremental losses, much as it had once flickered into existence some forty years before its 1801 founding. Shortly after the turn of the century, even the old timers would not be able to recall with precision where it had once been located.

# Chapter 12:

## Lost and Found

Exactly where was La Charrette Village located? We know the local streambeds with their associated banks and floodplains have since been transfigured. Original survey landmarks, the so-called bearing trees, have long since disappeared. Where were the little trading post, the syndic's home, Callaway's Fort, and the old river landing located before they became extinct? Where did Charrette Creek enter the Missouri when Lewis and Clark camped there overnight in 1804 and 1806? Is it possible for visitors to view this historical land site today? Can the exact location ever be reestablished for future generations to study and appreciate?

Today, the land sites once associated with the village represent portions of local Charrette Township farms. Private property is to the north of the old village. The waters of the Missouri River and Charrette Creek are to the south. Thus, as proposed by collaborator Jerome Holtmeyer to local historical society members, a motorboat excursion provides the most logical means to approach the site. Perhaps the most nostalgic approach to consider would be to embark at Colter's Landing into Little Boeuf Creek near Dundee on Highway 100, east of New Haven in Franklin County, as Colter himself would have done to visit the village.

## Redeemed Village Site with Lewis and Clark Campsites

Mr. H. A. Schoppenhorst (1840–1930), a Charrette Township farmer and a Missouri state legislator gave his best secondhand recollection on the location of La Charrette Village to Dr. E. B. Trail in 1926. Later, Warren County historian Ralph Gregory of Marthasville obtained the item from Dr. Trail, who then shared it with collaborator

Jerome Holtmeyer. The document, presently on file at the Missouri Western Historical Manuscript Collection in Columbia gives the location of this Warren County, Charrette Township site:

> The historic old French village of Charette was located in Township 45 Range one west of the 5th principal meridian Warren County, Missouri, one mile south of the present town of Marthasville, and 5 miles west of the 5th principal meridian on the North bank of the Missouri River. Charette Creek emptied in the Missouri River just above Charette Village. Charette Creek strikes the Missouri River Bottom in the south east corner of Section 23 T. 45 R 2 West of the 5th principal meridian in Warren County, Missouri. The old town of Newport was almost opposite to where Charette Creek strikes the river bottom.

The entry giving Section 23 is incorrect. It should read as Section 31. This description further dispels folklore indicating La Charrette Village was actually located at the mouth of Tuque Creek. That assertion was undoubtedly linked to the fact that Tuque Creek bordered the W. T. Lamme/Jean-Marie Cardinal Jr. farm in the early 1800s.

Collaborator Jerome Holtmeyer conceived the procedure to develop the map shown in Figure 5. His process was similar to that used by University of Missouri Geographic Resources Project members to reestablish the Wood Creek campsite Lewis and Clark occupied in the winter of 1803–1804.[1] Due to a drastic eastward shift of the Mississippi River, they claim the site is now positioned 328 feet inland from the west bank of the river in West Alton of St. Charles County, Missouri. Holtmeyer located La Charrette Village land claims to serve as his starting point by searching the microfilm records for each farm presented in Chapter 5. From the Jean-Baptiste Luzon property survey (Figure 6), he was able to position the Missouri River and Charette Creek as they were in 1806. Armed with this critical information, he pinpointed the location of the Lewis and Clark campsites and the village. He gratefully acknowledges assistance from professional engineers of the Warrenton, Missouri, firm of Lewis-Bade, Inc., in this effort. Details of the procedure are outlined in Appendix B.

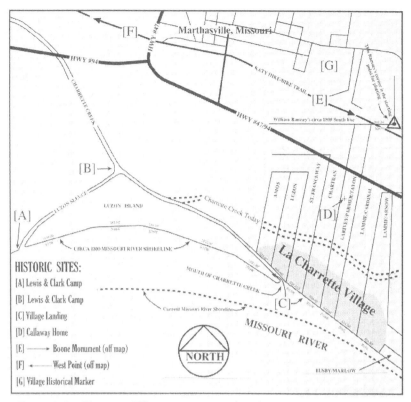

Figure 5. La Charrette Village superimposed with present-day Marthasville.

According to Sergeant Patrick Gass of the Corps of Discovery, the expedition camped a quarter-mile north of La Charrette Village in 1804. Lewis and Clark indicated their overnight camp was about a mile above the village at the mouth of Charrette Creek. The question then became: What may correctly be considered as the mouth of the creek in 1804 and again in 1806? Thus, either historic site A or B, as given in Figure 5, becomes the Corp of Discovery campsite. Historic site A is thought to be the most probable location because the expedition camped "above" the mouth of Charrette Creek.

The location of the village is thought to have represented an elongated cluster of homes along the north bank of the streams. The entire village represented 4,115 feet of stream frontage, nearly eight-tenths of a mile (Figure 5). The location of the trading post and the river landing are not known with certainty. In 1806, Canadian James Reed docked his five trading boats "opposite the village" on Luzon Island. Alternatively, the river landing might have been near the hub of the village on the Joseph Chartran farm, as suggested by site C. The trading post was most likely nearby. Callaway's Fort, constructed by early 1812, was probably located between site C and Callaway's log home, site D. Cart paths would have connected the homes, school, trading post, and Callaway's Fort with Charrette Landing. Sites E and F designate historical points of interests along the Katy Trail. Both are off the current map. Boone's Monument (site E) is a short distance east of Marthasville with School Number 1 somewhere nearby. West Point (site F) is an old Charrette Creek ford near the metal truss bridge on the Katy Trail, about two miles west of Marthasville. This site provides a unique opportunity to view the stream. Site G locates a La Charrette Village historical marker and a bousillage-style cabin in Marthasville, Missouri.

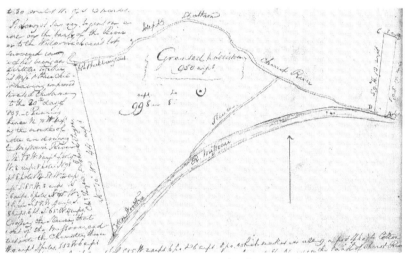

Figure 6. Jean-Baptiste Luzon land survey of 1806.

The February 28, 1806, land claim of Jean-Baptiste Luzon's farm shows the bifurcated mouth of Charrette Creek before it changed course (Figure 6). Note cottonwood and hackberry trees were survey markers on the west while Charrette Creek and the Missouri River served that purpose on the north and south with Luzon Sleuce crossing the farm from north to south. The slender column of land at the very eastern edge of Luzon's farm was typical of land assigned to each of the seven farms forming the village as depicted in Figure 5. Notice a similar column of land with the Busby/Marlow farm is excluded from the village. Apparently, the village was not subject to expansion.

# Part Three:

## Westward Bound

"Four days later they passed the last settlement on the Missouri, a miserable hamlet called La Charrette."

Gardiner, *West of the River* (1941)

The mass migration of settlers pushing farther into the American West is intimately associated with La Charrette Village history. Settlers would initiate new frontier villages while staking a land or mining claim; others would provide transportation or other support services essential to their undertakings. All came from points in the east, many as far away as Europe. Almost universally, they traveled on the available water routes, except for those forcibly relocated onto Indian reservations. Most walked. Steamboats embarked hundreds of immigrants at the port of call first known as Charrette Landing, later renamed Marthasville Landing. This old river landing exerted its second-generation influence beyond the life span of the village. Regardless, Americanization continued throughout the 1800s across lands once known as Louisiana.

Travelers navigating the Missouri often pushed off westward from La Charrette Landing to negotiate a difficult stretch of the river known as Charrette Bend while seeking Loutre Island. By 1808, Cote sans Dessein stood a bit farther upriver. But who would be encountered there? Would they be the same culturally rich families who once lived at

La Charrette, as others have suggested? Cote sans Dessein (the hill without design) history confirms La Charrette Village family members were indeed involved in this new settlement and they experienced similar outcomes while once again establishing the westernmost settlement on the American frontier.

# Chapter 13:

## Cote sans Dessein

Those who moved upriver with ties to La Charrette represented members of the Tayon, Cardinal, and Tebeau families who joined with others named Denoyer, Revard, Robidoux, and Roy to form the new community. Again, French-Canadian and Native American heritage predominated in this buffer zone of shared cultures. They continued trading in furs, as had been their custom since arriving in North America. Even the earliest Canadian records indicate many of these families frequently intermarried and a certain degree of intimacy existed between the Robidouxs, Tebeaus, and the others.[1] Jean-Baptiste Roy (Roi or LeRoy) founded Cote sans Dessein in 1808 with a 4,000-arpent Spanish grant approved by Pierre Chouteau Jr. Roy was illiterate, acknowledged as a "tall, robust, and fine looking man" whose bravery was exemplary. "A braver man never handled a western rifle," exalted one travel companion.[2,3] Contemporaries called this multilingual and successful community leader "Baptiste."

William Clark, as superintendent of Indian Affairs, licensed Baptiste and Joseph Robidoux II, his partner, as independent fur traders on the Missouri by 1827. In this capacity, Roy also trafficked liquor to Native Americans. He became sufficiently prosperous to own residential properties in St. Louis, where his wife and daughters eventually lived.

Like Roy, Robidoux had a reputation as a crafty Indian trader. His family previously held stock in the Missouri Company that sponsored the travels of Jean-Baptiste Trudeau, associated with the 1795 drowning of Joseph Chorette at Charrette Creek.[4] In 1799, Robidoux, along with other wealthy St. Louis citizens like Auguste Chouteau, Charles Gratiot, and Antonio Vincent Bouis, raised patriotic donations to assist Spain in its war effort. These experiences must have served Robidoux well because he is one of few who outwitted the foxy fur trader Manuel Lisa before his August 12, 1820 death.[5]

Baptiste's father, Andre Roy, was a French-Canadian. His mother was a French-Creole named Francoise Nicolle Chapart. By 1790, they lived with others of their family in St. Charles. Andre also had other children with Indian wives. The ecclesiastical marriage of Baptiste Roy to Cecile Reine Tayon was conducted in St. Charles when she was a minor of nineteen years, the daughter of La Charrette landholder Don Carlos and Cecilie Deschamps Tayon. They had four children born between 1808 and 1813. Louis Eugene, Emilia, and Brigette Martha survived into adulthood. Baptiste's brother and sister-in-law, Francis and Pelagie Roy, also lived at Cote sans Dessein with their son Francis Jr. Francis served as Baptiste's clerk. Two other Roy brothers, Joseph and Louis, also participated in the new settlement, as did La Charrette resident Charles Tayon, brother of Cecile Reine Tayon Roy. Francoise Roy, sister to Baptiste, resided there as well with her French-Osage husband Joseph Revard (or Revoir). His mother Catherine reared Joseph as an Osage. He later became a licensed trader financed by the Chouteau family of St. Louis. They were also from St. Charles, where they married in 1795. Their Cote sans Dessein home eventually served as the township polling place. Each of these families participated in frontier life with exceptional zeal and commitment. But what possessed them to depart St. Charles and La Charrette?

Failed land claims must have been a major factor prompting the four Roy brothers and the Tayons to move west and establish Cote sans Dessein. Each of the Roys had been denied 800 arpents of land in the District of St. Charles on August 7, 1807, according to the American State Papers. The United States agent noted all were minors five years before when their claims were staked and the land board required further proof before approving their grants. By this time, the La Charrette land claim of Charles Tayon had also fallen through. Later, his brother Louis Tayon and wife Louise also left Charrette Bottoms to join the new community.

Not only did Cote sans Dessein families share their heritage with one of the first settlers of La Charrette Village, but they were also its first squatters, dating from as early as 1763. For successive generations— from Montreal to Missouri—members of both the Tebeau and Cardinal families appear together on the Missouri frontier with their Native American wives. Two Denoyer nephews to Paul and Jean-Marie Cardinal Jr. of La Charrette Village resided at Cotes sans Dessin with their mixed wives, Margaret Barada (French-Omaha) and Margaret Dorion (French-Sioux), a likely relative of the Lewis and Clark

Expedition translator Dorion. Their mother was Ursule, also known as Charlotte Cardinal, daughter of Jean-Marie and Angelique Cardinal Sr. Ursule married Joseph Denoyer Jr., son of Joseph and Marie Josepha Noiselle Denoyer, on November 23, 1779. Joseph Teabo (Tebeau) Jr. and James Tebeau, the son and grandson, respectively, of Jose Tebeau Sr. associated with the Cardinal family at Prairie du Chien and La Charrette, also lived at Cote. Joseph Tebeau Jr. and his partner were involved in land speculation, selling lots 31 and 32 at Cote sans Dessein to Benjamin Sharp for $300 on November 24, 1811. According to the American State Papers, he also owned a lot in St. Charles at this same time.

The 1795 St. Charles marriage document of Joseph Tebeau Jr. and Marie Theresa Barada, daughter of Antoine and Marguerite Barada of St. Louis, gives Joseph's surname as Thibault. However, on April 10, 1805, Joseph married Marie Louise Vincennes. The possible relationship between Marie Theresa Barada Tebeau, Margaret Barada Denoyer, and Maria Louise Barada Tayon, wife of Louis Tayon of Charrette Bottoms, has not been revealed. From these accounts, it appears most accurate to state that one original La Charrette Village settler, members of his family, and descendants of its first squatters participated in the settlement of Cote sans Dessein as they continued living their closely intertwined lives.

Cote sans Dessein was located across the Missouri River, on the north bank, from the mouth of the Osage River. A unique river bottom hill served as its focal point. This narrow limestone outcropping of 600 yards in length is located along the Missouri riverbank, immediately south of present-day Tebbetts, Missouri. Brackenridge visited the village in 1811, describing it as "a beautiful place" consisting of "...thirteen French families, and two or three of Indians."[6] Seven years later, John Gale described it as consisting of "a tavern, a store, a blacksmith's shop, and a billiard table."[7] This first white settlement in Callaway County also boasted two blockhouses with palisades by 1812, Tebeau's Fort and Roy's Fort, which became the scene of many famous frontier Indian battles. As the aftermath of the War of 1812 continued, Julia Royer Roy became established as a frontier heroine when she successfully repelled an Indian attack on her fort with the aid of her sister-in-law, a few children, her husband Louis, and two other village men.[8] On April 4, 1815, fifty Sac and Fox Indians attacked while most of the others were out of town. The women hastily cast bullets for the men to fire at the warriors, but one of the three men was too distraught to fight. Instead, he prayed throughout the battle, lasting for several hours. Eventually, the fort was set afire, only to be extinguished several times with water. The judicious use of milk was then used after the water supply became exhausted. Julia finally filled the chamber pot and then strategically emptied the contents to save the fort. Her efforts were so exceptional that it was later proposed to honor her with a silver urinal, but pride interceded. So angered at the suggestion, Louis refused even to accept a silver mounted rifle to honor him for his role in repelling the siege. During the same year, four men were reportedly killed there in yet another Indian raid. Predictably, reports of highly emotional events such as these vary greatly in their detail from one account to another.

Nonetheless, the village, as well as the countryside, kept growing. When Brackenridge visited the village, he astutely predicted it would become an important place. Artist Titan Ramsay Peale came in 1819 and counted thirty log houses. The estimated local population soon approached some 800 souls because of the great western migration. A year before, Cote acquired its United States post office. Around 1820, Cote sans Dessein even rose to such prominence in Missouri that it became the penultimate alternative in contention to secure the state capital from St. Charles. The final selection was strongly—and more successfully—lobbied by land speculators allied with Jefferson City. By 1891–1892, the *Missouri Blue Book* documents a population of 1,600 residents in the township. During these prosperous times, it was likely prophesied to become the "New York of the West." But that was not to be. Today, after the demise of the town and its post office in 1907, Cote sans Dessein Township of Callaway County claims some 900 residents. Those old trapper and hunter families from St. Charles and La Charrette obviously loved north bank Missouri River villages, but, in spite of their efforts, not all of them would survive.

At the time of its founding, Cote sans Dessein became the farthest western American settlement on the Missouri frontier, supplanting that distinction from La Charrette. History also repeated itself in other ways. The two villages shared more than a common heritage, Indian raids, cultural diversity, a trading post, and an existence on the cutting edge of the American wilderness. The villagers remained as hunters, trappers, and traders. The Tayon family continued owning black slaves for at least a third generation. Irony also followed these upriver families. John-Baptiste Roy, son of Louis Roy, even served as the interpreter on the memorable 1821 Glenn-Fowler trapping-trading expedition to Santa Fe, twenty-four years after the Cardinal-Tebeau trio crossed the famous trail.[9,10] In spite of its near century-long existence, Cote sans Dessein, as with La Charrette, would not attain permanency beyond 1907. Today, the Katy Trail passes through the township, where the "hill without design" remains in view immediately south of Tebbetts, Missouri.

# Chapter 14:

## A Trail of Tears

Once again, relatives of Cecile Reine Tayon Roy and her brother Charles Tayon of La Charrette Village would participate in historic Missouri frontier events. This time, the focus becomes their Native American kin who continued to figure prominently in frontier politics. Authorities at all levels of government recognized the economic potential of settlers coming to the Missouri Territory. It was equally clear to them that the greatest single impediment in attracting settlers to "go west" was their fear of the warring Native Americans. The political tone of these considerations held root in the New England colonies, in the Federalist Papers of Hamilton, Madison, and Jay as well as in the Jefferson Administration administering the Louisiana Purchase.[1] Examples of this reality abound. Death was the prescribed punishment for Native Americans residing in today's liberal bastion of Connecticut during the late 1600s. President Jefferson even drafted a constitutional amendment that called for "the first direct and, at the same time, an official advocacy of Indian removal." Obviously, the proposed amendment never became law, but the concept held sanction within United States officialdom. Jefferson freely communicated his ideas to his colleagues and friends who continued embracing the concept of Indian removal well beyond his administration. Not only were Native Americans displaced, exasperated, and negotiated out of their tribal lands, but they were also greatly diminished in numbers by the processes of assimilation, the impact of war, excesses of alcohol, and the spread of European diseases. By the end of the nineteenth century, fully one-third of the Indian population was reported to have been of mixed heritage. Regardless, many would eventually be removed westward onto reservations.

Prospective settlers had all heard stories of brutal Indian raids and killings. Flocks of European immigrants considered Native Americans as hostile savages. However, by the 1830s, that fear was diminished.

The solution was, once again, remove all remaining Native Americans in Missouri farther westward. Such was the fate of about 2,000 Osages, along with members of other tribes, who were forced into present-day Kansas onto a reservation twenty-five miles beyond the Missouri boundary. Many Osages had already migrated west after the 1808 treaty negotiated by Indian Agent William Clark at Fort Osage was "interpreted" for them by Pierre Chouteau. By 1825, the Osage had signed yet another treaty with the United States surrendering all claims to their lands in Missouri. By 1830, the Indian Removal Act passed in the United States Congress, despite significant opposition. Congress next empowered a commission to handle the removal of Native Americans from east of the Mississippi while Black Hawk and his followers continued resisting, causing much concern to Missouri settlers. In 1832, Major Henry Dodge finally assigned Nathan Boone and his Company H of the Missouri Rangers to Fort Gibson (Oklahoma) to lead a program to pacify the Native Americans being relocated there. Boone and his men faithfully labored among the Native Americans until an August 1835 United States treaty established "initial" peace with them.[2] Now Boone and his men were free to offer protection to westward travelers, including those crossing the Santa Fe Trail.[3]

As before, these Indian relocation efforts were not totally effective. According to both the settlers and authorities, some Native Americans still remained scattered across twenty different states. A few Osages continued to return to Missouri to mourn at the graves of their deceased and hunt. Missouri Governor Bogg then ordered the militia to herd them onto the Kansas reservation. This forced the few remaining Osages in Missouri, along with their Missouri and Cherokee brothers, among others, to participate in the infamous Trail of Tears. The northernmost reaches of this trail passed from southern Illinois through central Missouri near Rolla into Oklahoma Territory during the winter of 1838–1839. Later, the discovery of oil on their reservation offered a bittersweet reprieve in their newly found wealth. Yet for the Osages, who seldom fought Americans or any European nation, their plight was ignominious. By now, Nathan Boone had moved his family to western Missouri near present-day Ash Grove. He and his dragoons continued quelling the Osages, as well as other Native Americans assigned to the reservations. Boone continued working to enforce Indian policy, establish peace, and fly the American flag across a vast, but hostile, western territory until 1848.

There were also Native Americans of mixed-blood heritage among those affected by these relocation policies. On the Ioway Indian Reservation, located in the corners of present-day northeast Kansas/southeast Nebraska, resided the family of Louise Roy (1843–1893), one of the wealthiest families living there in Nebraska Territory.[4] The full-blood Native Americans resented the presence of mixed-blood families like the Roys. Both held legal rights to life on the reservation, but the issue soon became a hot political topic. Louise and family were eventually assigned in 1854 to portions of sections 21 and 28 of Rulo Township, Richardson County, Nebraska. Louise was of only part Osage and Ioway heritage. As such, she was assigned to the Nemaha half-breed tract of the reservation. She reportedly ran her ranch with an iron hand and took great pride in educating her children. Her mixed heritage held its origins from Cote sans Dessein and in St. Charles before then. As the daughter of John-Baptiste and Parachenan Roy (he being the son of Louis and Julia Royer Roy), she also carried a French-Canadian genetic complement. In 1820, Baptiste and Cecile Reine Tayon Roy were the godparents to their new nephew, her father, John-Baptiste. Great-aunt Cecile was the daughter of Don Carlos and Cecilie Tayon of St. Charles and brother to the Tayons of Charrette Creek.

Previously, some Cote sans Dessein families, including Louis Roy, John-Baptiste Roy, and Joseph Revard, had chosen to move farther upriver in 1821 to establish the Kawsmouth community at the mouth of the Kansas River (Kansas City, Kansas). Here, they freely interacted with the local Native Americans, undoubtedly eventually prompting their identity with the reservation. On July 21 of that year, in a dispute over new government Indian relocation policies, Joseph Revard (1777–1821) paid with his scalp for the unpopular views he had expressed. The Cherokees, who fell into bitter conflict with the Osage over the half-breed issue, sought revenge upon half-French, half-Osage Revard. Revard's body was found two days later. By then, the Cherokees had returned to their village with fourteen of his horses and his scalp.[5] But not everyone residing on the half-breed tract was of French-Indian heritage. Joseph Vetter was a Civil War veteran of German-French heritage. He married Parachenan, the 1859 widow of John-Baptiste Roy. Vetter was now the stepfather to Louise Roy. He also lived on the reservation with his family and received quarterly annuity payments like the others. Descendants of these Roy families are known to have resided on the half-breed tract into the 1870s.

Many Native Americans from across the country, who were once so essential to the success of the gigantic fur-trading industry and played so many other vital roles in the development of the nation, were now relegated to reservations. With the fate of those issues resolved, Americans and newly arrived Europeans were now more at ease to migrate across the America West and settle with their families.

# Chapter 15:

## The Old Saxons

The area surrounding Charrette Creek once again experienced rapid transitions, even before the loss of old La Charrette Village. The two northern Missouri Territorial Districts of Howard and St. Charles were reorganized. In 1818, a new potential county, named Montgomery, was formed from western portions of the District of St. Charles before Missouri became the twenty-fourth state of the union in 1821. At this time, a new county road was laid out from Marthasville east to Femme Osage by Commissioners John Boone Callaway, a prominent justice of the peace, and William Hays Jr. In January 1833, Warren County was carved from eastern portions of Montgomery County that included present-day Charrette Township. The new county acquired its name from a prominent Boston physician and American patriot, Joseph Warren, who fell as a volunteer at the battle of Bunker Hill on June 17, 1775. He was allied with Samuel Adams and Paul Revere and a friend of John and Abigail Adams.[1] Abigail even took her seven-year-old son Johnny to see the battle smoke ten miles up the bay from Boston on the day when the thirty-four-year-old Warren was shot through the face, his body maimed by British bayonets. Abigail wrote John about the loss of one of their worthiest men in the province, "My bursting heart must find vent at my pen." Colonial patriot Warren committed his life to liberty, just as those of his namesake Missouri county, including the Ramsey family, John Busby, Captain James A. Callaway, and countless others.

As we know, sometime around 1825, the presence of La Charrette Village faded from prominence, if not existence. Old La Charrette Landing was soon renamed Marthasville Landing. Thus, the transition into statehood involved both La Charrette Village and Marthasville, each sharing the same river landing location assuming the name of its closest village. More guests and settlers than ever before, essentially all coming from the east, continued disembarking at the old landing as they participated in the development of the region now know as Charrette Township of Warren County. Indicative of the impact of this new wave of western migration was the growth experienced in St. Louis. During this same interval, old "Chouteau Town" grew from 5,000 people in 1823 to more than 65,000 by 1840. During the next decade or so, Missouri became home to more settlers than any other state. However, before many Germans arrived in Charrette Township, Marthasville was yet to be founded.

## Marthasville, Missouri, 63357…"It Will Hardly Grow"

Plate 8. Marthasville with old La Charrette Village farms in the background.

This southwesterly view across downtown Marthasville shows the fall 1895 harvest on land once owned by William Ramsey, Joseph Chartran, and widow St. Franceway, as indicated by shocks of corn between the village and Charrette Creek. Central Hotel is in the left-center of photograph, a two-story residence/store in the foreground with a two-horse buggy tied up at the hitching post. Note the casual village streets, cow pastures, and outhouses. Faintly visible in front of the corn shocks are the Missouri, Kansas, and Texas Railroad tracks, its depot and cylindrical water tank established in 1892. Its roadbed later became the Katy Hiking and Biking Trail.

Well before La Charrette Village became extinct, Dr. John Young laid out the village of Marthasville. In 1817, this Virginian chose a site on his farm within a mile north of La Charrette Village and named it for his first wife, Martha Fuqua. Previously, Young's farm had been part of Spanish Grant Number 1688 surveyed in the name of William Ramsey and bounded on three sides by the village farms of Chartran and Cardinal.[2] Although surrounded by hills on the north, east, and west, the downtown section was still subject to Missouri River and Town Branch flooding. Nonetheless, Dr. Young had selected a picturesque setting for his village, one of the few villages of those presented here to attain permanency.

His June 21, 1817, advertisement in the *St. Louis Missouri Gazette* proclaimed its virtues and welcomed all interested parties to settle. Even though only a few lots were sold at the public auction held on September 1, 1817, Dr. Young built a tavern while his professional peer, Dr. John Jones, established a medical practice, both representing the first of their profession living in the community. These frontier community leaders were busy men. Young, an obvious promoter, advertised items for sale in his store, Merchandise & Groceries, at ten to fifteen percent below prices in either St. Charles or St. Louis. He even took time to help cure a protracted illness of Reverend John M. Peck upon his arrival in St. Louis in 1818.[3] While the town was still in its infancy, Young also built water-powered mills on Tuque Creek. To encourage village growth even further, he traded a stud named Black Prince for four town lots to Benjamin Sharp. Horses of many colors—blacks, grays, sorrels, creams, and bays—were all important to the local economy. Local farmers came to town in horse-drawn wagons or buggies to sell their produce, attend church, or trade with the local merchants. Large draft horses or mules were hitched in teams to pull various farm implements while lighter saddle horses were ridden or hitched to the buggy. Young, like some of the other villagers and farmers, owned black slaves to assist with farm and household chores. Slave children attended the black school, separate from the school for whites, along with any free blacks residing there. By 1826, Young seemed to have lost interest in Marthasville. He then sold most of his Marthasville holdings to

United States Postmaster Harvey Griswold. Young then moved to St. Louis, where he died in 1832. It would not be long before his village would be described as a typical pioneer town boasting a steam-powered sawmill, flour mill, wagon factory, stores, and several churches. Before mid-century, a German school was added to the community.

Dr. Jones married Minerva Callaway, daughter of Flanders Callaway and granddaughter of Daniel Boone, and was Boone's physician in his later years. Jones desired to assist Boone record a narrative of his famous life while staying with his family at La Charrette. The narrative was never completed, and the portion that was became lost. Doctors like Young and Jones routinely obtained their professional training in a series of lectures totaling about twenty-five weeks supplemented with an apprenticeship. Future professional growth relied upon day-to-day experience and reading. Common texts of the day, not medical timely journals, included *Annuals of Medicine*, *A System of Surgery*, *Practice of Midwifery*, and *American Dispensatory*. These and twenty other books comprised the medical library of Dr. James R. Estes of St. Charles in 1819.

These frontier doctors were not only challenged by issues of health, but with current community issues as well, forever exposing them to great risk. By now, Missouri riverboats like the *St. Ange* were bringing fear and death to ports such as Marthasville Landing all along its river route, spreading smallpox, influenza, and Asiatic cholera.[4,5] In 1851, the *St. Ange* was described as a floating hospital with several deaths occurring every day, including Father Christian Hoecken, who had been traveling with Father De Smet and Captain La Barge during a cholera outbreak. Each evening, La Barge would dock the *St. Ange* to bury the dead by torchlight. Reporting on past community issues, the *Warrenton News-Journal* of May 20, 1887, credits Jones in seeking out local counterfeiters and horse thieves operating in and around Marthasville between 1835 and 1844, only to be shot and killed as revenge in his front yard on January 21, 1842. The perpetrators were purportedly from St. Charles.

The local citizens soon benefited from the improved medical training and services offered by their physicians. Once again, the influence of the Boone, Bryan, and Callaway families presents itself. Dr. Daniel Boone Jones, the first child born to John and Minerva, would carry on at least two family legacies: the name of Daniel Boone and a practicing physician. These family traditions also involved his younger brother Paul S. Jones, who took his apprenticeship under his brother, now practicing in

Newport, Missouri, before graduating from the medical department of the University of Missouri in 1854. Paul later became a practicing physician in Franklin County, according to Boone descendant J. T. Cotton.[6]

The spirit of adventure and the dream of riches had not died in Charrette Township following the departure of the French fur trappers and the demise of the fur trade. Local citizen Jacob C. Darst, along with others of his Darst-Callaway-Boone-Bryan family, became part of the expansionist movement into Texas largely influenced by favorable reports of Pike's Expedition. He left for DeWitt's colony following the death of his first wife Elizabeth Bryan, only to be killed in the battle of the Alamo in San Antonio on March 6, 1836. By 1849, word of gold discovered at Sutter's Mill near the Sacramento River lured Marthasvillians, just like thousands of others. Twenty-three local prospectors led by M. Jackson Lamme and Thomas Maupin formed a wagon train. The caravan started out in April of 1850 and arrived six months later in California. Lamme was reared at La Charrette Village as one of the sons of William T. and Frances Lamme. Committed to the proposition of "California or Bust," these prospectors were mostly descendants of Boone or his friends. Left behind was a Boone associate named Derry, the black slave who had faithfully trapped and hunted with Daniel Boone, Flanders Callaway, and W. T. Lamme. In June 1851, Derry died of the flux in Marthasville at seventy-two years of age.

Marthasville citizens also participated in other national events. Sometime in January of 1861, Marthasville slaveholders met and drafted a resolution.[2] The proclamation was printed and widely distributed. It accused abolitionists of being hostile to their institutions, referring to them as "offenders from foreign lands, who somewhere through deception became our fellow-citizens." Clearly, the newly settled Germans held views differing from those acceptable to the local slaveholders, who had preceded them to the community. Charrette Township was divided, just as was the nation during the Civil War.

Marthasville only grew at a modest pace from forty-seven residents in 1840 to more than 200 residents by 1900. Marthasvillians not only benefited from improved medical treatment and river steamboat travel, but they also came to appreciate the services of the Missouri and Western Telegraph Company since 1859. They later welcomed the Missouri, Kansas, and Texas railroad to town and, later still, the automobile. Missouri River ferries continued docking at Marthasville Landing well into the twentieth century. Over this same interval, Charrette Township's rural population grew more rapidly than the town of Marthasville, largely due to the influx of German farmers. Today, as in the past, local farm families of Charrette Township continue visiting, worshiping, and trading in Marthasville, now home to almost 900 Missourians as its bicentennial anniversary approaches.

# Arrival of Germans

Gottfried Duden, a man of letters, was from Remscheid, Germany. He settled at Lake Creek in 1824 near present-day Dutzow in Charrette Township. Duden became friends with Nathan Boone as they visited and traveled together through St. Charles, Howard, and nearby counties. Duden wrote many letters to friends in Germany, which were published as a book in 1829, recounting his three-year experience in Missouri. Duden enthusiastically endorsed what was soon to become southern Warren County. His comments subsequently attracted other Germans to Marthasville, in spite of one unflattering observation:

> [A] German mile from here (near Dutzow) an attempt was made to found a town. It is called Marthasville. Its location was chosen unwisely and it will hardly grow. It has only a few houses, but there are two stores, a post office, and also a doctor.[7]

Many consider his book as the major force in attracting Germans to migrate to "Duden's Eden." However, Professor Walter Kamphoefner, a preeminent authority on German migrations to Missouri, credits the sequential flow of many other letters from America to Germany, subsequently shared with friends and relatives there, as the major influence. He describes this process as one of chain migration of letters.

Heinrich von Martel, a First Lieutenant of the 8th Royal Hanovarian Battalion, left Germany with his father and brothers in 1832 seeking Duden's Eden. By October of that year, he was residing in Marthasville, sending letters back home.[8] Excerpts from several of his letters give insight into his activities in Charrette Township as its next cycle of settlers participated in chain migration:

Marthasville, October 27, 1832

> We have taken board with a Mr. Bryant, one of the oldest settlers in the region. He came with Colonel Boone from Kentucky, thirty years ago. For $1.25 a week we have a pleasant room and good board.

Martel was interested in farming, and after visiting several farms purchased one in St. Charles County, although he soon returned to Germany only to once again return to America where he lived in Texas, Colorado and Ohio. His newly purchased Missouri farm is described in another of his letters written while still at Marthasville:

November 3, 1832

A farm adjoining that of the Messrs. Mallinkrodt pleased us especially. We bought it for $1,200. We also bought the owners entire corn crop, twelve acres of wheat, 500 bushels of turnips, 100 hogs, 8 cows, 15 sheep, and a lot of chickens all for $300. The buildings on the property consist of several log houses. A new two-story dwelling house has to be finished on the inside. The farm contains 160 acres, of which 130 acres are in the Missouri bottoms and the rest upland. We shall buy 600 acres of government land which adjoins it.

One letter of November 14, 1832, described a local farming practice:

When they break prairie here, they use six yokes of oxen to one plow. The cost of breaking land is $2.00. One plow can usually break 1.5 acres per day.

His letter of January 30, 1833, relates impressions of the people of various cultures that had preceded him to the Missouri frontier:

On a journey to St. Charles, Corondelet, Belleville, Portage des Sioux, Florissant, and Kaskaskia I got acquainted with descendants of the French who immigrated many years ago. Although most of them are mixtures of French and Indian blood they seem nevertheless vivacious Frenchmen, with good and bad characteristics...

There are no jollier people in all the United States. They have preserved all the gaiete du coeur of their forefathers. The dance is their chief amusement...

At General Clark's, who is in charge of Indian affairs, I saw several Ottos from the upper Missouri. General Clark's museum contains many Indian curiosities, the greater part of which he gathered in the years 1804–6, when he and Captain Lewis and forty companions explored the Louisiana Purchase. When the seventy-year-old General Clark spoke of the daughters of the Mandans and other tribes, his eyes beamed with a youthful fire and he assured me that they were the handsomest women in the world.

Martel's letters, like those of Duden's and others, cast a spell upon the Germans. The power of suggestion combined with adventure, opportunity, and freedom were compelling forces they could not resist. By 1833, this new wave of German settlers began arriving by the shipload, and they continued to do so over the next twenty-five years or more. Not only were they enticed to come to "Amerika" by letters from friends and relatives, but they were intrigued by what they read in books written by American frontier travelers reporting upon their adventures and observations and, of course, what others retold them.

Most of these new residents of southern Warren County came from northwest Germany, almost exclusively from Prussia or its neighbor, the tiny principality of Lippe, also known as Lippe-Detmold. Hundreds and hundreds of German families first set foot in Warren County by disembarking at Marthasville Landing. Most had been German peasants of one description or another and were eager to farm the fertile land in the area, thereby overcoming their old country fears of overpopulation and subsequent Malthusian starvation. But not all were of peasant stock.

Emigrant aid societies were organized to assist some Germans with the biggest decision of their lives. One such group settled north of Dutzow in Charrette Township. Among them were Frederick Muench and Paul Follenius, who established the Giessener Emigration Society in 1833, greatly influenced by the earlier experiences of Dr. Duden and Ludwig Eversmann. Likewise, Wilhelm von Bock, along with fourteen of his friends, founded the Berlin Society in Dutzow. Members of the Solingen Emigration Society settled nearby at Lake Creek, while David Goebel chose to settle near Washington. The underlying theme of these so-called Latin Farmers was to establish a strict communal German lifestyle to eventuate in a German state as part of the United States of America. But those ideals were soon forsaken. These men trained in law, mathematics, geography, astronomy, and the classics experienced great difficulty adapting to the frontier and farming. Most soon relocated to life as professionals in St. Louis or other cities. However, Germans eventually became so prominent that, today, Texas A&M University professor of history, Walter D. Kamphoefner (from New Melle in St. Charles County and himself a product of this German migration) designated the region as the "Missouri German Belt." Fully one-sixth of all Germans in rural Missouri lived in St. Charles and Warren Counties by 1860. As might be expected, many of these German family descendants continue residing in the surrounding counties today. Friedrich Muench, an accomplished viticulturist, effectively summed up the outcome in 1870:

> In the course of a generation Duden's dream has, after all, become reality, and also the ideals of the founder of the Giessen Emigration Society, to establish a new German environment in this western part of the union has been fulfilled, though in a manner such as we had not anticipated or dreamed.[8]

Most of the arriving Germans were of the *heuerling* class of peasantry, a form of sharecropping with excessive taxation without representation passed from one generation to the next. They were less worldly and idealistic than the Latin Farmers. They were practical-minded and knew how to farm. Religion, hard work, education, and opportunity were their hallmarks.

Nicholas Hess came to Missouri during the initial influx of Germans in 1835–1837 to help others contemplating the move.[9] His commentary attempted to capture every aspect of frontier life by contrasting it with rural Germany. Local economic conditions were explained, including the cost of producing hogs and other livestock. He was impressed an individual Missouri farmer might own more than 200 hogs. For emphasis, he added that many also had fifty to one hundred sheep plus cattle and horses. To appreciate the contrast, a year's supply of meat for a typical German peasant family might represent only two or three hogs. Local opportunities for hunting and fishing were cautiously praised, suggesting "the new settler has so much hard work to do in farming." But there was no misunderstanding his contempt for bedbugs and ticks. "They more than take the place of German fleas…" Hess also explained in vivid detailed how he killed five rattlesnakes in the spring and summer of 1836 and concluded "…everyone should be warned not to walk along the road on summer evenings…" Some settlers were even leery of the Missouri climate and its effect upon health as previously surmised by scientist John Bradbury. Conventional wisdom of the day held that humid night air and drinking water obtained from shallow wells were threats to good health. Hesse thought the north winds "sharp and penetrating" and considered the weather "extremely changeable."

# Charrette Township Flourishes

The great westward migration had now hit full stride. German peasants arrived, ready to start life anew. Land was cleared to establish new farmsteads. Cabins, barns, and sheds were erected from the resulting timber—all of horizontal log construction—unlike the vertical log structures of the early French settlers. Zigzag rail fences surrounded the newly established fields and pastures. The new 1837 home of Herman and Sophia Ahmann was typical. It was constructed from hand-hewn logs at a total out-of-pocket cost of $1.50 to pay for nails, door hinges, windowpanes, and a gallon of whisky for the log-raising party. This eighteen-by-eighteen-foot one-room cabin remained as the last structure of its era on La Charrette farmland once owned by widow St. Franceway. The Ahmanns later added other rooms to their home, where they continued to live the remainder of their lives. A control burn on May 18, 2001 razed the entire home. During its waning years, the structure was used for storage. Oral history of the Kurt Schake family from Lippe includes an 1856 log-raising party to erect their new home with assistance from the black slaves owned by neighbor Frank Wyatt. Frank's father, Anthony, came from Kentucky and had settled there in 1808. The new Schake homestead neighbored the Robert Ramsey farm, scene of the brutal Indian raid of 1815. It was larger than most homes, featuring two fifteen-by-thirty-foot rooms, a dirt floor, and a loft for sleeping. It served as a residence for about 125 years before being razed.

Towns and villages sprang to life all across the Charrette landscape with churches, stores, shops, and schools providing the essentials for their lives. Towns named Holstein, Peers, Concord Hill, Lippstadt, Hopewell, New Boston, and Treloar were founded. Like La Charrette Village, some would not survive for long. Lesser places, often little more than a cluster of farmsteads at a crossroads with a store or blacksmith shop, acquired names such as Rekate's Store, Bierbaum Steam Saw and Grist Mill, or Kite's Mill. Each was possessed with a sense of community pride and filled with anticipation for a prosperous future.

Before there were local banks, these farmers secured their valuables in secret locations. Herman and Sophia Ahmann arrived from Lienen, Westphalia, Germany in 1836 seeking opportunity in America. Other than farm and hunt game for a living, Herman became more prosperous than most other immigrants did by selling farm produce in St. Louis at higher than local prices. On the return trip, he crossed over the Femme Osage road with his horse-drawn wagon loaded with wholesale goods for Merchandise & Groceries and other local stores. He eventually saved $2,000 worth of gold hidden in old shoes in his log home. Marthasville, Holstein, and Dutzow would later acquire banks to provide improved security for valuables along with other financial services.

New Catholic, Evangelical, Lutheran, and Methodist congregations were established throughout the township as their members strictly followed the tenets of their faiths as practiced in Germany. Many Germans were reluctant to learn English. Worship services were initially offered only in German. They were next offered as separate or mixed German and English services, which persisted into the mid-1900s. A sampling of church congregations established in the township include the 1842 log church called St. Peter and Paul, later to became St. Vincent de Paul Catholic Church of Dutzow. Others included the Liberal German Evangelical Church of Holstein, the Evangelischen St. Johannes Gemeinde of Pinckney, plus three Methodist Churches in Marthasville. A church-affiliated home for the unfortunates, Evangelisches Predigerseminar, was located between Marthasville and Femme Osage.

Around mid-century, those of German heritage began predominating in the community. These farmers were both highly traditional and forward-looking. From the Schwalenberg, Lippe, forest, they translocated an ancient German tribal hunting festival known as the Schutzenfest to Warren County. At the same time, they formed the Warren County Agricultural and Mechanical Association. Traditions and ambitions such as these gradually blended with existing cultures in the region as the frontier atmosphere began yielding to the pressures of development.

# Freedom of Expression

Even after the Germans had settled along the Missouri River, all was not as expected. Once a fiercely independent tribal people before Charlemagne began subjugating them in AD 772, they had experienced religious and political oppression for generations. They were now quick to express themselves in various public and political forums. Following a five-year residency, they could apply for American citizenship and were soon recognized as a major force at the ballot box. While slavery was taking shape as a national political issue, most German-language Missouri newspapers were voicing their protest against the practice. Conrad Mallinckrodt of St. Charles wrote editorials on this and other issues to the *St. Charles Demokrat*, an early German-language newspaper. On January 17, 1852, Mallinckrodt praised the newspaper for a recent piece on the unfair treatment of Germans by others in the county. He asked the German-Americans in neighboring counties to join him in his sentiments:

> We hope soon to hear the same also from the bordering counties so that we German-Americans, too, finally can realize the motto 'equal rights for all.' We do not want any special rights; we do not claim privileges. But only through general knowledge of all the civil rights due us, and mutually maintaining them, can we secure ourselves against injustice and achieve what is due us.

The first newspaper founded west of the Mississippi followed the establishment of La Charrette Village School by one year. Editor Joseph Charless negotiated with the governor of the Louisiana Territory, Meriwether Lewis, for the establishment of the *Missouri Gazette* in 1808. Governor Lewis wanted the first edition off the press by June when the territorial legislature would meet. Publication of the new, revised territorial laws would be essential. Lewis said, "I know not of any point in the U States where I concieve a country paper or printer would meet with more encouragement than in St. Louis."[10] The first edition to survive was printed on July 26, 1808, as Vol. I, Number 3. "St. Louis Louisiana. Printed by Joseph Charless, printer to the Territory" appears under the heading. During the second year of publication, it was renamed the *Louisiana Gazette*, reporting on the suspicious—and premature—October 11 death of Governor Meriwether Lewis in Nashville. By July 4, 1812, the United States Congress organized the Missouri Territory. Another name change ensued for the newspaper. This time, it was entitled the *Missouri Gazette and Public Advertiser*. The next year, the *Gazette* reported the president had appointed William Clark as governor of the newly designated territory. Other name changes and more newspapers followed, including *The Missourian*, published in St. Charles by Charless' stepson, Robert McCloud. Advertisements not exceeding "one square" cost one dollar for the first week and fifty cents for successive weeks. As late as 1810, the *Louisiana Gazette* accepted pork or flour as payment for the three dollar annual subscription.

Marthasville acquired its United States post office in 1818, the same year the request for a post office at La Charrette was passed over. During these times, papers from St. Louis or other eastern cities arrived by mail. In 1857, Robert E. Pleasants published the first Warren County newspaper, the *Nonpareil*. Chas. W. Rapp owned this Warrenton-based paper for two months in 1868 before reselling to Mr. Peers, who changed its name to the *Warrenton Missouri Banner*. German language newspapers, including *Die Washingtoner Post* published in Washington and the *Westliche Post* in St. Louis, gave Joseph Pulitzer his start as a giant among American journalists.[11] Later, with another St. Louis paper, he declared his political independence saying, "The *Post* and *Dispatch* will serve no party but the people..." Two long-standing local papers continue publication to the present. *The Missourian* was initiated in 1839. The *Marthasville News* (later *The Marthasville Record*) began in 1896. The subscription rate for the *News* was one dollar per year.

These newfound freedoms of expression were of great interest to the Germans, who considered themselves oppressed in many ways back home. Papers were initially under the sole control of the editor, often reporting misleading items, including the premature 1818 death of Daniel Boone. Even the September 1820 *St. Louis Enquirer* misstated that Boone had died at Charrette Village. But, in the course of time, the Missouri legislature placed restraints upon the pioneer editor. "He must be wary of charges of fornication and adultry; and he must not incite any Negro to rebellion."[9] Many forms of libelous, defamatory materials were published. Phrases and epithets such as toadies, dung hill breed, jackasses, this impertinent person, a base calumniator, and a dastard and a liar were crafted to slander anyone from politicians to those representing a social minority. Libel suits followed, fostering more legislative controls and improved professional management. By 1840, the editor of the *Missouri Argus* was even offering an international, though biased, perspective to its readership:

> No foreigners who come to add themselves to our population are more valuable than the Germans, and we sincerely rejoice to see from foreign papers that many thousand will leave the continent of Europe during the coming summer.

No single individual did more to raise editorial standards while simultaneously fervently addressing the difficult social and political issues following the Civil War than Pulitzer.[11] While serving both the *Post* and as a Missouri state representative, his message was to "abolish all disqualifications for voting—color and past disloyalty! Let every citizen cast his ballot."

# Stirring the "All-American" Melting Pot

In keeping with past trends, the ethnic composition of Charrette Township had once again undergone major transition. The Native Americans were obviously the original stewards of the land as part of their tribal heritage. Next, and almost concurrent with the 1801 settlement of La Charrette Village by French-Indian families, friends and members of the interrelated Boone-Bryan-Van Bibber-Callaway families and their black slaves arrived in Missouri. Some like Flanders Callaway and, after Rebecca's death, Daniel Boone, claimed La Charrette as their home. However, most, but not all, of the French residing at La Charrette began to move on between the visits of Lewis and Clark and the War of 1812.

Still, more Americans continued arriving. The October 28, 1825, *Missouri Intelligencer* claimed 300 wagons had already passed through St. Charles that year and as many more wagons were still on the way, each pulled by four to six horses or oxen. These families, many with up to a dozen black slaves, herded their cattle, hogs, horses, and sheep as they walked alongside their wagons. As the presence of black slaves increased, the Native American populations continued diminishing. Then, from the 1830s to the 1850s, German immigration began dominating setting the stage for a typical American cultural melting pot.

Local land ownership also reflected these ethnic migrations. The farms of our primary subjects of this work, the French-Indian families of La Charrette Village, were soon to be owned exclusively by those of German ethnicity. Given changes in farm size as influenced by stream erosion or other factors, the following unfolds. Various portions of the early 1800 farms once owned by Jack Amos, Jean-Baptiste Luzon, and "Vieuve" St. Franceway were owned by William Ahmann, Hermann Ahmann, and J. Ahmann by 1877. In the center of La Charrette Village was the farm of syndic Joseph Chartran, now owned by R. Hillermann. In 1884, Hillermann sold his farm to Karl Wilhelm Rocklage, whose son Karl Heinrich married Herman Ahmann's granddaughter, Maria Lavina Ahmann on August 30, 1887. About fifty years later, Mary (Maria) and Karl Heinrich Rocklage became my maternal grandparents. Farther to the east, farm boundaries had also undergone change. Cursively, the Tayon, Cardinal, and Lamme farms were now owned by German farmers named H. Hilgedick, George Kite, and H. Schwarze. Interspersed between the French and German owners of the village farmland were Flanders Callaway, W. T. Lamme, or James Bryan, all members of the Daniel Boone family.

The transfer of land ownership associated with the village farms became important in other aspects as well. All relied upon the same river landing to serve their mass transit needs. Most important to village history is the reality that much of what we have learned of La Charrette Village was recorded and passed on to us by this progression of new landholders and their neighbors. Within less than six decades, the once ethnically rich diversity of the area immediately surrounding La Charrette Village had been completely transformed. First- and second-generation German immigrants largely supplanted the unique diversity evidenced by the earlier squatters and settlers. Charrette Township as well as the nearby countryside underwent a similar transformation.[12] Census data for Warren and St. Charles counties in 1850 reveal that Germans owned fifty percent of the farmland, followed by forty-one percent for Americans. Old French, British, and the Irish round out the population of landowners. They also differed in their chosen occupations. The Old French, true to their traditions, predominated as riverboat pilots and buffalo hunters while Americans tended to serve more frequently as physicians, lawyers, teachers, clerks, justices of the peace, and other professionals. Germans predominated in the trades as distillers, blacksmiths, shoemakers, stonemasons, tailors, wagonmakers, millers, and cabinetmakers. These three ethnic groups shared in what today may be considered as the service sector of the economy represented by clergymen, merchants and grocers, carpenters, coopers, and saddlers. However, most Charrette Township families were now of German extraction working as grain and livestock farmers, establishing their hard-working frugal, clannish lifestyle as Missouri's German Belt.

According to the 2000 United States Census report, Missouri's total population stood at 5,595,211 citizens. Warren County represented 24,525 of these Missourians, of which approximately seventeen percent resided in Charrette Township. The ethnic composition within the county now stands at 95.9 percent white, 1.9 percent black, 0.4 percent Native American, and 0.2 percent Asian and Pacific Islanders. The remainder is either of mixed heritage or other ethnic categories. The once ethnically diverse settlement of La Charrette, the first attempted in today's Warren County by French-Canadians along with their customary Native Americans wives, had given way to a near monoculture of whites. Once rural Warren County with more than 1,400 farms in 1880 now records only 232 full-time farmers. All are white, except for two farms owned by African-Americans.

# Chapter 16:

## The Mighty River Highway

### Marthasville Landing

When Isaac and Nancy Murphy operated the ferry at Charrette Landing during the early 1800s, it served mostly local needs of commerce. However, around the time when it was renamed Marthasville Landing, it soon began serving as a major port of call for much of Warren County. Canoes, skiffs, barges, flatboats, ferryboats, and riverboats were all eventually maneuvered up, down, and across the river by rowing, poling, and cordeling. Even wind, animal, and steam power were employed. Marthasville Landing was one of eighty such river landings on the Missouri by 1838.[1] At that time, river steamers needed to travel eighty-nine miles from Chouteau's Landing in St. Louis to Marthasville Landing.

Washington Ferry Company began operation in 1822, connecting North Washington Landing at Lac's Point in Warren County to Washington Landing in Franklin County. Between 7:00 AM and 5:54 PM, according to an 1885 advertisement when Frank Hoelscher was ferrymaster, fifteen trips were scheduled across the river each day. To the west of Marthasville Landing in Pinckney Township were Pinckney and, later, Krusmeier's Landings. Christian Schwentker operated a mule-powered ferry between Pinckney and New Haven in the 1880s. As late as 1903, a steam-powered ferry, *The Dauntless*, transported up to twenty-six tons of cargo at a time between these river towns.

The date of origin and discontinuance of Marthasville (Charrette) Landing has apparently escaped recorded history. In all likelihood, it emerged as an interrupted continuum since before the founding of the La Charrette Village in 1801 and continued in service into the early twentieth century. Typical cargo of the day was unloaded at Marthasville Landing onto horse-drawn wagons headed to various destinations in the county crossing over Old State Highway 47. Farmers and merchants, of course, delivered their shipments in a similar fashion.

People from across America and beyond sought Marthasville Landing. Typical of Europeans seeking the landing were twelve Catholic families, who left their Hanover, Germany, village homes on July 25, 1833. According to St. Francis Borgia Parish history, these German immigrants sailed from the port at Bremen to New Orleans. By October of that year, they were making their way up the Missouri River after experiencing many stressful, yet exciting, happenings on their long journey to "Amerika." Upon boarding a Missouri River steamboat in St. Louis, they were asked their destination. No one had any place specific in mind except for one member of the party who recalled a favorable report from Dr. Duden's 1829 book, prompting the suggestion they disembark at Marthasville Landing. When they came near the landing, the riverboat captain said:

> Here is the landing place. But Marthasville is quite a distance to the north from the riverbank. Night is coming on; you cannot find the way and there is no house close by. I would rather land you on the opposite shore; there you will find a house where you can more safely stay overnight. And you can be taken across and be brought to Marthasville tomorrow.

This logical change in plans apparently suited everyone. That evening, October 28, was spent in Washington, Missouri, in the home and tavern owned by Bernard Fricke, a German.

They learned good land could be purchased in the community, so this party of twelve families collectively abandoned their Warren County plans in favor of Franklin County. Named by the head of these twelve German families, they were: Gerhard H. Trentmann, Frederick Bleckmann, Frederick Riegel, John H. Koering, Adolph Smertmann, Gerhard Uhlenbrock, Rudolph Uhlenbrock, John Henry Buhr, Herman Schwegmann, Wilhelm Weber, John Edelbrock (whose son later moved to Warren County), and John Matthias Hustermann.

Still, other German families experienced various degrees of success upon disembarking at Marthasville Landing. Three Ahmann brothers from Lienen, Westphalia, also followed the advice of Dr. Duden. Friederich and Jacob Ahmann arrived via the "Duden Route" through Baltimore in 1833. The same year, Warren County's 3,500 citizens carved their new county out of Montgomery Country. They arrived successfully at Marthasville Landing and then married and settled in

Warren County, soon to be joined by their little brother Herman and his future bride, Sophia Suhre. Not only did he choose to leave Germany, but he left much of his inheritance and his entire military obligation behind. Sophia was of a lower class of peasantry than Herman, thereby disqualifying their marriage unless a fine was paid. Instead, this couple paid a forty-dollar fare for their sixty-one-day passage from Bremen to New Orleans. They were heading up the Missouri River toward Marthasville Landing on June 23, 1836. Being a very dry season, the boat captain belatedly informed them the river was so low that he could not make their destination. Sophia and Herman, along with their wooden trunks, were disembarked on the riverbank just east of Marthasville Landing. Leaving their belongings behind, they started walking toward the hills. They soon encountered a local farmer. He directed them to Friederich and Jacob, who lived nearby in Charrette Township. By September, the romance of Sophia and Hermann was sealed in marriage.

Marthasville Landing not only served as a means of ushering in another tier of ethnic diversity to the region, but it also served many other purposes, most notably that of supporting local commerce. Fifty years after Lewis and Clark visited La Charrette, Johann Cord "Kurt" and Friedericke Kuhfuss Schake and their family of three daughters and two sons, Adolph and Frederich, left Humfeld, Lippe, Germany, to later disembark at Marthasville Landing. Unlike the early French settlers who relied upon acorns to fatten their free-ranging hogs, the Schakes fed theirs. Their fertile land produced an abundance of corn and turnips that allowed the hogs to grow rapidly. They initially herded their hogs to markets in St. Louis, stopping overnight at the farms of their friends along the way. Next, they decided local processing of their hogs, along with those purchased from neighboring farmers, would be more profitable. The Frederick Schake and Brother Pork Packers was located on Front Street in Washington, immediately east of the Buescher Corn Cob Pipe factory, from 1885 to 1891. The transport of live hogs across the Missouri River for slaughter and further processing was largely a winter enterprise. If the river was frozen, the hogs would be herded across the river to Washington. If not frozen, Marthasville Landing and Ferry was utilized.

Martin Kite of Virginia, who also claimed German heritage, came to Warren County in 1835 and developed the area's first sawmill on Charrette Creek some four miles above Marthasville Landing. Timber was both an abundant and highly valued commodity of many uses. Just as when the fur trade was the basis of the local economy, timber remained as the fuel and construction material of choice. Trees were harvested from the woods and trimmed of limbs, mostly used for firewood. The resulting tree trunks were typically sawed into eight-, ten-, or twelve-foot segments, which were removed from local forests by teams of oxen or horses, loaded onto log wagons, and delivered to the mill. The Kite sawmill, powered by Charrette Creek water, supplied an abundance of lumber to the community, especially for the construction of buildings, flatboats, and wagons. Some of the resulting lumber and wooden products were shipped to other river markets from Marthasville Landing. Firewood was sold to river steamboats now docking there as well. Before Kite's Mill, all the splitting and sawing of lumber was done by hand. One walnut tree on Loutre Island allegedly produced 200 fence rails, eleven feet long by four to six inches thick. Some 30,000 shingles were obtained from one cottonwood tree, the same variety of cottonwood Corps of Discovery leader Meriwether Lewis recorded as the fourth plant specimen while at La Charrette:

> No. 4. Was taken at a small Village North side of the Missouri called Sharett, on the 25th of May 1804. this is the last settlement on the Missouri; and consists of ten or twelve families mostly hunters. this specimine is the seed of the Cottonwood which is so abundant in this country, it has now arrived at maturity and the wind when blowing strong drives it through the air to a great distance being supported by a parrishoot of this cottonlike substance which gives the name to the tree.

Downriver passengers departed Marthasville Landing. Captain Joseph La Barge, the acknowledged dean of Missouri River boat captains, was once retained by eastern politicians to escort them to Marthasville Landing. On July 17, 1845, the "Master River Pilot" docked the *Kansas* at the old Warren County port of call. On board was a delegation from the Kentucky legislature. Led by the Honorable John J. Crittenden, United States senator, attorney general under President Harrison and soon-to-be governor of Kentucky, they proceeded to trudge over old La Charrette Village farms toward Bryan Cemetery, the village's multiethnic resting place. They unceremoniously exhumed the remains of Daniel and Rebecca Bryan Boone. Local black slaves, King Bryan, Henry Angbert, and Jeff Callaway had opened the graves. Upon completion of the ill-advised task, La Barge turned the *Kansas* around and headed downriver with the Kentuckians. Also on board were the remains of the preeminent American wilderness icon and, by now, an internationally famous frontiersman as well as his beloved wife. All this in spite of the fact that Daniel Boone said when he left Kentucky, according to his son Nathan:

> [H]e did it with the intention of never stepping his feet upon Kentucky soil again; and if he was compelled to lose his head on the block or revisit Kentucky, he would not hesitate to chose the former.[2]

The remains of Daniel and Rebecca Boone, surrounded by a state monument, were interred in the Frankfort Kentucky Cemetery.

## Romantic River Steamboats

Marthasville Landing, also known as Charrette Landing, could not have contributed what it had to the commerce and ethnic mixing of the region without the presence of steamboats. This exciting chapter of Missouri River history allowed for more rapid transportation and communication for its citizenry than ever. Once loaded, boats and barges on the Missouri-Mississippi River system could navigate to markets in less time than ever before, opening new opportunities for numerous commodities and services. The first steamboat, named the *General Pike*, arrived in St. Louis in 1816, cutting travel time to a fraction of previous schedules. But an important question remained. Could steamboats successfully navigate the more treacherous Missouri River besieged with sandbars, mud flats, snags, and floating obstacles such as ice, water-logged tree trunks, and bloated buffalo carcasses? The *Constitution* is recorded as the first steamboat to enter waters of the Missouri on October 1, 1817, while the *Independence* navigated the first roundtrip from St. Louis to Franklin and on to Chariton in just twenty-one days. A little later, the *Washington* negotiated the same route in only six days. A local paper, the *Missouri Intelligencer and Boonslick Advertiser*, itself a little over a month old, reported on this momentous event on May 28, 1819:

> With no ordinary sensations of pride and pleasure, we announce the arrival, this morning, of the elegant STEAM-BOAT INDEPENDENCE, Captain NELSON, in seven *sailing* days (but thirteen from the time of her departure) from St. Louis, with passengers, and a cargo of flour, whiskey, sugar,

iron, castings, etc., *being the first Steam Boat that ever attempted ascending the Missouri.* She was joyfully met by the inhabitants of Franklin, and saluted by the firing of cannon, which was returned by the *Independence.*

The grand *desideratum,* the important fact is now ascertained, *that Steam Boats can safely navigate the Missouri River.*

A new era of Missouri history had been announced with overstated optimism. Later in the same year, an even more impressive steamer trudged slowly upstream under the command of the United States military. Christened the *Western Engineer,* it was part of the 1819 Scientific Expedition headed by Major Stephen H. Long. It was designed to impress, if not scare, the Native Americans along the route. The engines were disguised below deck, the helmsman's house was bulletproof, and an attempt was made to subdue the paddle wheels from view. The bow, combining questionable engineering with atrocious aesthetics, was shaped into the head of a black serpent, serving as an additional smoke stack with its red tongue protruding—all to create the illusion of a powerful mechanical river monster belching ashes and smoke as it swam by. While the illusion may have been impressive, its performance was dismal. Part of its problem was the sludge clogging the boilers as silt-laden river waters were heated to produce its steam. By the time they approached La Charrette, the crew had learned how to insert a tube into the boilers to remove the muddy sludge under steam pressure. This procedure, when repeated every day or so, allowed the Long Expedition to travel a little faster than the Lewis and Clark Expedition had journeyed fifteen years earlier. With these conditions prevailing, it is easy to understand why Gottfried Duden wrote in 1827 that "Steamboat navigation on the Missouri River is not very flourishing as yet."[3]

This soon changed. Some even thought steamboating might be romantic. William H. Gray and his bride chose to join three other honeymooning couples in New York City in 1838.[1] Upon arrival in St. Louis that spring, they enthusiastically boarded the *Glasgow* and headed up the Missouri into Oregon Territory to serve as missionaries. The brides maintained journals recording their shock upon learning the chambermaid was a slave and disappointment when unexpectedly transferred to the *Howard,* a new boat too "small and crowded." By Sunday, the brides expressed disbelief their boat traveled on this day of rest. "I believe they generally acknowledge that almost all steamboat accidents happen on the Sabbath," recorded one. Later in the day, another bride noted in her journal, "Never before did I heard so much profanity or seen as much wickedness on the Sabbath." Romance aside, these youthful missionary couples had apparently discovered an abundance of opportunities for their chosen calling on the frontier.

By the 1840s, Missouri riverboats had greatly enhanced trade over the Santa Fe Trail, provided support for the Mexican War, and aided settlers on their way to Oregon as well as gold rush prospectors seeking their fortune in California. Improved river steamers of the 1850s, now costing between $12,000 and $20,000, saw traffic at its peak. Most of the Missouri River traffic moved between St. Louis and Omaha, costing about eighteen dollars for one-way passage. During the land rush era into Kansas and Nebraska, boats began providing luxury dining saloons, brass and string bands, a ladies' cabin, and, of course, drinking, gambling, and prostitution. Some of the fur-trading companies of days past had by now diversified into running packet riverboats. St. Louis alone had close to 3,000 steamboat arrivals in 1850. Indeed, Robert Fulton's steamboat had revolutionized river travel. But risks were involved.

Missouri River traffic associated with St. Louis included forty-four steamboat collisions, 166 fires, 209 boiler explosions, and the sinking of 576 steamboats, the result of hitting objects in the water. All within thirty-nine years of river traffic! Another account of this era reports $8,823,500 of property lost due to sunken or damaged boats on the river. The first Missouri River steamboat victim was the *Thomas Jefferson* (of the 1819 Long Expedition flotilla) when it struck a snag in Osage Chute. The *Emile* was one of the first riverboats to depart St. Louis following the break up of the spring ice on the river in late March 1843. All went well until it hit a snag as Captain John Keiser was maneuvering her around Charrette Bend on the western edge of where the old village once stood. The *Old School Democrate* of April 5th reported, "No fatalities were suffered by the crew or passengers, however the boat and cargo were a total loss." Another steamboat, also named *Emilie*, was engaged in a steamboat race with the *Spread Eagle* in 1862.[4] Passengers on both crafts wanted to win this upriver contest by enthusiastically egging on the captains. The boats abruptly collided in midstream, but they managed to survive, even though *Emilie's* Captain La Barge "swore a big French oath" while aiming his rifle at the head of Captain Bailey on the *Spread Eagle*. No shots were fired as the passengers intervened, but Bailey lost his license on a recklessness charge. Two years later, the *Spread Eagle* sank at Pinckney Bend, a few miles above Marthasville Landing.

On the other hand, Captain La Barge was no saint. Previously in 1843, La Barge was caught shipping an excessive quantity of liquor for James John Audubon. Within hours, Audubon records, "I was on excellent and friendly terms in less time than it has taken me to write this account of our meerting" after offering his credentials to the lieutenant in charge. [4] But La Barge thought Audubon's behavior belittling and overbearing. A little earlier, Baptiste Roy, the founder of Cote sans Dessein, and his partners had "flagrantly traded in alcohol" all along the Missouri. He was licensed to trade with the Ioway, Sac, Otoe, and Pawnee tribes as far upriver as the Little Platte. Brother-in-law Francis Tayon, along with others, functioned as middlemen in this highly lucrative trafficking business delivering whole cargoes of liquor to the Native Americans. During the winter of 1830 alone, forty-three Otoe and Ioway Indian alcohol-related deaths were reported. Aside from the harm contributed to Native American society, these ventures held collateral consequences for Roy and Tayon—both with family connections to La Charrette. While partying at their trading post near St. Joseph with 300 Otoe and Ioway Indians in 1836, an intoxicated Francis caused a fracas when frantically dancing. Tempers flared, and knives flashed. In an instant, Francis Tayon grabbed his bloody face, only to contemplate his future without a nose.[5] The episode continued to include the suggestion from the son of Baptiste Roy's partner, Joseph Robidoux III, to have a local physician stick it on again, but, by then, the nose was lost! But Roy, who was an acknowledged drunkard by both missionary Samuel Allis and fur trader Ramsey Cooks, was still sufficiently prosperous to extend a loan to Captain La Barge in 1841. The loan must have sufficed, as La Barge, "the old explorer of the Missouri," continued running boats into the 1880s. Joseph Robidoux III eventually became credited as one of the founders of St. Joseph, Missouri, where he established his Blacksnake Hills trading post.

Captain Joseph La Barge (1815–1899) had a distinguished sixty-year career as a pilot and navigator on the Missouri. He not only docked many of his eighteen packet boats at Marthasville Landing, but he also held claim to the largest number of passengers ever on the Missouri when some 900 souls were cramped on board the *St. Mary* in 1856.[6] Seven of his boats burned. Two apiece either snagged or lost in ice. One apiece hit a rock, broke in two, or was lost to a tornado. He named three of his boats after his daughters, Martha, Emilie, and Octavia as well as one for his missionary friend, De Smet. Only days before his death, congenial Father De Smet blessed his namesake boat owned by his "most intimate personal friend" in 1873.[7]

Joining La Barge as a famous river captain in 1855 was Arch S. Bryan, a local man, son of John "Long Jack" and Hulda Lamme Bryan of La Charrette and Marthasville extraction. Captain Bryan had just returned from South America after seeking his fortune in California gold along with others of his adventurous Boone-Bryan-Callaway-Lamme clan.[8] He traveled the Missouri River from St. Louis to the Yellowstone for thirty-six years. His packet line also serviced the Osage and other rivers of the Midwest. Byran lived in Washington when the *Helena* snagged for the second time on Bonhomme Island and finally sunk there on October 23, 1891. This 194-by-33-by-4.5-foot stern wheeler is most remembered for the many Sioux delivered to Indian reservations.

There were still other river adventures and mishaps of local interest. The *Ben West*, a 241-ton side-wheeler loaded with $5,000 worth of timber, hit a river snag in 1855, while the eighty-five-ton center wheel ferry *Bright Star* was impaled by running ice in 1873 before they both sank at Washington. During the Civil War, the *Bright Star* was one of the boats used to evacuate Washington. At daybreak on October 2, 1864, it transported Union troops, government property, and civilians to St. Charles. When they passed South Point, Price Raiders fired some seventy-five rounds at her. As recent as January 22, 1877, the *Dora* was sunk by ice at the mouth of Charrette Creek, perhaps while departing Marthasville Landing and preparing to negotiate the now-infamous and treacherous turn in the river known as Charrette Bend. It was raised and repaired at a cost of $1,500 before being sold to the Washington Ferry Company. Apparently, submerged sandbars and snags in the river accounted for about seventy percent of these river mishaps.

Most frequently, steamers sank in waters shallow enough to allow passengers to gather personal belongs and wade to shore, leaving the upper deck, pilothouse, and smokestacks protruding above the water. Even so, river travel was not safe by any standard, as indicated by an 1856 report claiming 2,035 lives had been lost to wrecks and explosions on the Missouri.[8] Starting in 1838, the Corps of Engineers began clearing channel impediments from the river. Snagboat crews cleared the cluttered stream of 17, 676 snags in one thirteen-year period, cut many dangerous overhanging trees from the riverbank, and began the processes of encouraging stream channelization. These efforts would become more extensive (and expensive), including the comprehensive 1944 flood control act of the United States Congress to improve river commerce.[9] Barge traffic was introduced to the river in 1819 and continues to the present.

Typical cargo on an 1840 steamboat included 311 hogsheads of tobacco, twenty-four bales of hemp, fourteen casks of bacon, eleven kegs of lard, forty-nine barrels of wheat, forty-five barrels of flour, six barrels of beef, one keg of butter, one pack of peltries, and one sack of feathers. Other items of the day included beeswax, tallow, and, eventually, railroad ties. Passengers, in addition to local citizens, included Native Americans on their way to territories and reservations, troops with weapons and ammunition being transported to military forts, plus immigrant families with their trunks and other possessions headed to new settlements along the route. In one way or another, all of the cargo was related to development of western frontier agriculture and settlement activities.

Other modes of transportation to compete within the industrial revolution soon emerged. All would compete with the horse. The famous Boonslick Road had intersected Marthasville Road since 1824 as it passed through northern Warren County. A four-horse stagecoach left St. Louis at four o'clock in the morning and arrived two days later in Franklin at seven o'clock in the evening. Before Boonslick Road becoming a $60,000 planked tollway between St. Charles and Warrenton in the early 1850s, Washington Irving crossed it. He left St. Charles in September 1833, describing the undulating, thickly forested countryside beginning to shed its gorgeous and brilliant hues of the fall season, while enjoying the easy, lavish, and hearty hospitality of his host. They covered about thirty miles each day. The intercontinental railroad and the automobile soon superseded the short-lived Pony Express started at St. Joseph, Missouri, in 1860 to connect with westward destinations. Each would challenge and then surpass the other in rapid succession. But the railroad, combined with truck freight, eventually undid the era of steamboats on the Mighty Missouri.

# The Katy Trail

The rich history of the Katy Trail reaches further back in time than the founding of the Katy Railroad. The North Missouri Railroad was extended to St. Charles from St. Louis in 1855. In 1892, the Missouri, Kansas, and Eastern Railroad finally passed through downtown Marthasville, soon connecting it with the greater Southwest and other destinations across the nation. Construction crewmembers were offered food and lodging plus a $1.50 a day to build the new line. It was soon renamed the Missouri, Kansas, and Texas Railroad with rails and telegraph lines extending from St. Louis westward following older routes here and there variously associated with La Charrette into Waco, Texas. Represented, from east to west, lay the trail to the Village of Missouri, Boonslick Trail, Osage Trace, Santa Fe Trail, and the Texas Road, first blazed in 1832 by Captain Nathan Boone.[10,11] The oldest of these trails, the Trail to the Village of Missouri, the Santa Fe, and the Osage Trace were obviously of Native American origin. The main Katy line followed closely along these trails of the lower Missouri before crossing the river at Booneville and heading southwest from Sedalia.

The MK&T Railroad, also known as the Katy, was no less than fundamental to the development of the entire region. The Katy transported farm implements, feed grains, coal, cattle, hogs, timber, and many, many other products of commerce serving the communities along its route, mostly small towns like Marthasville, Peers, and Dutzow. According to one 1917 report, about thirty percent of the freight traffic in 1905 was of animal and other agricultural origins. Thirty-two percent represented mineral products. Ten percent represented forest products, and twenty-eight percent represented manufactured goods.[12] Its interconnected 3,856-mile network of cross ties and rails was serviced with special cars supportive of each function—box, flat, coal, furniture, refrigerator, livestock, automobile, ballast, dump, plus more than 400 passenger cars. Of these, ten were dining cars. Another sixty cars were devoted to carrying the mail and baggage. Passenger cars offered a convenient means for Charrette Township citizens to access St. Louis or other points beyond to include the transport of servicemen and women during the World Wars. Typical turn of the century fares for a Marthasville passenger to St. Charles was $0.76, $1.46 to St. Louis, or $2.22 for a westbound passenger to New Franklin.

The Katy railway system was a major economic engine. It reported $20 million in gross earnings in 1905 and grew at an annual rate of $1.3 million for the next decade. Locally, many people worked for the Katy. Like other hard-working section gangs, those headquartered at Marthasville Depot were responsible for their stretch of railway. The Marthasville Depot stationmaster and his staff were responsible for all incoming and outgoing rail shipments, twenty-four hours each and every day. His staff sold tickets to prospective passengers, loaded bags of mail, and provided oversight of the arrival and departure of each train. All was aided by telegraph and telephone lines. The trains were so dependable that their familiar "woo-woo" whistle sounds served as the community clock.

To provide efficient and safe service to their customers, crews like these were expected to perform their assigned duties with distinction all along the Katy. Ever present were supervisors, inspectors, detectives, and lawyers to assure compliance. At least the Marthasville Depot staff avoided any embarrassing mishaps during 1916, unlike their neighboring stations. In June of that year, the only month reported in detail, investigations at Treloar revealed one case of "concealed damage" for a freight shipment while the Dutzow Depot was cited for two errors in loading, four billing errors, and one case of carelessness. In the St. Louis District alone, a total of 1,197 such citations were reported for the month.

After almost a century of faithful service, like the Santa Fe Trail and the Missouri River steamboats preceding it, the Katy Railroad was discontinued, only to then yield its roadbed in support of a unique hiking and biking trail in 1987. The Katy Trail comes within less than a mile of where La Charrette Village homes once stood. This most famous hiking and biking trail in Missouri crosses portions of the farms settled by the "Ancient Syndic" Joseph Chartran, widow "Vieuve" St. Franceway, William T. Lamme, and the Jean-Marie Cardinal family. State Highway 94, designated as the Lewis and Clark Trail, comes even closer to old La Charrette Village immediately south of both Marthasville and the Katy Trail, where it passes through the northern portions of these old village farms. State Highway 47 crosses over the same roadway as State Highway 94 between Dutzow and Marthasville as it connects Washington of Franklin County to the county seat of Warrenton in Warren County (Figure 5). All of these routes offer ready access for exploring this historic region today.

Present-day Washington Bridge opened for traffic on May 28, 1936, and soon replaced Harry Schaefer's river ferry service between Washington and North Washington Landings in Charrette Township, operating since 1822. The bridge cost $400,000. On opening day, approximately 3,000 automobiles and 12,000 local citizens crossed over the bridge. Round-trip tolls were assessed at twenty-five cents for each foot passenger and seventy-five cents for autos to retire the remaining $200,000 debt. The one-way fare for each sheep or hog was five cents. Today, as one crosses Washington Bridge, traveling north into Warren County on State Highway 47 and looking westward as far up the north Missouri River bank as possible, a glimpse of the historic La

Charrette Village site and its old river landing may be approximated. The mouth of the combined channels of Charrette, Tuque, and Lake Creeks is clearly visibly from this same vantage point.

# Chapter 17:

## Visiting Charrette Township

The popular Katy Trail provides an exceptional opportunity to relive frontier happenings while hiking, jogging, or biking along its easy-to-navigate route. Participate in the grand tradition of spending a night or two in Charrette Township, just like members of the Lewis and Clark Expedition, the English naturalist John Bradbury, Captain Zebulon Montgomery Pike, the Duke of Wurttemberg, and so many others. Take time just to stop and visit, like squatters named Cardinal and Tebeau might have done with New Spain explorer Pedro Vial or as fur traders Joseph Chorette, Jean-Baptiste Trudeau, and the Chouteau brothers did some 200 years ago. Continue the ageless tradition of walking trails once traveled by those of Native American heritage named Angelique Burgiere Cardinal, Nicholis Colas, Paul Ramsey, and Charles "Indian" Phillips or frontiersmen Boone, Derry, Kinkead, and Colter. Challenge your vital cardiovascular functions by jogging at a brisk pace, just as if in training at La Charrette for the epic expedition as originally planned by Lewis and Clark as "We proceeded on."

At whatever pace you progress along the trail, create your own memorable experiences, as have Tom Uhlenbrock of the *St. Louis Post-Dispatch* staff, Brett Dufur of Rocheport, and many, many others. Uhlenbrock called upon Jane Glosemeyer, a hog farmer on Charrette Creek at long-forgotten West Point just east of Peers. Farther west, at milepost 131, Dufur recalls returning to times past at Turner's Store in Tebbetts located within eyeshot of old Cote sans Dessein.[1] Mrs. Turner made the sandwiches and sold antiques in her spotless store. Others often become nostalgic as they amble cross the trail to reconnect with their genetic roots, their youth, and history. For those traveling with handheld Global Positioning Satellite (GPS) systems, the coordinates of N 38 degrees 37.611' by W 091 degrees 03.635' will assure your arrival at Trailhead 31 in Marthasville. To avoid becoming known as a "Lost

Pathfinder" like Captain Pike, maintain your own journal entries with accuracy.

Bring family and friends on your expedition over the Lewis and Clark Trail while you enjoy a relaxing weekend at a local bed-and-breakfast to fully absorb La Charrette history. To rest or seek directions, visit the State Park's Department's information depot in Marthasville. Located on the Katy Trail, it is designed to resemble the old-fashioned depot once there. *The Complete Katy Trail Guidebook* offers an array of excellent options to plan and schedule each day's event.[1] Enroll the children in special education events scheduled for "Katy Kids" managed by the Katy Trail State Park. Contemplate the old sugar camps, Indian raids, and hunting wildlife inhabiting the hills beyond the beautifully sculptured and rugged limestone bluffs as you proceed over this public trail. Don't forget the cameras or sketch pads to capture the scenic beauty of nature, as the first western artists George Catlin and Titian Ramsay Peale did during the romantic riverboat era. Schedule your visit to coincide with the blossoming of the dogwoods, or capture the colorful fall foliage Washington Irving once described. Alternatively, visit a local historical museum in any season.

As you cross the Katy Trail, as your thoughts return to these historic lands, gaze to the south from Marthasville at milepost 78 to envision La Charrette villagers prodding their oxen along on a sultry summer day while tending to crops. Enjoy today's lush fields of corn and soybeans in season, and contrast them in your mind's eye to the poorly tended crops of the settlers. Save time to dream, too. Dream about floating downstream to La Charrette Village from the long-extinct West Point ford on Charrette Creek at the MK&T metal truss railroad bridge about two miles west of Marthasville. Waters typically remain shallow enough here to accommodate horses crossing the stream on the way to nearby Peers and Treloar, the same trail Reverend Peck crossed in 1819. Or cruise past the village site by crossing the Missouri River in a motorboat launched from Colter's Landing in Franklin County. As you cross the wide Missouri, call to mind steamboats piloted by Captains La Barge and Bryan docking at the old river landing or attempting to negotiate the treacherous currents of Charrette Bend. Conjure up the picturesque scene of French trappers named Luzon, Cardinal, Tayon, and Chartran rowing their dugouts up and down Charrette Creek.

Plate 9. Westbound Katy Trail hikers approaching the MK&T metal truss bridge near old West Point. They are crossing lands once owned by the author's family.

Continue west of Marthasville 53 miles to Tebbetts, where Cote sans Dessein of Callaway County was once home to frontier heroine Julia Royer Roy, who lived there with families from La Charrette. Remember the ethnic and cultural richness of their villages and the frontier challenges they overcame. Back in Marthasville, read about La Charrette Village, as described on an historical marker posted near the Katy Trail. Proceed to the east of Marthasville where the Katy Trail passes Boone Monument and crosses Tuque Creek approaching Hancock Bottoms so exalted by Dr. Duden. While on your way to Dutzow, visualize a Katy section gang working the rails in vivid contrast to the idealistic Latin Farmers. While there, envision how differently a westbound trip by canoe, horseback, covered wagon, stagecoach, and riverboat, or even on the Katy might contrast with the travel alternatives of today.

Relax with a glass of local vintage wine just as the French Creoles of La Charrette Village did in their humble village homes. Alternatively, select a hearty brew preferred by the frugal German farmers. Contemplate the past, and anticipate the future to assure that we "will [continue to] make the most of it." Wherever you stay, take time to sign the guestbook as you continue the grand tradition of visiting Charrette

Township. And remember, even though La Charrette Village is no longer visible, it holds vivid contributions to the development of the Missouri frontier now universally recognized by a single journal entry, "the last settlement of whites on this river" once serving as the "advance guard of civilization."

To assist with planning a visit to Charrette Township, the following activities are among those to consider while exploring this historic region. Arrive at Marthasville by way of either State Highway 47 or 94. State Highway 47 connects Washington with Warrenton to the north, both with historical societies and museums that house archives of local history. State Highway 94 follows along the north bank of the Missouri River while repeatedly crisscrossing both the ancient Trail to the Village of Missouri and the Katy Trail. This east-west route links St. Charles to Tebbets in Cote san Dessein Township of Callaway County. Amtrak arrives at Rennick Riverfront Park in Washington, offering another opportunity to view the old village site. RailCruise America even offers their unique Charrette Creek car from St. Louis to Washington for private parties to enjoy the scenic route along the Missouri. By way of the Katy Trail State Park, the towns nearest Marthasville are Dutzow, 3.4 miles to the east, and Peers, four miles to the west. Visit Daniel Boone's Monument immediately east of Marthasville. Daniel Boone Monument Road intersects the Katy Trail 1.5 miles east of Marthasville. Proceed north toward the hills, and turn left when the road Ts for 1.2 miles. The monument appears on a small knoll to the right. Visit the 2,250-acre Daniel Boone Memorial Forest on Tower Ridge Road in western Warren County or any of the local wineries.

In Marthasville Park, visit syndic Chartran's re-created bousillage La Charrette Village cabin used in the National Lewis and Clark Bicentennial Commemoration. While in Dutzow, stop by Blumenhof Vineyards and sip some Missouri semisweet La Charrette wine. Purchase several bottles labeled with artist Billyo O'Donnell's rendition of Lewis and Clark departing La Charrette, all created to celebrate this special frontier village. Enjoy your time at La Charrette—once the village gateway to the American West.

# Epilogue

Undeniably, La Charrette Village citizens played a unique role in a brief but exciting moment of American history. Perhaps it was only a tiny ripple upon the larger pond of historic events representing the struggles of frontier families desirous to survive on the very cusp of the known world. During that brief moment, it was as if all significant happenings related to westward expansion somehow involved the village—seeking advice, transacting business, staying overnight, or just acquiring a little map—before proceeding on. Their role among the giants of western exploration was exemplary. This crossroads of varied cultures and famous expeditions attained a peerless station during its seven-year life as America's westernmost frontier settlement. Even before it became extinct, some of its family members founded Cote sans Dessein as the next westernmost settlement on the frontier and, once again, distinguished themselves. Logically, the argument could be advanced that the village's life was unfulfilled. If only Lewis and Clark had trained their crew here, if its first land claims had been granted, or if a post office was established, it might have been spared the fate of extinction. But that was the reality of fate.

Yet, with a bare minimum of historical information and even less physical evidence to document the location of the village and the Lewis and Clark campsites, the village residents emerge across history with enduring legacies. Representing only seven families and their neighbors, once described as indolent, they emerge as a unique mixture of multiethnic and culturally diverse frontier settlers. With apparent enthusiasm, they were among the first citizens of Louisiana to participate in our great American melting pot experiment. Interestingly enough, this folding together of cultures, man's most important instrument of adaptation, had been underway for thousands of years in Native American society. In many ways, their achievements in this sphere of society were exemplary and, at the same time, dismal. Perhaps the greatest irony befell the Native Americans who were both freely accepted into village life but simultaneously brutally excluded from mainstream society. Nonetheless, within the span of a century, the village farm sites reverted from one monoethnic heritage of Native

Americans to another exclusively of German heritage with the multi-ethnic diversity so abundantly observed throughout the life of the village sandwiched in between. Of course, both Africans and Europeans also represented an amalgamation of people and cultures from times previous, supporting contemporary thought renouncing the existence of race.[1]

Many quests remain unresolved and deserve further research. Perhaps most exasperating is the lack of insight into the emotions and thoughts of the village citizens while participating in their frontier struggles. How did they look upon their lives and times? Regrettably, little or nothing is known about most of the women, the children, the nine or so orphans, the Native Americans, or the slaves. Exceptions include only Indian Phillips, Julia Royer Roy, Rebecca Boone, and little else but the mournful plea of Paul Ramsay's brother, "Daddy, the Indians did scalp me." Sadly, they largely represented a group of silent participants in the village community. What little has been learned in this regard comes largely from a few vibrant men. John Colter has been credited with a "quick and ready thoughtfulness and presence of mind in a desperate situation, and the power of endurance, which characterizes the western pioneer."[2] Extrapolating from this, we may safely conclude most village citizens must have been eager to explore and live in worlds new to them. Certainly, they could rightfully be described as committed, determined, brave, and resourceful, while simultaneously possessing the usual frailties of humankind. In most ways, they were ordinary men and women who were well-adapted to the times. Predictably, most may not have thought their daily experiences differed greatly from their contemporaries. While most of their individual contributions remain obscured by time, collectively, they accomplished what must be considered as both unique and yet typical in the annals of the western frontier life. However, of one thing we may be certain, they each contributed to a small, but important, building block in the shaping of the American West to advance the American Dream.

To each of these frontier family heroes and heroines, those known by name as well as the unnamed, we offer our belated gratitude for their faithful contributions to the development of the Missouri frontier. Yet, it is prudent to remember that only select fragments of their frontier lives have been portrayed based almost entirely upon what others chose to record on their behalf. Only with properly managed archaeological digs and additional research on village history will additional fragments of their lives become more fully established.

Recalling the fate of the blue buck antelope of the Introduction, it may be instructive again to draw parallels to the insights of Professor Stephen Jay Gould. He writes, in part, about the plight of curators:

> What can be more noble than faithful preservation and accurate documentation of often pitiable fragments? This sadness spawns a respect for our later compassion and need to preserve—tawdry fragments in one sense, yet magical in another, and therefore of precious rarity...

La Charrette Village, in one sense, was also once alive. But, all too soon, it was lost. This old French-Indian village not only served as the ancestral and historical foundation of this earliest of Missouri outposts, but it was also the gateway to new and unfathomable western horizons for many, many immigrants and others, who now hold ties to and an interest in their village and its legacies. A precious rarity indeed.

Two centuries later, we may only speculate if French foreign minister Talleyrand might acknowledge Jefferson struck the better deal when the United States acquired the Louisiana Purchase. Assuredly, Talleyrand would be proud of his Frenchmen at La Charrette as elsewhere along the frontier while Jefferson may boast that they, as other Americans, have made the most of it.

# Appendix A.

## District of St. Charles Property Tax Records, 1804–1830

Select entries from annual property tax records were obtained from microfilm reel number S 245, Missouri State Archives of Jefferson City. Volume I represented the first tax year of 1804–1805 for the district. These microfilm ledgers were largely illegible, greatly limiting a complete portrayal of the village tax roles. The next available records were for 1814–1815 through 1830. They offered more complete entries than for the 1804–1805 tax year. These later reports were presented by county and within county categorized by watershed areas such as Chorette (Charrette) or Duke (Tuque) Creek or as numbered tax divisions. The area about La Charrette Village represented Divisions 1 and 2, but the village residents were not listed separate from other taxpayers, thus offering no clue on the date of demise of the village. Data, when available, are presented here only for La Charrette Village landholders and prominent village neighbors representing the cast of characters of the text.

### Tax Year 1804–1805

Apparently, two tax forms were used as many property holders are listed twice in the ledgers, each including slightly different data. One appears to represent a censuslike form. The other form appears to have been used exclusively for tax purposes. Data presented here were obtained from both forms. The tax schedule of September 1805 assessed each single adult male resident living with a family at $1.00, each mature servant (slave), $1.00, and all cattle and horses over three years of age, $.50 each, although most landholders apparently paid less tax than their inventories of taxable property would indicate. Some landholders were granted various exemptions as ordered by the court and administered by the five-member tax board and the sheriff.

213

**Flanders Callaway.** This future villager reported seven members in his family. He owned five slaves, six horses, and eighteen cattle. His ownership of slaves was consistent with other members of the Boone family. He may have paid $11.00 in taxes, although that entry appeared to have been struck out.

**Jean M. Cardinal Jr.** No family statistics were reported, but he declared six cattle and one horse, requiring him to pay $1.10 in property taxes. He resided in Division 1.

**Joseph Shattrow (Syndic Chartran).** Chartran indicated he had three members in his family, including son Joseph Jr. He was taxed on one single man (Pierre Blanchet) residing in his home, four horses, and ten cattle. He paid $2.30 in taxes. (The orphans mentioned with his land claim process do not appear).

**William Hancock.** This Hancock family residing in Hancock Bottoms consisted of six members. They had one slave, six horses, and four cattle. According to the tax schedule, William should have paid $7.00, but the record does not reveal what taxes, if any, were assessed.

**William and David Kinkead.** David was the father of the "Mountain Man" from Charrette Creek, Matthew Kinkead. There were six members shown in William's family and nine for David's.

**William T. Lamme.** The Lamme family consisted of three members. They had two horses and paid $1.00 in taxes.

**Adam McCord.** This early surveyor reported three members in his family. He claimed three cattle, but no tax payment is indicated.

**Anthony Palmer.** An unnamed single man was residing in the Palmer home in Division 1. This soon-to-be La Charrette Village schoolteacher paid $11.00 in taxes, among the highest taxes in the district, even though no inventory of taxable property was listed.

**Charles Tyon (Don Carlos Tayon).** Sons Charles and Louis are shown living in the home of Don Carlos Tayon, even though Charles was residing at La Charrette Village at this time. He claimed five slaves, nine horses, and twenty-five cattle, requiring him to pay $12.00 in property taxes.

**Joseph Tebo (Tebeau).** This 1763 partner of Jean-Marie Cardinal Sr. at Prairie du Chien (or his son, Jr.) owned three cattle and paid $.30 as district property taxes. It is not indicated where within the district he was residing.

**Francis Roye (Roy).** This brother of Cote sans Dessein founder, Jean-Baptiste Roy, lived in District 1 of St. Charles. Francis also settled at Cote sans Dessein in 1808. Other Roys of this family are also listed.

## Tax Year 1814–1815

This tax reporting form for the Territory of Missouri, County of St. Charles was structured differently than the first one. Handwritten column headings on the form included the following items (left to right): 1) Name of persons charged with taxes, 2) Confirmed land, 3) Unconfirmed land, 4) County in which the land lies, 5) Situated on the watershed of what stream, 6) Original claimants, 7) Town lots-Valuation, 8) Dwelling houses in the county-Valuation, 9) Slaves, 10) Pleasure carriage, and 11) Aggregate amount of taxes plus one column provided for Remarks. Taxes were no longer assessed upon livestock. County Clerk J. William Christy Jr. oversaw the collection of $878.58 of property taxes for the year with support provided by the sheriff and five senior justices, one representing each township. These records reflect that six landowners now resided on Charrette Creek watershed, seventeen on Tuque Creek, and numerous others on the Missouri River watershed.

**Flanders Callaway.** By now, Callaway had 400 acres of confirmed land on the Missouri River (at La Charrette Village) with Joseph Chartran listed as the original claimant of the property. Callaway possessed one dwelling (the log house pictured in Chapter 5) assessed at $25.00, but no longer owned any slaves. Nor did he own a pleasure carriage. Total taxes paid were $2.47.

**William T. Lamme.** Lamme now claims 300 acres of confirmed land on the Peruque watershed, one town lot assessed at $60.00, one dwelling valued for tax purposes at $125.00, and one slave. His property tax for the year was $0.62.

**John McKinny.** McKinny, like Adam McCord, was a surveyor and land speculator. He owned 800 acres on the "Chorette" watershed without a dwelling and paid $1.62 in property taxes on this property. He also owned seven other land parcels in excess of 3,500 acres, representing one of the largest landholders. He and five others are the only ones reported as holding property on the "Chorette" watershed. Other members of this family, Alexander and Alexander McKinny Jr., owned land nearby on the Dardenne and Missouri River watersheds.

**Charles (Anthony C.) Palmer.** This former La Charrette Village schoolteacher now holds 640 acres of confirmed land on the Dardenne watershed with one dwelling valued at $25.00. He paid $3.01 in property tax.

**Charles Phillips.** Charles "Indian" Phillips declared forty acres of confirmed land located in the "public field" at St. Charles. It may represent the same plot of public land supported by the testimony of Pierre Blanchette earlier in the century. He owned four town lots valued at $300, one dwelling valued at $20, and paid $0.84 as property tax.

**William Ramsey.** This same William Ramsey enrolled his children in the La Charrette Village School in 1807. His 640 acres of confirmed land was located on Duke (Tuque) Creek where he had one dwelling assessed at $150. He declared three slaves. His property tax payment for the year was $5.86.

**Charles and Louis Tayon.** Charles Tayon (Don Carlos) was now residing on the Dardenne watershed. He owned 448 acres of confirmed land, one town lot assessed at $50.00, and one dwelling valued at $25.00. His property tax assessment was $15.00. Louis held 1,550 arpents of land on the "Charotte" watershed.

## Tax Years 1817–1830

In 1818, La Charrette Village became part of Montgomery County.

**Anthony C. Palmer.** By 1817, Palmer, the former village schoolteacher and first teacher of what became Warren County in 1833, is now serving as sheriff of St. Charles County, assisting with the administration of these tax laws.

**Doctor John Young.** The founder of Marthasville paid $11.65 in property taxes in Montgomery County in 1822. He claimed one dwelling assessed for tax purposes at $150, twelve slaves assessed at $2,275, plus horses and cattle, among other holdings.

**Joseph Shartrain (Joseph Chartran Sr.).** The village syndic claimed 640 acres of land in Montgomery County in 1830 designated as "not surveyed." No taxes were assessed.

**William T. Lamme.** The 1830 Montgomery County tax report indicates Lamme now owns 1,275 acres previously held by James Bryan, Jean M. Cardinal, Joseph Arno, John Busby, John Haun, and Gabrial Marlow, all early Charrette Bottom landholders. These and other records fully confirm the changes in ownership of village land as previously described.

# Appendix B.

## Procedure Employed to Locate the Original Village Site

Collaborator Jerry Holtmeyer consulted the following sources as he developed the procedure to locate the original village site. Land transactions from circa 1800, such as land parcel claims and survey drawings, were obtained from the Linnemann Library of St. Charles and the Missouri State Archives of Jefferson City. Microfilms were reviewed and assigned a farm-family name corresponding to each microfilm reel and page designation as follows: Luzon (B40–p. 190), Franceway (B41–p. 522), Shattrows/Chartran (B40–p. 219), Larivey/Palmer/Tayon (B41–p. 366), and Lamme/Cardinal/Arnow (B41–p 11). United States land surveys from 1853 were also scrutinized, but they proved to be ineffective for this purpose. A plat for the Jack Amos (Ameys) farm was never discovered in these records, thus reel and page designations for that property are not available. Each village farm was connected either to Charrette Creek or Missouri River bank frontage from its larger acreage extending inland farther to the west, north, or east, forming the village waterfront hub of 4,106 feet. This total footage of water frontage was derived as follows: Amos—558.60 feet, Luzon—660.00 feet, Franceway—577.50 feet, Chartran—558.00 feet, Tayon—442.66 feet, Cardinal—654.50 feet, and Arnow—654.50 feet.

The above documents frequently designated property corners by land features such as trees. Because these land features no longer exist, commercial computer programs plotted compass heading and distance coordinates between property corners on current Warren County aerial photo section maps. The starting or reference point for these computer plots was the southeast corner of the William Ramsey survey. At this point, only one obstacle remained, namely that of convincing local scholars and abstract professionals of the existence of a linear arpent as a unit of French land measurement. Eventually, it was

217

documented a linear arpent represented 192.5 feet, or 2.916 chains. The squared unit represents 0.8507 acre. With the appropriate input data, computer-generated surveys were then produced as portrayed in Figure 5.

# Endnotes

## Introduction: Dreams and Legacies

1. J. M. Faragher, "More Motley than Mackinaw," in *Contact Points*, eds. A. R. L. Clayton and F. J. Teute (Chapel Hill: University of North Carolina Press, 1998).

## Part One: Engaging the Wilderness
## Chapter 1: Louisiana, a Historical Sketch

1. C. A. Milner, C. A. O'Conner, and M. A. Sandweiss, eds., *The American West* (New York: Oxford University Press, 1994).

2. R. Carse, *The River Men* (New York: Charles Scribner's Sons, 1969).

3. *Encyclopaedia Britannica* (Chicago: The University of Chicago, 1973).

4. J. S. C. Abbott, *The Adventures of the Chevalier De La Salle and his Companions* (New York: Dodd and Mead, 1875).

5. A. Cooke, *America* (New York: Alfred A. Knopf, 1974).

6. H. Folmer, "Entienne de Bourgmound in the Missouri Country," *Missouri Historical Review* XXXVI (1942).

7. R. V. Hine and J. M. Faragher, *The American West* (New Haven, Ct.: Yale University Press, 2000).

8. M. A. Stoddard, *Sketches of Louisiana* (Philadelphia: Mathew Carey, 1812).

9. E. M. Coyle, *Saint Louis, Portrait of a River City* (St. Louis: The Folkstone Press, 1970).

## Chapter 2: The Geographic Landscape

1. G. Duden, *Report on a Journey to the Western States of North America* (Columbia, Mo.: University of Missouri Press, 1980).

2. J. A. Caruso, *The Mississippi Valley Frontier* (Indianapolis: The Bobbs-Merrill Company, Inc., 1966).

3. E. L. Harrison, "The Place Names of Four River Counties in Eastern Missouri" (master's thesis, University of Missouri-Columbia, 1943).

4. R. L. Ramsey, "Our Storehouse of Missouri Place Names," in *Missouri Handbook Number Two*, vol. 53, no. 44 (University of Missouri: 1952).

5. J. B. Trudeau, *Journal of Jean Baptiste Trudeau among the Arikara Indians in 1795*, trans. H. T. Beauregard, *Missouri Historical Society Collections* 4 (1911).

6. "Trudeau's Journals," *South Dakota Historical Collections* 7 (1908).

7. A. P. Nasatir, *Before Lewis and Clark*, vol. I, St. Louis Historical Documents Foundation (St. Louis: 1952).

8. J. F. McDermott, ed., *The Early Histories of St. Louis*, St. Louis Historical Documents Foundation (St. Louis: 1952).

9. N. de Finiels, *An Account of Upper Louisiana*, eds. C. J. Ekberg and W. E. Foley (Columbia, Mo.: University of Missouri Press, 1989).

## Chapter 3: Adventuresome Squatters of 1763

1. P. L. Scanlan, *Prairie du Chien: French, British, American* (Menasha, Wisconsin: The Collegiate Press, 1937).

2. J. A. Caruso, *The Mississippi Valley Frontier* (Indianapolis: The Bobbs-Merrill Company, Inc., 1966).

3. J. S. C. Abbott, *The Adventures of the Chevalier De La Salle and his Companions* (New York: Dodd and Mead, 1875).

4. A. H. Abel, *Tabeau's Narrative of Loisel's Expedition to the Upper Missouri* (Norman, Okla.: University of Oklahoma Press, 1939).

5. J. B. Musick, *St. Louis as a Fortified Town* (St. Louis: R. F. Miller Press, 1941).

6. W. Brandon, *Quivira*, (Athens, Ohio: Ohio University Press, 1990).

7.  D. Jackson, *The Journals of Zebulon Montgomery Pike*, vol 1 (Norman, Okla.: University of Oklahoma Press, 1966).

8.  C. I. Wheat, *1540–1861 Mapping the Transmississippi West* (San Francisco: The Institute of Historical Cartography, 1958).

9.  "Documents, Papers of Zebulon M. Pike, 1806–1807," *The American Historical Review* 13 (1908).

10. L. Martin, and C. E. LeGear, comp., *Noteworthy Maps* Library of Congress, Maps Division. 1927–28. No. 3. LCCN: sn 89029712.

11. R. L. Duffus, *The Santa Fe Trail* (New York: David McKay Company, Inc., 1930).

12. H. E. Bolton, "Material for Southwestern History in the Central Archives of Mexico," *The American Historical Review* XIII, no. 3 (1908).

13. E. A. H. John, *Storm's Brewed in Other Men's Worlds* (College Station, Tex.: Texas A&M University Press, 1967).

14. N. L. Loomis and A. P. Nasatir. *Pedro Vial and the Roads to Santa Fe* (Norman, Okla.: University of Oklahoma Press, 1967).

15. L. F. Burns, "The fur trading ventures of Auguste Pierre Chouteau and Pierre "Cadet" Chouteau" (master's thesis, Kansas State Teachers College, 1950).

16. H. Inman, *The Old Santa Fe Trail* (Minneapolis: Ross & Haines, Inc., 1966).

17. J. Ashton, "History of Jack Stock and Mules in Missouri," *The Monthly Bulletin* XXII, no. VIII (1924).

## Chapter 4: Resident Native Americans

1.  C. H. Chapman, *Osage Indians, The Origins of Osage Indian Tribe*, vol. III, Garland American Indian Ethnohistory Series (New York: 1974).

2.  A. Debo, A *History of the Indians of the United States* (Norman, Okla.: University of Oklahoma Press, 1970).

3.  G. C. Din and A. P. Nasatir. *The Imperial Osages* (Norman, Okla.: University of Oklahoma Press, 1983).

4.  F. W. Hodge, *Handbook of American Indians North of Mexico* (Totowa, N.J.: Rowman and Littlefield, 1979).

5. B. B. Chapman, *The Otoes and Missourians* (Norman, Okla.: University of Oklahoma Press, 1965).

6. T. C. Thorne, *The Many Hands of My Relations* (Columbia, Mo.: The University of Missouri Press, 1996).

7. J. A. Maxwell, ed., *America's Fascinating Indian Heritage* (Pleasantville, N.Y.: The Reader's Digest Association, Inc., 1978).

8. J. D. Hunter, *Reflections on the Different States and Conditions of Society; with the Outlines of a Plan to Ameliorate the Circumstances of the Indians of North America* (London: J. R. Lake, 1823).

9. E. G. Chuinard, *Only One Man Died* (Glendale, Calif.: The Arthur H. Clark Company, 1980).

10. F. A. Sampson, "Glimpses of Old Missouri Explorers and Travelers," *Missouri Historical Review* 68 (1975).

11. G. Foreman, *Indians & Pioneers* (Norman, Okla.: University of Oklahoma Press, 1936).

12. C. J. Latrobe, *The Rambler in North America* (London: Seeley and Burnside, 1970).

13. K. L. Gregg, "The History of Fort Osage," *Missouri Historical Review* 34 (1940).

14. J. M. Faragher, *Daniel Boone, The Life and Legend of an American Pioneer* (New York: Henry Holt and Company, 1992).

15. J. M. Faragher, *Note files* (New Haven, Conn.: Yale University Department of History, 2000).

16. C. T. Foreman, "Nathan Boone: Trapper, Manufacturer, Surveyor, Militiaman, Legislator, Ranger and Dragoon," *Chronicles of Oklahoma* 19 (1941).

17. N. O. Hammon, ed., *The Draper Interviews with Nathan Boone. My Father, Daniel Boone* (Lexington, Ky.: The University Press of Kentucky, 1999).

# Part Two: Frontier Village Life
## Chapter 5: The Village of La Charrette

1. M. Perrin du Lac, *Travels through the Two Louisianas* (London: Richard Phillips, 1807).

2. L. Houck, *The Spanish Regime in Missouri* (New York: Arno Press & The New York Times, 1971).

3. F. C. Shoemaker, *Missouri and Missourians* (Chicago: The Lewis Publishing Company, 1943).

4. W. F. Foley and C. D. Rice, *The First Chouteaus* (Urbana, Ill.: University of Illinois Press, 1983).

5. Wm. S. Bryan and R. Rose. *A History of the Pioneer Families of Missouri* (St. Louis: Bryan, Brand & Co., 1876).

6. H. L. Conrad, *Encyclopedia of the History of Missouri* (New York, Louisville, Ky., and St. Louis: The Southern History Company, 1901).

7. *History of St. Charles, Montgomery and Warren Counties, Missouri* (1885; St. Louis: Paul V. Cochrane, 1969).

8. R. G. Thwaites, *Journal of a Voyage up the river Missouri* (Cleveland: A. H. Clark Company, 1904).

9. W. E. Foley, *The Genesis of Missouri* (London and Columbia, Mo.: University of Missouri Press, 1989).

10. R. B. Roberts, *Encyclopedia of Historic Forts: The military, pioneer, and trading post of the United States* (New York: Macmillan Publishing Company, 1988).

11. D. D. March, *The History of Missouri* (New York: Lewis Historical Publishing Company, 1967).

12. A. P. Nasatir, *Before Lewis and Clark*, vols. I and II (St. Louis: St. Louis Historical Documents Foundation, 1952).

13. E. M. Violette, *A History of Missouri* (Cape Girardeau, Mo.: Remfre Press, 1953).

14. R. D. Thomas, "Missouri Valley Settlement—St. Louis to Independence," *Missouri Historical Review* 21 (1927).

15. L. K. Richardson, "Private Land Claims in Missouri (Part I and II)," *Missouri Historical Review* 50 (1960).

16. G. Duden, *Report on a Journey to the Western States of North America* (Columbia, Mo.: University of Missouri Press, 1980).

17. *An Illustrated Historical Atlas, Warren County, Missouri* (Philadelphia: Edwards Brothers of Missouri, 1877; Warren County Historical Society, 1989).

18. R. E. Oglesby, *Manuel Lisa* (Norman, Okla.: University of Oklahoma Press, 1963).

19. T. E. Spencer, *The Story of Old St. Louis* (St. Louis: St. Louis Pageant Drama Association, 1914).

20. E. M. Olson and R. G. Sperandio, *Historic St. Charles, Missouri* (St. Charles, Mo.: McElhiney Publishing Company, 1993).

21. Jr. Bryan, "C. W. Flanders Callaway, A Frontier Type," *Missouri Historical Society Collections* VI, no. 1 (1928).

22. J. M. Faragher, *Note files* (New Haven, Conn.: Yale University Department of History, 2000).

23. H. Wish, "The French of Old Missouri (1804–1821): A study in assimilation," *Mid-America, An Historical Review* 23 (1941).

## Chapter 6: Forts and a Trading Post

1. L. Houck, *A History of Missouri* (Chicago: Donnelley and Sons Company, 1908).

2. *Writers' Program of the WPA in the State of Missouri. Missouri, a guide to the "Show Me" state* (New York: Duell, Sloan and Pearce, 1941).

3. R. L. Nichols, *The Missouri Expedition, 1818–1820* (Norman, Okla.: University of Oklahoma Press, 1969).

4. R. G. Thwaites, *Original Journals of the Lewis and Clark Expedition* (New York: Arno Press, 1969).

5. M. Lewis, *Lewis and Clark Codices*, compiled by E. Coues in 1892 (Philadelphia: American Philosophical Society, 2000).

6. G. Catlin, *North American Indians* (New York: Dover Publications, Inc., 1973).

## Chapter 7: Charrette's First School and Post Office

1. E. R. Liljergren, "Frontier Education in Spanish Louisiana," *Missouri Historical Review* XXXV (1941).

2. J. B. Musick, *St. Louis as a Fortified Town* (St. Louis: R. F. Miller Press, 1941).

3. H. H. Dugger, *Reading Interest and the Book Trade in Frontier Missouri* (Ph.D. diss., University of Missouri, Columbia, 1951).

4.  R. G. Schultz, *Missouri Post Offices* (State College, Penn.: American Philatelic Society, 1981).

## Chapter 8: Frontier Hostilities

1.  G. C. Din and A. P. Nasatir. *The Imperial Osages* (Norman, Okla.: University of Oklahoma Press, 1983).

2.  J. A. Van Fleet, *Old and New Mackinac; with copious abstracts from Marquette, Hennetin, La Houton, Aldeabe, Henry, and others* (Woodbridge, Conn.: 1973).

3.  J. D. Hunter, *Reflections on the Different States and Conditions of Society; with the Outlines of a Plan to Ameliorate the Circumstances of the Indians of North America* (London: J. R. Lake, 1823).

4.  K. L. Gregg, "The War of 1812 on the Missouri Frontier (Part I & II)," *Missouri Historical Review* 33, 1939.

5.  Wm. S. Bryan and R. Rose. *A History of the Pioneer Families* (St. Louis: Bryan, Brand & Co., 1876).

6.  J. Sugden, *Tecumseh* (New York: Henry Holt and Company, 1997).

7.  C. J. Latrobe, *The Rambler in North America* (London: Seeley and Burnside, 1970).

8.  E. B. Wesley, "James Callaway in the War of 1812," *Missouri Historical Society Collections 5* (1927).

9.  D. Meyer, *The Heritage of Missouri—A History* (St. Louis: State Publishing Company, Inc., 1963).

10. R. D. Hurt, *Nathan Boone and the American Frontier* (Columbia, Mo.: University of Missouri Press, 1988).

## Chapter 9: Living at the "Last Settlement of Whites..."

1.  A. W. Greely, *Explorers and Travelers* (New York: Charles Scribner's Sons, 1893).

2.  R. D. Hurt, *Nathan Boone and the American Frontier* (Columbia, Mo.: University of Missouri Press, 1988).

3.  H. M. Brackenridge, *Journal of a Voyage up the Missouri; Performed in eighteen hundred and eleven* (Baltimore: Coale and Maxwell, 1816).

4. F. L. McCurdy, *Stump, Bar, and Pulpit. Speechmaking on the Missouri Frontier* (Columbia, Mo.: University of Missouri Press, 1969).

5. Jr. Bryan, "C. W. Flanders Callaway, A Frontier Type," *Missouri Historical Society Collections* VI, no 1. (1928).

6. H. M. Anderson, "Missouir, 1804–1828: Peopling a Frontier State," *Missouri Historical Review* XXXI (1937).

7. Wm. S. Bryan and R. Rose. *A History of the Pioneer Families* (St. Louis: Bryan, Brand & Co., 1876).

8. P. De Smet, *Life, Letters and Travels of Father Pierre-Jean De Smet*, ed. H. M. Chittenden and A. L. Richardson (New York: Francis P. Harper, 1905).

9. J. O'Fallon, "Three Early Letters," *Missouri Historical Society Collections* VI, no. 3 (1931).

10. S. E. Ambrose, *Undaunted Courage* (New York: Simon and Schuster, 1996).

11. T. Flint, *Recollections of the Last Ten Years (in A Series of Letters)* (Boston: Cummings, Hillard, and Company, 1826).

12. Eighteenth Annual Narrative of Missionary Labors, *Missionary Society of Connecticut* (Hartford, Conn.: Gleason and Company, 1817).

13. J. M. Peck, *Annals of the West: Principle Events, Western States and Territories*, 2nd ed. (1851); 1st edition by J. M. Perkins. Published privately by James R. Albach, St. Louis, Missouri.

14. J. M. Peck, *Forty Years of Pioneer Life, Memoir of John Mason Peck, D.D.* ed. R. Babcock (Philadelphia: J. P. Lippincott and Company, 1864).

15. K. L. Gregg, "The Boonslick Road in St. Charles County," *Missouri Historical Review* 27 (1933).

16. P. C. Phillips, *The Fur Trade*, vol. I and II (Norman, Okla.: University of Oklahoma Press, 1961).

17. Gen. T. James, *Three Years among the Mexicans and the Indians* (Chicago: The Rio Grande Press, 1962).

18. J. C. Luttig, *Journal of a Fur-trading Expedition on the Upper Missouri, 1812–1813*, ed. S. M. Drumm (St. Louis: St. Louis Historical Society, 1920).

19. L. F. Burns, *The Fur Trading Ventures of August Pierre Chouteau and Pierre "Cadet" Chouteau* (master's thesis, Kansas State Teachers College, 1950).

20. T. C. Thorne, *The Many Hands of My Relations* (Columbia, Mo.: University of Missouri Press, 1996).

21. L. Kinnard, *Annual Report of the American Historical Association* (Washington, DC: United States Government Printing Office, 1945).

22. J. J. Holmberg, "I Wish You to See & Know All," in *We Proceed On*. An address delivered at the 23rd Annual Meeting of the Lewis and Clark Trail Heritage Foundation, Louisville, Ky., November 1992.

23. E. Casselberry, "The Discovery, the First Settlements, and the First Laws of the Mississippi Valley (Part III)" *The Western Journal* (1848).

24. C. E. A. Gayarre, *History of Louisiana*, vol. IV (New York: AMS Press, 1972).

25. H. M. Brackenridge, *Recollections of Persons and Places in The West*, 2bd ed. (Philadelphia: J. P. Lippincott and Company, 1868).

## Chapter 10: The Village Guestbook

1. C. L. Goodwin, "Early Explorations and Settlements of Missouri and Arkansas, 1803–1822," *Missouri Historical Review* 14 (1920).

2. D. Lavender, *The Way to the Western Sea* (New York: Harper & Row, 1988).

3. D. Jackson, *Letters of the Lewis and Clark Expedition* (Urbana, Ill.: University of Illinois Press, 1962).

4. S. E. Ambrose, *Undaunted Courage* (New York: Simon and Schuster, 1996).

5. E. S. Osgood, *The Field Notes of Captain William Clark* (London and New Haven, Conn.: 1964).

6. G. E. Moulton, ed., *The Journals of the Lewis & Clark Expedition* (London and Lincoln, Neb.: University of Nebraska Press, 1993).

7. W. B. Douglas, "Manuel Lisa," *Missouri Historical Society* 3 (1911).

8. R. G. Ferris, *Lewis and Clark* (Washington, DC: United States Department of Interior, National Park Service, 1975).

9. B. DeVoto, ed., *The Journals of Lewis and Clark* (Boston: Houghton Mifflin Company, 1953).

10. D. L. Hastings. "La Charrette: Was it a Winter Encampment of the Lewis and Clark Expedition?" *Journal of the Illinois State Historical Society* 97 (2004).

11. E. C. McReynolds, *Missouri, A History of the Crossroads State* (Norman, Okla.: University of Oklahoma Press, 1954).

12. D. Duncan, *Lewis and Clark; The Journey of the Corps of Discovery* (New York: Alfred A. Knopf, 1977).

13. J. Bakeless, *The Journals of Lewis and Clark* (New York: Penguin Group, 1964).

14. W. E. Foley, "The Lewis and Clark Expedition's Silent Partners: The Chouteau Brothers of St. Louis," *Missouri Historical Review* 77 (1983).

15. K. L. Gregg, *Westward with Dragoons* (Fulton, Mo.: The Ovid Bell Press, Inc., 1937).

16. R. G. Thwaites, *Account of an Expedition from Pittsburgh to the Rocky Mountains*, vol. 3 (New York: Ams Press, Inc., 1966).

17. M. Villiers, "Le Massacre de l'Expedetion Espangnole du Missouri," *Journal de la Societe des Americanistes de Paris* 13 (1921).

18. E. Coues, *History of the Expedition under the Command of Lewis and Clark* (New York: F. P. Harper, 1893).

19. W. H. Goetzmann, *Exploration and Empire* (New York: Alfred A. Knopf, 1966).

20. H. M. Chittenden, *The American Fur Trade of the Far West* (Fairfield, Conn.: Augustus M. Kelly, 1976).

21. J. F. McDermott, ed., *The Western Journals of Washington Irving* (Norman, Okla.: University of Oklahoma Press, 1966).

22. H. M. Brackenridge, *Journal of a Voyage up the Missouri; Performed in eighteen hundred and eleven* (Baltimore: Coale and Maxwell, 1816).

23. J. Bradbury, *Travels in the Interior of America: in the Years 1809, 1810, and 1811* (London: Sherwood, Neely, and Jones, 1819).

24. Washington Irving, *Astoria* (Norman, Okla.: University of Oklahoma Press, 1964).

25. B. Harris, *John Colter: His years in the Rockies* (New York: Charles Scribner's Sons, 1952).

26. E. Coues, *The Expeditions of Zebulon Montgomery Pike* (New York: Francis P. Harper, 1895).

27. *Zebulon Pike's Notebook of Maps, Traverese Tables, and Meteorological Observations, 1805–1807*, National Archives Microcopy Number T361, Roll 1 (1955).

28. D. Jackson, *The Journals of Zebulon Montgomery Pike*, vol. 1 (Norman, Okla.: University of Oklahoma Press, 1966).

29. W. E. Hollon, *The Lost Pathfinder* (Norman, Okla.: University of Oklahoma Press, 1949).

30. E. H. Shepard, *The Early History of St. Louis and Missouri* (St. Louis: Southwestern Book and Publishing Company, 1870).

31. D. L. Morgan, ed., *The West of William H. Ashley* (Denver: The Old West Publishing Company, 1964).

32. R. L. Nichols and P. L. Halley, *Stephen Long and American Frontier Exploration* (Newark, Del.: University of Delaware Press, 1980).

33. A. O. Weese, ed., "The Journal of Titan Ramsay Peal, Pioneer Naturalist," *Missouri Historical Review* 41 (1947).

34. M. Benson, ed., *From Pittsburgh to the Rocky Mountains* (Golden, Colo.: Fulcrum, Inc., 1988).

35. W. R. Nitske, *Travels in North America 1822–1824* (Norman, Okla.: University of Oklahoma Press, 1973).

36. B. DeVoto, *Across the Wide Missouri* (Boston: Houghton Mifflin Company, 1975).

## Chapter 11: Beginning of the End

1.   C. L. Goodwin, "Early Explorations and Settlements of Missouri and Arkansas, 1803–1822," *Missouri Historical Review* 14 (1920).

2.   R. J. Gerber, "Old Woman River," *Missouri Historical Review* 61 (1962).

3.   J. Viles, "Old Franklin: A Frontier Town of the Twenties," *The Mississippi Valley Historical Review* IX, no. 4 (1923).

4.   D. C. Peattie, *Audubon's America* (Cambridge, Mass.: The Riverside Press. 1940).

## Chapter 12: Lost and Found

1.   T. Hillig, "Trail of evidence has Missouri, Illinois claiming Lewis and Clark" *St. Louis Post-Dispatch*, 26 August 2001.

## Part Three: Westward Bound
## Chapter 13: Cote sans Dessein

1.   A. H. Abel, *Tabeau's Narrative of Loisel's Expedition to the Upper Missouri* (Norman, Okla.: University of Oklahoma Press, 1939).

2.   O. Bell, *Cote sans Dessein, A History* (Fulton, Mo., 1930).

3.   J. Anderson, "Jean Baptiste Roy—St. Louis Fur Trader," *Missouri Historical Society* 4 (1947).

4.   J. B. Musick, *St. Louis as a Fortified Town* (St. Louis: R. F. Miller Press, 1941).

5.   S. Vestal, *The Old Santa Fe Trail* (Cambridge, Mass.: The Riverside Press. 1939).

6.   H. M. Brackenridge, *Journal of a Voyage up the Missouri; Performed in eighteen hundred and eleven* (Baltimore: Coale and Maxwell, 1816).

7.   R. L. Nichols and P. L. Halley, *Stephen Long and American Frontier Exploration* (Newark, Del.: University of Delaware Press, 1980).

8.   L. F. Burns. *Osage Indian Bands and Clans* (Fallbrook, Calif.: Ciga Press, 1984).

9.  L. R. Hafen, *The Mountain Men and the Fur Trade of the Far West* (Glendale, Calif.: The Arthur H. Clark Company, 1966).

10. E. Coues, *The Journal of Jacob Fowler* (Minneapolis: Ross & Haines, Inc., 1965).

## Chapter 14: A Trail of Tears

1.  T. C. Thorne, *The Many Hands of My Relations* (Columbia, Mo.: University of Missouri Press, 1996).

2.  R. D. Hurt, *Nathan Boone and the American Frontier* (Columbia, Mo.: University of Missouri Press, 1988).

3.  L. M. Upton and J. K. Hulston, *Nathan Boone, the neglected hero* (Republic, Mo.: Western Printing Company, Inc., 1984).

4.  A. H. Abel, *The History of Events Resulting in Indian Consolidation West of the Mississippi* (New York: AMS Press, Inc., 1908).

5.  G. Foreman, *Indians & Pioneers* (Norman, Okla.: University of Oklahoma Press, 1936).

## Chapter 15: The Old Saxons

1.  D. McCullough, *John Adams* (New York: Simon & Schuster, 2001).

2.  R. Gregory, *A History of Early Marthasville, Missouri* (Marthasville, Mo.: Three Pines Publishing Company, 1980).

3.  R. Babcock, *Memoir of John Mason Peck, D.D.* (Philadelphia: American Baptist Publication Society, 1864).

4.  H. M. Chittenden, *History of Early Steamboat Navigation on the Missouri River. Life and Adventures of Joseph La Barge* (New York: Francis P. Harper, 1903).

5.  S. Vestal, *The Missouri* (Lincoln, Neb.: University of Nebraska Press, 1945).

6.  L. H. Oliver, *Some Boone Descendants and Kindred of the St. Charles District* (Burlington, Vt.: Cheduvato Service, 1964).

7.  G. Duden, *Report on a Journey to the Western States of North America* (Columbia, Mo.: University of Missouri Press, 1980).

8. W. G. Bek, "The Followers of Duden" *Missouri Historical Review* 17 (1923).

9. W. Bek, "Nicholas Hesse, German Visitor to Missouri, 1835–1837" *Missouri Historical Review* 41 (1947).

10. W. H. Lyon, *The Pioneer Editor in Missouri 1808–1860* (Columbia, Mo.: University of Missouri Press, 1965).

11. W. A. Swanberg, *Pulitzer* (New York: Charles Schibner's Sons, 1967).

12. W. D. Kamphoefner, *The Westfalians* (Princeton, N.J.: Princeton University Press, 1987).

## Chapter 16: The Mighty River Highway

1. J. S. Pope, "A History of Steamboating on the Lower Missouri: 1839–1849" (Ph.D. diss., St. Louis University, 1984).

2. N. O. Hammon, ed., *The Draper Interviews with Nathan Boone. My Father, Daniel Boone* (Lexington, Ky.: The University Press of Kentucky, 1999).

3. G. Duden, *Report on a Journey to the Western States of North America* (Columbia, Mo.: University of Missouri Press, 1980).

4. H. M. Chittenden, *History of Early Steamboat Navigation on the Missouri River. Life and Adventures of Joseph La Barge* (New York: Francis P. Harper, 1903).

5. J. Anderson, "Jean Baptiste Roy—St. Louis Fur Trader," *Missouri Historical Society* 4 (1947).

6. F. Way Jr., *Way's Packet Directory, 1848–1994* (Athens, Ohio: Ohio University Press).

7. P. De Smet, *Life, Letters and Travels of Father Pierre-Jean De Smet*, eds. H. M. Chittenden and A. L. Richardson (New York: Francis P. Harper, 1905).

8. *Biographies of Franklin, Jefferson, Washington, Crawford and Gasconade Counties, Missouri* (The Goodspeed Publishing Company, 1911; Bowie, Md.: Heritage Books Inc., 1995).

9. R. K. Schneiders, *Unruly River* (Lawrence, Kan.: University Press of Kansas, 1999).

10. V. V. Masterson, *The Katy Railroad and the Last Frontier* (Norman, Okla., University of Oklahoma Press, 1952).

11. W. T. Walker, "Nathan Boone: The Forgotten Hero of Missouri," *Journal of the West* 28 (1979).

12. J. W. Kendrick, *A Report Upon the Missouri, Kansas & Texas Railway System* (Chicago, 1917).

## Chapter 17: Visiting Charrette Township

1. B. Dufer, *The Complete Katy Trail Guidebook*, 5th ed. (Rocheport, Mo.: Pebble Publ., Inc., 1999).

## Epilogue

1. N. Zack, *Thinking About Race* (Belmont, Calif.: Wadsworth Publishing Company, 1998).

2. M. H. Brown, *The Plainsmen of the Yellowstone* (New York: G. P. Putnam's Sons, 1961).

In addition to the references cited, select microfiches and microfilm tapes from the Draper and other collections were reviewed. The resources of The Warren County Historical Society; The Washington Historical Society; The Missouri State Archives; the Palace of the Governors Fray Angelico Chavez Library of Santa Fe, New Mexico; and the Santa Fe Chamber of Commerce were visited. The University of Missouri Ellis Library, The State Historical Society of Missouri, The Western Manuscript Collection, Lindenwood University Butler Library of St. Charles, and the Southwest Collection of New Mexico State Library in Santa Fe were also called upon. The French and Spanish Archives of the St. Louis Historical Society; St. Louis Public Library; Missouri Linnemann Library of St. Charles; Eden Theological Seminary Archives of St. Louis; Louisiana State Museum, New Orleans, Louisiana; the Family History Center of the Mormon Church, Salt Lake City, Utah; The Lutheran Historical Society of Pennsylvania; the Internet, among other sources, were also consulted.

# About the Author

The author was born in 1938 on a Charrette Township farm in Warren County, Missouri, first surveyed by Adam McCord, an early La Charrette Village neighbor. The farm was first owned by John McKinney, father of Aleck McKinney of the "Indian War" era of Warren County, and shared its east border with widow St. Franceway's farm of La Charrette Village.

In his youth, Lowell M. Schake learned much of Charrette Creek, the Missouri River, and Charrette Township. Charrette Creek borders his family farm for most of two miles on the south and west. His German ancestors all entered Charrette Township by disembarking at Marthasville Landing. They eventually owned much of the farmland where La Charrette villagers St. Franceway, Luzon, and Chartran once resided. As a lad, he fished, hunted, trapped, swam, explored, and even ice-skated Charrette Creek. Like the children of La Charrette Village, he walked across neighboring farms to his one-room school and farmed with a team of horses. He collected Indian artifacts from an Indian campsite on his farm where his Grandfather Schake, once operated an old sugar camp. He and his wife lived their first year of marriage within a few yards of Charrette Creek. Today, Schake enjoys hiking the Katy Trail across his family farm between mileposts 79 and 80, as many others do.

For thirty years, Schake was a professor and administrator of animal and food science departments at Texas A&M University, the University of Connecticut, and Texas Tech University. Now retired, he resides at Royal Sands on Mustang Island, Port Aransas, Texas, with his wife, Wendy. Recognized as an innovative teacher, he has published more than 300 technical articles on the behavior, energy management, and nutrition of cattle. His hobbies include researching genealogy, writing, hiking, tutoring, fishing, and otherwise enjoying the beaches of the Gulf of Mexico.

His first post-retirement activity, which lasted five years, was a comprehensive study of his family genealogy and ethnohistory. His research took him to the farms of his peasant ancestors who lived in the German villages of Betzen, Humfeld, Lemgo, and Ludenhausen in Lippe-Detmold and to Leinen, Lengerich, and Versmold in Westphalia.

Find *The Schakes of La Charette* posted at www.rootsweb.com/~mowarren/schake/intro.html. To remain current on his latest five-year project regarding the events and history of La Charrette Village, visit http://fpl.centurytel.net/lacharrette and http://lacharrettevillage.blogspot.com/. He is currently compiling a biography about a Michigan dentist who, as an amateur ornithologist, was instrumental in saving three endangered species, including the whooping crane and Kirtland's warbler.

# Index

## Numbers

## A

# M

# O

# P

# Q

# R

# T

# U

# Y

978-1-58348-483-8
1-58348-483-3

Made in the USA
San Bernardino, CA
01 December 2016